CHASING
THE
DREAM

B A N T A M   B O O K S

New York   Toronto   London   Sydney   Auckland

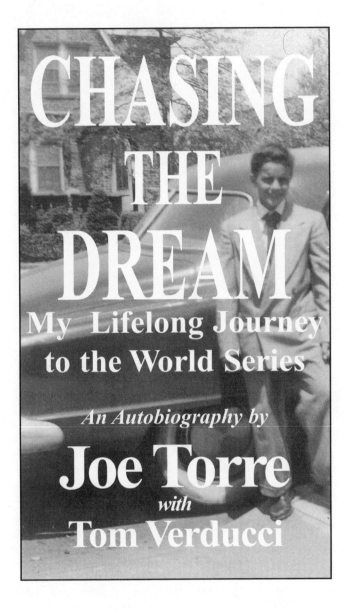

CHASING THE DREAM

DREAM

My Lifelong Journey
to the World Series

An Autobiography by

Joe Torre

with

Tom Verducci

CHASING THE DREAM
A Bantam Book / April 1997

All insert photographs not otherwise credited are from Joe Torre's collection.
Title page photographs are by Steve Crandall and from Joe Torre's collection.

BOOK DESIGN BY GLEN EDELSTEIN

Library of Congress Catalog Card Number: 97-070309

ISBN: 0-553-10658-9

Published simultaneously in the United States and Canada

Bantam Books are published by Bantam Books, a division of Bantam Doubleday Dell
Publishing Group, Inc. Its trademark, consisting of the words "Bantam Books" and
the portrayal of a rooster, is Registered in U.S. Patent and Trademark Office and in
other countries. Marca Registrada. Bantam Books, 1540 Broadway, New York, New
York 10036.

PRINTED IN THE UNITED STATES OF AMERICA
BVG   10 9 8 7 6 5 4 3 2 1

To my wife, Ali, for renewing my faith in life, giving me inspiration to live and believe in myself, being my best friend, and encouraging me to chase my dream.

—J. T.

For Kirsten, my love and inspiration.

—T. V.

Acknowledgments

Many people have helped me put this book together. I would especially like to thank Irwyn Applebaum, Bantam's publisher, whose commitment and enthusiasm for this book has been unwavering. Brian Tart, my editor, is Bantam's Derek Jeter, in that he never faltered in his "we will win" attitude. He along with his hardworking assistant, Ryan Stellabotte, made the perfect double-play combination. Chris Tomasino, my literary agent and bench coach, who is a lot easier on the eyes than Don Zimmer, was tireless in her drive for perfection. I thank Bob Rosen, without whom this project would not have gotten off the ground. Tom Verducci deserves all my appreciation for the constant calm, eloquence, and style with which he handled the madness of *Chasing the Dream*. He is my MVP.

I truly value the contributions of the following people, not only to this book, but in my life: Rae, Sister Marguerite, Frank, Ali, Matt Borzello, Bing Devine, Bob Gibson, Jack Kennedy, George Kissell, Stan London, Ed Maull, Dal Maxvill, Tim McCarver, Jim McElroy, Marvin Miller, Dale Murphy, John Parascandola, Joe Ponte, Arthur Richman, Arthur Sando, Daniel "Rusty" Staub, and Bob Uecker.

Contents

CHASING
THE
DREAM

CHAPTER 1

Brotherhood

N THE COOL OF A BREEZY OCTOBER Sunday afternoon, I sat next to my mother in the upper deck of Milwaukee County Stadium—between home plate and third base—as my brother Frank prepared to bat in the fourth game of the 1957 World Series against the New York Yankees. The Yankees were leading the Series two games to one. Frank was a first baseman for the Milwaukee Braves, having made it to the big leagues only the year before. I was a chubby seventeen-year-old kid, and I'd never seen anything this exciting in all my life.

I had been to World Series games before this trip to Milwaukee, but all of them had been back home in New York. I had seen my beloved New York Giants lose at the Polo Grounds to the Yankees in 1951—the last World Series for Joe DiMaggio and the first for Mickey Mantle and Willie Mays. I had been at Yankee Stadium for Game Five of the 1956 World Series, when Don Larsen of the Yankees pitched his perfect game against the Brooklyn Dodgers. And I had watched the Yankees and the Milwaukee Braves split the first two games of the 1957 World Series at Yankee Stadium. I had always looked forward to going to the ballpark to watch a World Series game in New York. But it also felt like business as usual—like another day at the office. Because of the great successes of the Yankees, Giants, and Dodgers, the World Series almost never left the boroughs of New York City in the years I was growing up. From the time I was nine years old, in 1949, to that first time the Braves brought the World Series to Milwaukee, all but four of the forty-six World Series games in that span were played in New York. The Phillies managed to host two games in Philadelphia in 1950, and the Indians hosted two games in Cleveland in 1954. Otherwise the World Series was as New York as an egg cream and Coney Island.

Only when I went to Milwaukee did I really learn just how precious and thrilling the World Series is, especially when my own brother made his first World Series start in Game Four. The town was absolutely nuts about the Braves. For Milwaukee fans it was a time as special as your first love. The ball club had moved there from Boston only four years earlier. The streets and stores of the downtown area were covered with banners and signs wishing their team good luck. Many of the signs said "Go Bushville" because some of the Yankee players, apparently not enamored of having to go to a small midwestern city, had referred to Milwaukee as "the bushes." The truth is, the Braves had outdrawn the Yankees during the season by more than 700,000 people. It was a great baseball town that called itself "Baseball's Main Street." I never had liked the Yankees—everybody in my family grew up fans of the Giants and the National League—and it really angered me that they looked down on having to go to a small town to play the World Series.

I had been to County Stadium before, to visit Frank during the 1956 regular season, but this was very different. I never had before felt this kind of electricity in the air. Before the game I was in the Braves clubhouse talking with Frank when I happened to look up and see Desi Arnaz, one of the biggest television stars of the day, standing right there next to me. I never had seen County Stadium packed like this before either. Every seat was filled. There were 45,804 people there for Game Four. Almost every one of the men wore a jacket and tie—some of them wore an overcoat and hat as well—and just about all of the women, my mother included, wore a dress and hat. My mother, who was fifty-two years old at the time, had come to Milwaukee on the first plane ride of her life. My sister Rae also sat with us. Another sister, who was born Josephine but took the name Sister Mary Marguerite when she became a nun in the Ursuline order, was in a convent and unable to make the trip.

The stadium, built for the Braves in 1953, still sparkled with newness. As Frank came to bat in the fourth inning, I could see the red, white, and blue bunting gently billowing all around the ballpark on the railing to the first row of the stands—and even on the outfield fences. I could see the spruce and fir trees, called Perini's Woods, behind the center-field fence and the Veterans Administration Hospital on Mockingbird Hill overlooking right field. The patients watched the games for free from there. And I could see the Yankees' pitcher, a right-hander named Tom Sturdivant, who had won sixteen games that year, wind up and deliver a pitch to my brother. Frank connected so solidly that I could hear the crack of the bat even in the upper deck. The baseball flew high toward right field. Frank wasn't a home run hitter. He had hit only five home runs all year, three of them with help from the cozy dimensions of the Polo Grounds. But the baseball kept carrying and carrying and carrying until it finally disappeared into a jubilant mass of people in the bleachers. My brother had just hit a World Series home run.

Everybody screamed with joy. My mom shot up out of her seat with such force that her hat flew off her head. "That's my son!" she yelled. A man sitting near us said, "You can't be his mother. Why would you be sitting up here in the upper deck?" My mom, ever the generous person, had given the better tickets we got from Frank down in the field-level boxes to some friends. I felt enormous pride as I watched my brother run around the bases. I got choked up. I couldn't wait to go back to my neighborhood in Brooklyn and talk to all those Dodgers fans about my brother and his World Series home run. Frank was a clutch player. He had proved himself under the ultimate test.

Frank's home run gave Milwaukee a 4–1 lead. The Yankees, though, tied the game with two outs in the ninth inning on a three-run home run by Elston Howard. When the ball cleared the fence, I grew sick to my stomach. I felt even worse in the tenth inning, when Hank Bauer hit a triple off Warren Spahn to knock in Tony Kubek to give the Yankees a 5–4 lead. The Yankees were three outs away from taking a three-games-to-one lead in the Series. But then Nippy Jones was hit in the foot by a pitch—reaching first base only after he showed umpire Augie Donatelli the shoe polish on the baseball. Johnny Logan doubled home the tying run. And then Eddie Mathews whacked a home run, and the place went crazy. The Braves won, 7–5.

After the game I went into the Braves clubhouse. It was the happiest time of my life. The clubhouse looked spacious and new, even though by today's standards it is considered lacking for its current tenants, the Brewers. It reminds me of the way I look at the house where I grew up in Brooklyn on Avenue T. I always thought that house was big. I look at it now—Rae still lives there—and I can't believe how small it seems.

From the dugout the Braves players walked up a concrete ramp and a small flight of steps to enter the clubhouse at a back corner. The manager's office, belonging to Fred Haney at the time, was on the immediate right. Farther into the room, on the same side as the manager's office, were the sinks and shower room. The lockers lined the perimeter of the room. The players seemed huge to me, much larger in the clubhouse than on the field. Joe Adcock, the regular first baseman who had been replaced by Frank that day because of a slump, was six foot four inches and 210 pounds. Eddie Mathews, the third baseman, was six foot one, 190 pounds, and strong as a bull. Catcher Del Crandall was six foot two and 180 pounds. Henry Aaron, the team's star twenty-three-year-old outfielder, seemed to be the only one who was slightly built, but even then I noticed how powerful his hands and wrists looked.

The players were elated. They grabbed bottles of Coca-Cola and beer out of a metal tub in the center of the room. They didn't have refrigerated dispensers then. They'd just unload the bottles from wooden boxes into a large metal tub with a drain at the bottom, then put in a big block of ice and an ice pick. Whenever a player grabbed a soda or beer, he'd put a mark next to his name on a big piece of cardboard tacked to the clubhouse wall. He was billed later according to how many marks were next to his name.

There were no postgame spreads of food in those days either. In fact, the Braves were the only team I knew of at the time to make anything available for the players to munch on. They had a bunch of crackers and a crock of cheddar cheese. It was, after all, the dairy capital of the world. Nowadays every home and visiting clubhouse serves a catered full-course meal to the players after each game.

During the Braves' postgame celebration, a fan came to the clubhouse door looking for Frank. He was holding a baseball. The fan explained that this was the baseball he had hit for the home run. Frank traded two tickets to Game Five for the baseball. Later Frank had every one of his teammates sign the ball. When he brought it home to Brooklyn, Rae preserved the cherished family heirloom with a coat of her clear nail polish.

I spent just about all my time in that exuberant club-house trying to be as inconspicuous as possible. I was a timid kid, and I kept my mouth shut, hanging close to

Frank's locker. My eyes were wide open, though. I'll never forget how I felt in that Braves clubhouse after a World Series win. I knew right then it was the only place I ever wanted to be. I was lucky enough to get a peek behind the thick velvet curtain—to go backstage at the World Series— and it inspired me. That's when the World Series became my dream. I fell asleep that night dreaming about it.

I was a decent sandlot player at the time, but I knew I had many, many miles to travel to get from where I was playing to where Frank was playing. Dreaming about getting to the World Series was the same as dreaming about becoming president of the United States. It seemed so far away. You had to be blessed enough and lucky enough to get there. But I was having a hell of a good time living my dream through my brother.

Early the next morning my mother appeared on the *Today* show. Frank accompanied her on the trip to a Milwaukee TV studio. My mother was so nervous that, when they asked her who her favorite ballplayer was, she didn't say Frank. She said Gil Hodges of the Brooklyn Dodgers.

The Braves won again that day, 1–0, behind Lew Burdette's pitching. The Series then returned to Yankee Stadium for Game Six. We had better seats there, the box seats behind home plate. Yankee Stadium was a museum to me— a museum of baseball. When I walked in, I thought about all the great teams and athletes who had played there. A couple of years ago I played a round of golf at Augusta. I had the same feeling walking that course: like I was in a golf museum. The surroundings and the knowledge of all the people who had walked there before me were humbling.

In the fifth inning, with the Braves losing 2–0, Frank tagged a pitch from Bob Turley. Hank Bauer, the Yankee right fielder, drifted back to the three-foot outfield wall, near the 344 feet sign. He put one hand on the wall, stood on one leg, and reached for the ball with his glove. But the baseball sailed well over him and into the bleachers. Frank had hit another home run. This time I felt like running all the way home to Avenue T right then and there to tell my friends about it.

The Yankees won that sixth game 3–2, bringing the 1957 World Series to a seventh game. Warren Spahn was supposed to start that final game, but he was sidelined by the flu. So Haney gave the ball to Burdette, asking him to pitch on only two days of rest. I knew Burdette was tough. While shutting out the Yankees in Game Five, he took a wicked line drive off his chest. I was in the clubhouse after that game, and I saw on his chest the imprint of commissioner Ford Frick's autograph, which was on the World Series baseballs. Burdette pitched one of the greatest games in World Series history, shutting out the Yankees 5–0 in the deciding game.

My brother was a world champion—and he had the ring to prove it. It was one of the most beautiful things I had ever seen. It was a heavy gold ring with four rubies on top in the shape of a baseball diamond, with a large diamond stone in the middle. Around the rubies, inscribed in a square, it said "Milwaukee Braves. World Champions." On one side of the ring it said "1957," above the Braves' Indian logo. On the other side it said "Frank Torre. 1B." Frank wore it proudly every day.

Amazingly, Frank and the Braves made it back to the World Series against the Yankees again in 1958. Milwaukee took a three-games-to-one lead in the Series. The Braves' wives were so confident of victory, they started talking about how to spend the World Series winners' shares. One of them, Darlene McMahon, the wife of pitcher Don McMahon, bought a fur coat in New York in anticipation of the $8,000 winners' paycheck. After the Yankees won Game Five 7–0, Don didn't talk to her all the way back to Milwaukee. He knew the Series wasn't over. Sure enough, the Yankees won the last two games in Milwaukee to win the world championship.

Frank, a hero in the 1957 World Series, committed two errors at first base in the 6–2 loss in Game Seven. I waited for Frank in the clubhouse after that game. He barely spoke as we drove back to his apartment. He was so angry at himself that he was speeding through Wisconsin Avenue in downtown Milwaukee at about sixty miles per hour. A policeman stopped the car. When he walked up to the driver's window and saw who it was, the officer said, "Just take it easy, Frank, okay?" and let us go. I thought that was real nice. Frank's day was bad enough already.

Every player, manager, coach, trainer, and executive who gets to the World Series gets a ring. The winners' rings say "World Champions" and the losers' rings say "League Champions." I've seen enough other people wearing them to know that they are more elaborate these days than when Frank played. Many of the recent ones feature words or a phrase that embodies the team's season. The Atlanta Braves' 1995 world championship ring, for instance, is inscribed

"Team of the '90s." Frank's 1958 World Series ring had smaller stones than the 1957 ring. It had an oval face rather than a rectangular one and it too featured the Braves' Indian logo. It was inscribed "Milwaukee Braves. National League Champions." Frank decided to turn his 1958 ring into a pendant for our mother. A jeweler removed the sides of the ring and used only the top. My mom, though, never wore jewelry, and it sat in her dresser for a while. After a couple of months I asked her if I could have it. She said sure. I brought it to a jeweler and had it turned back into a ring.

I wore that ring for several years, including during the early part of my playing career in the big leagues. My teammates and other people would see this big World Series ring and ask, "Where'd you get that?" and "What team did you play on to get that?" I got tired of having to explain that I didn't earn it, my brother did. So finally I just put the ring in a small jewelry travel pouch and left it there. Then one day in 1972 I reached into the pouch for a pair of cufflinks and noticed that the ring was gone. I figured out that while I had been at a New York hotel three or four days before that—I was there for the players' ratifications vote concluding the 1972 players' strike—someone had stolen the ring. It must have been an inside job, because nothing else in the room was disturbed. The thief must have known we were out of the rooms at 1:00 P.M. taking the vote.

Ever since I lost the ring, Frank would tell me, "You've got to replace that ring." And then when his son, Frankie, was born in 1976, he would say, "I want you to get a ring and give it to my son." That was his way of telling me that eventually my dream would come true—that I was going to get to the World Series. Though I doubted it many times, my brother was right. At 10:56 on the night of October 26, 1996, I rushed out from the dugout onto the field at Yankee Stadium a World Series champion. Thirty-nine years after I had watched Frank hit those two World Series home runs, the same two clubs, the Braves and Yankees, had staged another grueling, unforgettable Fall Classic. This time, as manager of the Yankees, I was a part of the celebration.

As I took my team on a victory lap around Yankee Stadium, I thought, This is what I waited for my whole life. It felt even better than I ever imagined. It had taken me until I was fifty-six years old. It had taken me 4,272 major league games as a player and manager—no one had ever waited longer to get to the World Series. It had taken getting traded twice and getting fired three times. Both my parents had died years before they could have seen me celebrate the victory. And in the end it had taken the most emotional twelve months of my life: the birth of my daughter Andrea Rae; the shocking death of my brother Rocco; and a life-saving heart transplant for Frank on the eve of the clinching game of the World Series. I never expected that chasing the dream would bring me to so many magical moments, or that the road to get there would be so long and so often painful.

CHAPTER 2

Our House

AE WAS WIELDING A KITCHEN KNIFE when my father reached for the gun. I was nine or ten years old at the time, standing between the two of them, and scared as hell about what might happen. My father, Joe, was a New York City detective with a mean streak he never hesitated to show around the house. Lord knows my mother felt the sting of his hand more than once. She was there, too, that day at our brick row house on Avenue T in East Flatbush, Brooklyn. My father was raging at Rae, threatening her and yelling at her to put down the knife. She wouldn't put it down. So my father turned and began to reach into a dining-room drawer. I knew that was where he kept his revolver.

I didn't know what he planned to do. I didn't know what he was capable of, though I was so terrified of the man, it was easy for me to imagine the worst. Either way, I didn't want to find out. I couldn't let this madness play out any further. I grabbed the knife out of Rae's hand and put it on the dining-room table. "Here!" I said to him. And with that the confrontation ended and a calm fell over the house somehow. I don't recall what had provoked that fight, and it hardly matters because such confrontations were all too common. As long as my father was under our roof, those interludes of calm were charged with tension and anxiety, the same way that storm clouds building with rain and thunder inevitably burst forth.

Growing up, I was a nervous, self-conscious kid with hardly an ounce of confidence. I was the baby of the family, the youngest of five children, all of whom were at least eight years older than me. My shyness occurred partly because I was a fat kid. But I know I was skittish because of the threat my father represented to me as well. I know he used to hit my mother, even if I can't recall if I was present when he did. To this day I can see him raising the back of his hand to her, and then . . . I see nothing. Maybe I've just blacked out the rest in my mind. He never hit me. But sometimes that's worse than actually getting hit, especially for a child. I was always thinking, What is he going to do to me?

My father used to come home at two or three in the morning after work. I'd hear him come in, and just his presence in the house would be enough to make me nervous. He would sleep until the early afternoon. On weekends and days when there was no school, I walked around the house on eggshells, trying not to wake him. If I did make too much noise, he would pound the wall next to his bed three times slowly: Boom! Boom! Boom! That was his warning signal from his upstairs bedroom.

He usually would leave the house around four or five in the afternoon. The first thing I did when I came home from school was check to see if his car was parked outside our house. If I saw the black Studebaker out front, there was no way I was going home. I'd go to a friend's house or stay outside and play.

I remember one time—I couldn't have been more than five or six—when my parents had some friends over. I was in the upstairs bathroom urinating, except that I didn't close the door, and the acoustics were such that the sound carried extremely well. My father was so embarrassed, he flew into a rage, yelling so viciously at me in front of everyone that even my older brother Frank was afraid for me. That was pretty typical. Although he never physically hurt me, he verbally abused me often.

That's what it was like at the Torre house, at least when my father was around. Don't get me wrong—our home was filled with plenty of love too. In fact, I was smothered with attention and affection because I was so much younger than my siblings. I'll admit it—I was spoiled. Sister Marguerite thinks that my mother doted on all of us, especially me, because she lived with such pain and unhappiness in her marriage. I think she's right. I think the nervousness that pervaded our house made us cling to one another a little more tightly. Of course, my mother was especially protective of me in that environment because I was the youngest. This much I know for sure: I was loved very much, but my father frightened me.

I was born Joseph Paul Torre on July 18, 1940, in Madison Park Hospital in Brooklyn, the first in our family to be delivered in a hospital. My mother had my four brothers and sisters in the bedroom of an apartment in the Greenpoint section of Brooklyn, where my family had lived before I was born. My mother was a strong, stubborn woman who didn't like doctors. Six years earlier she had given birth to a baby girl who died almost immediately from complications, but only after she was baptized and named Theresa. Doctors advised my mother not to have any more children. I guess I was the mistake, the one who wasn't supposed to be here. I know from stories Frank told me that my father was angry when he found out my mother was pregnant with me. She was thirty-five years old.

From the moment I came home from the hospital, my mother and sisters devoted themselves to making sure I was happy. Rae, who was fourteen when I was born, and Sister Marguerite, who was ten, used to sit around and wait for me to cry, then pounce immediately with love and hugs to soothe me. Frank was the next youngest to me—although he was eight and a half when I came along. Rocco was twelve. At the end of our block, no more than a hundred yards from our house, was Marine Park. Rocco would be rushing out of the house to go play baseball there with his friends from the neighborhood, and my mother would say, "If you want to play, you have to bring Joey along." Rocco and his friends would have to push me in the baby carriage to the park. So you see, I grew up around baseball from a very early age.

My mother was born Margaret Rofrano in Italy in 1905

and came to this country as an infant. I remember asking her about our heritage, "What are we? Neapolitan? Sicilian?" She said, "You're American." That was a time when you were embarrassed about being "from the other side," especially during the war years. One memory stands out about being a kid in wartime. We used to have mandated blackouts at night in Brooklyn, where every house would have to cut its lights and draw the shades, in case the enemy was looking for land during an invasion from sea. In those days we worried that at any moment the war could spread to our shores. My brothers, sisters, and I would huddle in a tiny nook—it was no bigger than a small closet—outside our first-floor bathroom. Being the nervous kid that I was, I was petrified of the darkness and what might be out there, so sometimes Sister Marguerite would allow me the tiny concession of lighting a small votive candle in that nook.

My mom lavished her children with love and attention. At Christmastime she used to make sure we had the best presents. We would go to my grandmother Torre's house on Christmas Eve. She lived in my family's old apartment house in Greenpoint on Lorimer Street. It would always take my sisters longer than me to get in the car, for what are now obvious reasons. Before they left the house, they would throw the presents under the tree so that when we came back home later that night, it would look like Santa Claus had already made his drop. I remember one Christmas getting a Howdy Doody doll, which was *the* toy to have at the time. That was my mom—nothing was too good for us, especially me. When I attended elementary school—it was about a one-mile walk from our house—I used to come home for lunch. All the other kids were at school eating sandwiches out of brown bags. My mother would cook me eggs and a hamburger patty. I had home-cooked hot meals for lunch every day. Other times I'd come in from playing outside, and my mom would have a fresh fruit salad waiting for me in a bowl. I must have been an adult by the time I knew cantaloupe actually comes with a skin on it.

In a lot of ways my mother was a typical Italian mother. She was a fabulous and prodigious cook (my early physique was a walking, irrefutable testament to that talent) and a devout Catholic who always put her family first. She could also be very tough, although I only remember her hitting me once. I know, however, that the thought occurred to her often. Whenever she did raise her hand to strike me, she would stop herself by biting her index finger. That was my cue to get out of her reach. In those days such parenting methods weren't so unusual, at least from what I knew in Brooklyn. But mostly my mother was a loving, stabilizing influence, who always was there for me. She worked some as well. She used to earn money crocheting clothes, especially for infants. She'd sit in front of the television set and do her work. And she loved to play casino with us. You could always tell when she had good cards and was going to make a big hit on you because she would straighten them per-fectly in her hands, as if proudly dressing up her children to go out on Sunday.

Sister Marguerite often said to Mom, "Oh, Frank is your favorite." And Frank used to think I was her favorite. But my mother used to have a saying whenever anybody thought she had a favorite. She'd hold up her hand with her palm open and say, "See these fingers? Cut off any of them, and it hurts just the same." Five fingers for five children. The 1996 World Series made me think of another one of her favorite lines. She always used to tell me, "Don't worry, Joe. Good things come to those who wait." And she was right about that.

Sister Marguerite says she doesn't know how my mother endured my father for so long. I think she stuck it out because she didn't want me to be harassed or embarrassed by the other kids in grammar school. Divorce was not as convenient in those days as it is now, especially for someone as religious as my mother. She went to mass every day at Good Shepherd Church, always walking through Marine Park to get there. Of course, I was really too young at that time to understand how bad things were between my parents.

My father, an Italian-American who was born in New York, actually was a very shrewd, brilliant man with a charismatic side. His mother once gave him the money needed to apply to the police academy. My father kept the money but never went. He did, though, show up for the police exam and passed it anyway. He rose quickly through the department with the kind of sharp mind and gruff manner that earned him the nickname Joe the Boss. That's what his friends would call him off duty, too, while he engaged in his two favorite pastimes: playing the horses and playing cards. He was never really a drinker. I'm not sure what caused his rage, but I know it wasn't a drinking problem.

My dad always had his ways of making people feel obligated to him. He used to carry around Italian candy, nuts, little miniature bottles of cognac, and stuff like that in boxes in the trunk of his car. He'd always be dropping off gifts to people, but not always to spread joy; he didn't mind knowing that his gift-giving would make others feel indebted to him. At Christmastime he would wrap these small gifts in packages, write little notes with them, and send them out to hundreds of people. I mean hundreds of people. He was very meticulous about it. He anticipated that some might do favors for him in return.

I used to look forward to the month or two after Christmas, when my father would be in Florida for his winter getaway. That was great for me because the house was calm without him. I didn't find out until much later that he would make these trips to Florida with a woman, whom he would eventually marry after he and my mother were divorced. I later met her and found her to be a nice woman. Unfortunately, my father abused her too. I wasn't observant enough as a child to notice that after my father spent two months in Florida he never came home with a tan. He was always playing cards. He'd go to a golf course and play cards all day with his friends.

Frank was never afraid of my father, even if he did catch his share of beatings. Frank was a street-tough kid who never took any money from him because he didn't want to feel indebted to him. When Frank was older, my father tried to use his car as leverage against him, always threatening Frank by saying he wouldn't let him use it for one reason or another. Finally one day Frank threw the keys at him and said, "Keep it. I don't want your car." By then Frank had grown to be a pretty big kid, and my father would never mess with Mom as long as Frank was in the house.

I don't think Sister Marguerite was afraid of my father either. Actually, he was rather affectionate toward her. She happened to be terribly sick with pneumonia when she was two years old. My parents thought she was going to die. My father later told her that he made all kinds of promises to Saint Theresa, his favorite saint, if only his daughter would live. Because of that episode my father treated her very well, although she grew up to resent him because of how he treated the rest of us. Now she says she's amazed that Rocco, Frank, and I grew up to be decent fathers at all, with that kind of role model. She used to use the expression "My father has loused up three lives," referring to my two brothers and me, because for a while I was irresponsible and immature. But I was lucky enough to have Rocco and Frank, both of whom were considerably older than me, as strong male figures in my life. I grew up in my teenage years with Rocco as a beat policeman and a solid family man and Frank as a professional ballplayer: two strong men in uniform. I was very proud of them and gained a respect for authority and our family name because of them. I never wanted to embarrass them by any of my actions. I drew strength, love, and friendship from Rocco and Frank—a lot more than from my father.

Rocco probably was the best ballplayer among the three of us brothers. He was a right-handed power pitcher whom the Brooklyn Dodgers wanted to sign. My father, though, refused to grant the parental permission required for any prospect under the age of twenty-one. He insisted Rocco go to college—he wanted him to become a lawyer—even though Rocco didn't care for school. He was lucky to get through high school because of his poor grades. Rather than argue with my father, he joined the navy and served in World War II. After his service time he enrolled at St. John's University for a year or two, married at twenty-two, and took a job as a policeman in Brooklyn.

Rocco was a tremendous influence on me because he was such a responsible family man. He had a completely different agenda from Frank. Frank was single through his baseball-playing days, and he was the one who always liked the action. He'd go to the horses during the daytime and the trotters at night. He loved to play cards. He had no responsibilities. Plus, my relationship with Frank was more of a professional one right up until a couple of years ago, when he became sick. Only then were you allowed to show your emotions to him.

It was tough for me to get close to Frank because he was so critical of me all the time. Rocco was a lot easier to be around and talk to. I looked forward to occasionally eating Sunday dinner at Rocco's house in Flushing. His wife, Rose, was a great cook, and later Rocco was too. In fact, as adults Rocco and I used to trade recipes. It was a very comfortable feeling to be around Rocco and to be at his happy home. I also liked to catch up with Rocco at the moonlighting jobs he would take from his police work. He worked at a gas station for a while. And he worked a couple of nights a week at the Colonnade liquor store on West Fifty-sixth Street near Eighth Avenue. I'll never forget that place because they filmed the movie *The Hustler* right across the street.

There's no question that Rae and my mother took the brunt of my father's boorishness and saw more of his dark side than the rest of us. Rae is an absolute sweetheart, the one who grew closest to my mother as an adult because she lived at home while working for the phone company. Rae is such a kind, generous woman that most people thought, if anyone in our house would become a nun, it would be her. She was so honest that in all those years at AT&T, and later at Nynex, she refused to take home from work so much as a pencil or pad of paper—not that I didn't try planting larcenous thoughts in her brain. I'd often ask her to bring home that kind of stuff. On the whole, though, Rae passed on her trait for unabashed honesty to me. I remember one time when I was ten, going to the movie theater to see a film that required a child to be eleven years old. The clerk asked me how old I was. I was so honest that I blurted out my real age, thereby assuring that I would be denied a seat in the theater. I walked home by myself.

Another time when I was ten, my mother had to go out somewhere, and she told Sister Marguerite to baby-sit me. Sister Marguerite, though, had an interview scheduled with the Trinitarian nuns about the possibility of joining them. She did not, however, tell my mother about that. She wasn't ready to tell her she was thinking about becoming a nun, for as religious as my mother was, she probably would not like the idea of "losing" one of her daughters. It's not as if my mother would have expected her to make such a decision either. Sister Marguerite was a typically devilish, precocious, boy-crazy young woman. So now she had to make a decision: baby-sit me or go to the interview. She decided to do both. She brought me along to the interview; then, in an attempt to ensure my secrecy about this misbehavior, she bought me an ice cream soda and took me home in a taxi, which was an extravagance for us. "Now whatever you do, don't tell Mom about this," she instructed me. Of course, when my mother came home and asked me what we did, I promptly told her the whole story. Sister Marguerite was livid, but that's me. I just can't lie, I guess.

Because Rocco, Frank, and Sister Marguerite eventually moved out of the house and because I was so young, only Rae and my mother were around to deal with my father. That's probably why Rae is the only one of the children who never came to any kind of reconciliation with him. I understand that. It must have been hell. I don't remember my dad actually striking Rae, but I know many times my sister put herself in harm's way by physically defending my mother against him. I remember all the yelling going on between the three of them, and that scared me. I guess that day when Rae picked up that knife and pointed it at my father, she had reached the breaking point.

Then one day, mercifully, the terror finally ended. It was 1951, and I was eleven years old. Sister Marguerite had left home to become a nun earlier that year. The day she left, she bought me a present.

"I was going to buy you rosary beads," she said, "but I figured I might as well give you something you'd use." And then she gave me a beautiful and rather expensive baseball glove. "Every time you use it," she instructed me, "say one Our Father."

And then she was gone, semicloistered in the convent, which meant she could have visitors but she couldn't come home. She spent many of those nights crying herself to sleep over what my father was doing to our mother and our family. Rocco was out of the house too; he was married. Frank had spent most of the year playing minor league ball in Denver, where he had received many late-night telephone calls from my distraught, weeping mother. Frank's always been a tough son of a gun, a straight shooter who's not afraid to tell it like it is. And when he returned home from Denver after his season ended, that's how he laid it out to my mother.

"Mom, I'm tired of getting these phone calls in the middle of the night a thousand miles away," Frank said. "Now, listen. He has to go. And you either make the move now—because he won't do anything with me around—or when I leave for next season, I'm never coming back. Because I can't put up with this stuff anymore."

My mother agreed. It was time for them to split up. But she couldn't bring herself to tell my father. So she, Frank, Rae, and I all gathered around the dining-room table one day and called my dad in. Frank did most of the talking. He told my father that this marriage wasn't working out for anybody. The whole family wanted him out. He wouldn't have to pay any alimony or child support or anything like that. All we wanted was for him to sign the house over to my mother. That was it. My father had bought the house brand new, back in 1935, for $5,900. We still had a mortgage on the place. Grudgingly, my father agreed. I think, inside, he was relieved because he knew our family was not a happy one. He moved out to another part of Brooklyn. I didn't speak another word to him for six years, and neither did my siblings. The little brick row house on Avenue T became a much happier place. There would be no more storms.

It turned out that I would have two failed marriages myself. Was that my father's fault? I don't think so. I made those mistakes because I was spoiled and irresponsible, though I have three wonderful kids from those marriages: Michael, Tina, and Lauren. I love them unconditionally and always have been a part of their lives. Everybody in my family was telling me in those days not to get married. That was all I needed to hear—I'd do the opposite. I thought I could do anything I wanted. I look back, and I really hate myself for the way I was. Totally spoiled. I'm sure I hurt my mother deeply with my first two marriages. In both cases I married outside the Church, without anyone from my family in attendance. I wish she had lived long enough to have known Ali, my present wife, and been there the day we walked down the aisle of the Lady Chapel behind the main altar at St. Patrick's Cathedral in Manhattan.

After my father left, I really didn't see him again until I was seventeen years old. Sad to say, he started to show up at some of my baseball games once word got out that professional scouts were looking at me. Being the kind of wheeler-dealer that he was, he wanted to be in on the action. My dad also began coming to my games because he was loosely affiliated with the Braves as a scout. In 1950 he had worked a deal with the Braves, who were based in Boston then, that he would give the club permission to sign Frank only if they gave him a scouting job. He later scouted for Baltimore. It wasn't as if we renewed our relationship right away. That happened later in the winter, when Frank was home from playing ball. Frank had the same love for card playing that my father did. And he knew that every Tuesday night my father would play gin rummy in a back room of Sirico's restaurant on Thirteenth Avenue in Bay Ridge. They'd have a dozen guys back there, smoking and gambling. They didn't play for big stakes; it was more the ritual of getting together with the guys that was important. My dad would run the whole show. Joe the Boss would scream at anybody who made a dumb move, no matter who he was.

Frank would sit in on these card games. Naturally, I always wanted to tag along with my big brother, so Frank started bringing me. He thought it was important that all of us come to some sort of peace with my father. Frank was the first of the children to begin speaking again with Dad (though it was never a full reconciliation). That was very big of him, considering he was the one who finally had had the guts to kick my father out of the house. Later on Sister Marguerite also came to an understanding with him. He would visit her at the convents, and she developed what she calls "a special love" for him. It was a love, she said, that didn't blind her to the reality of what she knew him to be: a terrible father and a dreadful husband.

With Frank's help I also developed a friendship with my father, though it was never a very close one, and I didn't see him often. I don't think he ever knew me well. I remember one time when I was in my early twenties, he gave me a leather belt as a gift. The belt was way too big for me. He had remembered me as being such a fat kid, which I no longer was.

When my mother found out that Frank and I were hanging out with my father at these card games, she was furious. Understandably, she didn't want us to have anything to do with him, and I don't believe she ever forgave him for what he did to her. Rae was the same way. I guess I managed to keep most of the feelings I had about my father repressed for many years. I just never acknowledged to myself what impact my childhood years had on me as an adult. I'd always been a very guarded person. Then during the week after Thanksgiving in 1995, only three weeks after I accepted George Steinbrenner's offer to manage the Yankees, Ali asked me to come with her to a four-day seminar on self-improvement. It was being held at a Holiday Inn in Cincinnati, her hometown. I had no idea what it was all about. I didn't know if it was about business, about life outside of baseball, or what.

"I'll go with you," I said. "I don't want you to go alone."

"Don't go just because you want to go with me," she said. "I want you to go because you want to go."

"I'll go," I insisted.

So I went. And as soon as I got there and got a sense of what it was about, I said, "Oh, shit."

Since I married Ali in 1987, I've slowly gotten a little better about expressing myself, but it hasn't been easy. Over the years she's frequently said to me, "We've got to talk." And whenever I heard that, immediately I could feel myself tense up. For some reason that was like death to me. That's why I panicked when I walked into that ballroom at the Holiday Inn and found out what was about to happen. There were about fifty people there, and they promptly broke us up into groups of six. There was one hitch: You were not allowed to sit next to your spouse or anyone else you knew. And you weren't allowed to talk with your spouse about what happened when you went home during the training. I found myself having to talk about myself and my feelings to complete strangers over the next four days. I was in agony.

On the first day I began to open up—reluctantly, but I did it. We had to stand up and answer questions like "What do you want to accomplish here?" and "What don't you like?" When it came my turn, I got up and said, "I don't like confrontation. I am uncomfortable with it." And over the course of group sessions during the next three days and nights, I gradually bared my heart and my tears to these strangers. They had ways of drawing out the emotions from everyone, including myself. You had to hold each other and look into each other's eyes. It was very emotional.

I began to understand why I never liked confrontations. I talked about my father and the way he dominated our house and abused our mother. Because of his behavior, yelling and loud noises always made me uncomfortable, and I did whatever I could to avoid those kinds of situations. As we started to dig out those kinds of things—carefully and gradually, like archaeologists—I telephoned Sister Marguerite, on the morning of the third day of the seminar, to confirm some of my findings.

"Did Dad really hit Mom?" I asked her.

"Oh, did he ever," she said. "Joey, I'm surprised you turned out as well as you did, growing up in that house."

As we talked some more about my dad and our childhood, I started crying on the telephone. Then I rejoined my

29

group and told them about the phone call, and I got all choked up just talking about it again. It made me feel better. I began to understand. It seems as if everybody thinks they're the only ones who have something wrong with themselves. It's like you're in a dark quiet room, thinking you're alone, but a light goes on, and you see you are surrounded by people just like you, who felt they were alone too. I get a kick out of that concept, because it helps me as a manager to understand players. I laugh, for instance, at players who want to tell you how good they are. I think what they're really trying to do is convince themselves, not you. Michael Jordan doesn't tell you how good he is. I mean, he knows he's good, and he won't back off from it. But he doesn't have to do what Dennis Rodman does, to get the attention he gets.

That weekend in Cincinnati actually helped me become a better manager. It helped my approach going into the 1996 season with the Yankees. It taught me how to relax myself by putting everything into its proper category rather than thinking I could just take on all my problems at once, which is how you get overwhelmed.

Once my father left the house in 1951, my brothers became even more important to me. Frank became especially influential because he was a professional baseball player. He had signed his first professional contract in 1950, the year I turned ten. Milwaukee Braves scout Honey Russell, the former Seton Hall University basketball coach, gave him a six-thousand-dollar bonus. Frank was such a terrific hitter in high school that he swears he never struck out, not once. He played first base and pitched. In fact, Frank pitched the

Brooklyn Cadets sandlot team to a national title in 1950 at the All-American Amateur Baseball Association tournament in Johnstown, Pennsylvania. He threw a no-hitter in the final game, even though his eyes were nearly closed because of an allergy. I was in awe of my own brother.

Frank began his 1951 season in Hartford before the Braves assigned him to the Denver Bears, a Class A club in the Western League. He invited me out to Colorado to join him. I traveled from New York to Denver by train with my aunt Ella, cousin Carmela, and Rae. My life was about to change in a big way. I went to Denver as something of an average-sized ten-year-old and came home a little more than one month later an eleven-year-old blimp. I mean, I just blew up. I always had a pretty good appetite, and my mother always did a fine job attending to it. But in Denver I ate all the time.

Frank used to hang out at this place called Richard's Steak House. I can remember having my birthday party there—I had a cake as big as a desk. I used to go to the ballpark with Frank every day. But first, at about one or two in the afternoon, we'd go to Richard's for lunch. I'd devour a huge meal, usually a steak. I'd shag flies and work out at the ballpark, then eat some more during the game—maybe a hot dog or two and something else. And then after the game we'd go back to Richard's, and I'd eat another big meal— usually another slab of steak and some sort of mountainous dessert.

One thing everyone should know about Frank is that he's a world-class needler. He is always stirring the pot. And after I became this fat kid, Frank did more than needle me.

31

He rode me mercilessly. He would call me a fat slob repeatedly, tell me what an embarrassment I was to him and the family. I hated him for this for a long time. I was a chubby kid and felt ashamed of it. One time I played a special sandlot game at Ebbets Field in which Pee Wee Reese served as our manager. I must have made a big impression on the great Dodger shortstop. Later on Pee Wee said to Frank, "Oh, your brother likes the groceries, doesn't he?"

Another time Frank invited me back to Ebbets Field to work out with the Braves before a game against the Dodgers, playing catch and shagging flies. I must have been fifteen or sixteen. Frank, of course, had been getting all over me for years about my weight and nothing much had changed, so I guess he thought he had to enlist some help. So he told the real needlers on that Braves team—guys like Warren Spahn, Lew Burdette, and Bob Buhl—to get on my case about being so fat. He figured if I didn't believe him, maybe I'd get the message through these other guys. So when I showed up and started changing into a Braves uniform, those guys were all over me, calling me "Spaghetti Bender" and things like that. I felt so terrible that after the workout I waited until after the game started to take a shower to make sure no one would see me naked.

I really did hate Frank because he was so vicious in the way he'd get on me. I'd show him trophies that I'd won playing ball, and he'd just grumble, "Those things are worthless. They don't mean anything. You'll never be a ballplayer. You're too much a fat slob to be a ballplayer." But Frank was definitely my idol. He was doing what I wanted to do: He was a ballplayer. And that meant I had to keep jumping back in with him. I was always looking for his approval. So even though he was tough on me, the only way I was going to get that approval was to be around him and do things to make him proud of me.

But I also knew this: Frank's bark was a lot worse than his bite. He was very generous. Even when he was in the minor leagues, he'd send my mother a couple hundred dollars a month, which was big money in those days. And he'd give her a lump sum at the start of winter too. Frank would always bitch about something, but then he'd give you whatever you asked for or, usually, more than you asked for. I remember when he went off for a two-year hitch in the army during the Korean War. He actually played some ball over there while he was in Seoul. In fact, that's how he became such a good fielder; he used to take grounders on these rocky open fields in Korea. (He also volunteered for night duty over there, after a couple of nights when he awoke to discover huge rats milling around inside the tents. The rats weren't such a problem during the day, with more people walking around.) Anyway, I'd write to Frank once in a while over there. My letters to him didn't go much beyond this: "Dear Frank: Can you send me fifty bucks? Joe." Frank never failed to come through with spending money for me even from that far away. And when he came home from Korea, he paid my way through a private high school, even though all my brothers and sisters had attended public school.

There's no doubt that Frank is the most different among the Torre children. Though I'd have to say that all the brothers grew up with a chauvinistic attitude—Sister

Marguerite believes that the girls in the family waited on us boys—Frank has the strongest feelings of male superiority. He's a softie inside, but he has a gruff exterior. About five years ago, before he got sick, Sister Marguerite said to him, "Do you tell your children that you love them?" And Frank looked at her like "What are you, nuts?" He said, "Why do you think I'm doing everything I do for them?" Sister Marguerite said, "But Frank, you've got to say the words." Frank had been the family's protection against our father, but he did it in the same intimidating, gruff manner my father had. He'd hate for me to say it, but I believe Frank is most like my father among the Torre boys.

Frank always had a hard edge about him. With him there's no middle of the road: people either love him or hate him. See, Frank's been a fighter his whole life. One of the best stories I know about his feistiness involves his first heart attack, right before Thanksgiving back in 1984 in Las Vegas. He'd played tennis that day with a good friend of his, Alex Failoni. He got tired a lot during the match. Several times he would have to take a break, sit down, then get up and play some more. Later, at dinner, Frank wasn't hungry and told Alex he was going back to his room. Alex thought he didn't look so great but, knowing my tough brother, said, "Ah, you'll feel better in the morning." But the more Alex thought about it, the more he grew worried. Finally, he called up Frank and said, "Let's go. I'm taking you to the doctor."

And so they jumped into a cab and went to the hospital. Frank was in pretty bad shape by then. They put him on a gurney—he was semiconscious—and he heard one doctor say, "I think we're losing him." Thankfully, they managed to stabilize him. A little while later they allowed Alex in to visit him. Frank was lying there on the table with tubes up his nose. All of a sudden, when he saw Alex, he burst out laughing.

"What the hell are you laughing about?" Alex said.

"Here I am having this massive heart attack," Frank said, "and I beat you six–love!"

There's nobody like Frank. He's always been so competitive and one of the all-time agitators, whether it's tennis, golf, or just playing gin. What he's great at is unsettling people to the point that they change their game. And he'll never give you any credit when you do something well. Whatever team I was involved in, as a kid, a pro ballplayer, or a manager, Frank would always find something to complain about. Actually, that's how I knew Frank was getting sicker in recent years. I'll never forget calling him from Hawaii before the season started in 1994, when I was managing the Cardinals. We were talking about the team, and he would just say, "Oh, that's good," and, "That sounds fine." He never argued with me. So right away I started thinking, I know he's really not feeling well. This is serious.

It's great to see Frank back to his crusty self now. He's back to agitating people, which means he's feeling a lot better. In fact, he started to feel better once we got him stabilized at Columbia-Presbyterian Medical Center in Manhattan, before the heart transplant. Sister Marguerite found that out the day we clinched the East Division. She had called me up that morning from the Nativity of the

Blessed Virgin Elementary School in Queens, where she's the principal, and said, "I really can't come to the game today. I have a faculty meeting." Then she saw a picture of me on the back of *The New York Post.* I guess I must have looked pretty bad. She said later that she saw such a sadness in my face, brought on by Frank's illness, that she called up Rae and said, "Call Joe and get tickets. We're going to the game."

We won in a rout over Milwaukee, and Sister Marguerite called Frank the next morning to tell him about what happened: the blizzard of confetti at the stadium; me coming over to the stands to give kisses to Ali, Andrea, Rae, and her; the way all of us were crying; and how we all felt Rocco's presence there with us.

"Frank," Sister Marguerite said, "I'm telling you, it was an emotional high. It was the greatest moment of my life."

Frank listened as my sister gushed on about this incredible moment. And then it was his turn.

"It was nothin'," he barked. "They've still got three rounds of playoffs to get through. That was nothin'." Leave it to Frank to snap you back to reality.

I'm forever grateful that Frank is a little rough around the edges. He was exactly what I needed, especially when our father left. I was this shy, overweight kid with terrible self-confidence who was being coddled by his mother and sisters. Frank was the kick in the butt I needed to amount to anything in life. It was Frank who toughened me up, Frank who turned me into a catcher, Frank who put me through high school, Frank who used to send me spending money even when he was off fighting in Korea, and Frank who was everything I ever wanted to be. He was a ballplayer. I may not have had a father in my life then, but I sure as hell had a hero.

CHAPTER 3

The Wonder Years

RANK IS THE ABNER DOUBLEDAY OF paperball. Maybe no definitive proof exists that establishes him as the first person to come up with the game, but as far as I'm concerned, he was its founder. Frank always was inventing games in our neighborhood—games he passed on to me proudly, like heirlooms. One of those treasures was paperball. I'd take a brown paper bag, newspaper, or some similar paper product and roll it up into a ball. Then I'd wrap lots of rubber bands around it. The ball was nearly as hard as a rock. My buddies and I would go over to East Thirty-fourth Street, which in those days wasn't paved yet, and we'd play baseball between the houses—with specially modified rules.

The bat was a sawed-off broomstick. You had to bat on the opposite side of your natural hitting stance. The pitcher would have to lob the paperball in. If you hit the ball over a first-floor window, it was a double. Over a second-floor window was a triple. Anything on the roof was a home run. But if one of the fielders caught the ball on the fly after it hit a house, you were out. The kind of ball we used made for some interesting games. It wasn't perfectly round, so when it bounced off a house, the carom was a lot more unpredictable than one off the Green Monster in Fenway Park. Also, the ball was so hard, we did break our share of windows. The neighborhood always was alive with games like that. I lived in a neighborhood that consisted predominantly of Italian and Jewish families, with a scattering of Irish families too. It was a tight-knit neighborhood where everyone seemed to know each other and look out for each other. I hung out for years with the same group of eight to ten boys, spending much of our time playing games in the street and the park.

Frank kept us busy with his inventions, including another game in our driveway, which declined steeply from the street down to our garage. A short porch hung over the garage. Someone would throw a ball toward the top of the garage, and you'd have to jump as if you were trying to take a home run away from the other guy. Frank also showed me how to play stoopball, bouncing a rubber ball off the front steps of our house. Even though he was so much older than me, I'd play with him and his friends sometimes. I'd tag along with him as much as I could. If they happened to be one man short, I'd get to play with them. Even after Frank reached the big leagues, he'd play stickball in the street with me and my friends after the season.

The little automobile traffic we did get on Avenue T in

those days knew to slow down whenever it ventured down our block. Even though the park was so close to us, we seemed always to have a punchball, slapball, touch football, stoopball, or most likely, stickball game going on in the street. A home run in stickball was a ball that traveled two sewers. When darkness came, we'd move the game closer to the streetlights and just keep on playing. Every once in a while, especially when you'd have to go fetch a foul ball out of somebody's geraniums, a cranky neighbor would bark, "Why don't you kids go play in the park?" And we'd always have a simple, logical answer: The ball doesn't bounce nearly as well in the park as it does in the street.

The Brooklyn of my youth was a place where baseball was king. Nothing compared to it. Football was a game played mostly between the twenty-yard lines with very little scoring. We would play touch football in the street and have an annual Thanksgiving Day touch football game in the park, coming home all filthy dirty and bruised for the turkey dinner. But football had yet to ignite a real interest in most people. Basketball? Sure, we played it sometimes, and I gained great fame around the neighborhood for being able to palm a basketball at an early age with my big hands. But basketball as a spectator sport was nothing. Hockey? That was another boring sport, with most games ending up 0–0 or 1–0. Of course, my friends and I played just about any kind of game, including roller hockey. I couldn't skate, so I'd always be the goalie whenever we played in the street.

Baseball was our love, plain and simple. Until Frank left to play ball himself, he and I shared a tiny bedroom upstairs in our house. The place was wall-to-wall bed, so Frank and I slept next to each other, sharing the same covers. You couldn't fit two beds in that room. I never worried about being pushed out of bed by Frank because I slept on the side against the wall. The one bookshelf in the room was filled mostly with Frank's trophies; mine were scattered around the downstairs of the house. We had one closet that barely was deep enough to accommodate hangers. We'd put ourselves to sleep talking baseball. It was a time when America's passion for the game still ran deep, but nowhere with greater fervor than in New York. We always had at least one, usually two, and sometimes three big league teams involved in heated pennant races. Most people in Brooklyn were Dodgers fans, of course, but many in the borough rooted for the Yankees, who played in the Bronx—probably because the Yankees seemed to win every year. And then there was the Torre family. We were some of the few people in Brooklyn who rooted for the Giants, who played at the Polo Grounds in upper Manhattan. For reasons that are unclear to me, my brothers and sisters were Giants fans. And so I grew up a Giants fan too. Willie Mays and Don Mueller were my favorites. I hated the Yankees because they won every year. Every once in a while I sit back and laugh that my greatest accomplishment in baseball came with a team I despised as a kid. But deep down I admired them because I knew how good they were.

Every Giants fan who grew up in New York at that time knows exactly where they were the day Bobby Thomson hit his famous home run off Ralph Branca in 1951 to win the pennant over the Dodgers. It was my happiest moment as a Giants fan. The Dodgers held a thirteen-game lead over the

Giants that season as late as August 11. I found out about big leads with the Yankees: They never seem to be big enough. The Giants caught Brooklyn by finishing the season with a 37-7 run. In the last inning of the deciding game of a three-game playoff—it was 3:57 on the afternoon of October 3—Thomson hit a fastball from Branca into the left-field seats of the Polo Grounds to eliminate the Dodgers and put the Giants in the World Series. Ralph Branca's name became synonymous with being a goat while Bobby Thomson's name epitomized delivering in the clutch. I was eleven years old, talking on the telephone with Rae, who was at work, while watching the game on television. I immediately put the phone down and ran into the streets of my neighborhood, looking for any Dodgers fans I could find to gloat about my team's victory. I saw a car parked on the street, all soaped up in anticipation of a Brooklyn victory. It said "Brooklyn Dodgers. National League Champions." I got a kick out of that.

I followed baseball religiously. We were one of the first families on our block to get a television set. It must have been around 1947. I remember watching baseball games on that black and white set all the time. The New York teams would broadcast their home games. It wasn't until I left home as a ballplayer myself that I found out that not every team did that.

Despite our allegiance to the Giants, my father did take me on occasion to Ebbets Field. Though I was afraid of my father inside my house, those rare trips with him to the ballpark were great. I remember walking into this beautiful cathedral of a ballpark—and I'm amazed how the sounds of baseball there still ring clearly to me after all these years. The starting pitchers in those days would warm up right between the dugout and home plate. I can still hear the echo of the ball popping into the catcher's plump mitt as I walked up a tunnel to my seat, even before I could see the field. To a kid who was seven or eight years old, it sounded like a firecracker going off. My dad would buy me these five-by-seven pictures of the Brooklyn Dodger players that came inside white envelopes. I remember tearing open those envelopes and seeing Campanella, Hodges, Reese, Cox, Robinson, and the like. Though I wasn't a Dodgers fan, I respected anyone who wore a big league uniform.

Later on, when my brother played for the Braves, I became a real die-hard Milwaukee fan. In fact, when the Giants bolted for San Francisco and the Dodgers took off for Los Angeles after the 1957 season, I wasn't too angry about losing my favorite boyhood team and my hometown team. I was most upset about the fact that now I would have to go to Philadelphia, which was the closest National League city, to watch Frank and the Braves play. I used to feel sick when the Braves lost. I let myself get into a situation that I sometimes do now as a manager—thinking that somehow you can influence every pitch.

One of the most painful summers I recall was 1956, when the Braves squandered their lead in the pennant race to the Dodgers. I was riveted to the radio that September, rooting for the Braves to win. The Braves had a great rivalry with the Dodgers in those years. I'll never forget being at Ebbets Field one day in 1956 when Bill Bruton of Milwaukee hit a home run off Brooklyn's Don Drysdale. Johnny Logan was the next hitter. Drysdale knocked him down with a fastball. The next time around Bruton hit another home run. This time Drysdale responded by hitting Logan with a pitch, so Logan charged the mound. Logan never reached Drysdale, but Eddie Mathews did. Mathews popped Drysdale with a punch I could see clear as day even from the stands. I can still see him throwing that punch as if it was yesterday.

Although my life revolved around baseball, I did take on some odd jobs as a teenager to earn a little money. I worked for a while as a gofer in a printing shop owned by George Russano, the father of Richie and Robbie Russano, good friends and sandlot teammates from my neighborhood. I delivered the *Brooklyn Eagle* newspaper for a short time. I also had hung out at an amusement place on Avenue S and Flatbush Avenue long enough to get some work from the owner. He'd ask me and my buddies to set up the duckpins in his bowling alley. And he had us paint the golf balls for the miniature golf; we'd dip them in buckets of paint, roll them in our hands to make sure every dimple was covered, and then place them on a bed of nails to dry. I worked briefly at the Byhoff Brothers record store on Kings High-way—not that I remember coming home with any money. I came home with albums instead. I wasn't an Elvis Presley fan. That's because all the girls liked him. I liked the rock-and-roll singers like Buddy Holly, Lloyd Price, and the Big Bopper, as well as Johnny Mathis and Bobby Darin.

Mostly, though, my brief and unproductive periods of employment served only to get in the way of my playing baseball. If I couldn't be outside playing ball, then I'd be inside playing baseball board games with my friend Johnny

Parascandola, who lived around the block from me on East Thirty-fourth Street. We started out playing Ethan Allen's All-Star Baseball—a game with spinners—and then graduated to APBA, a dice game that included strategic options and cards of major league players with numerical designations that were supposed to reflect their actual performance. I can remember my mother stepping over us as we spent rainy days playing on the floor of our house. She'd be praying that the weather would break so that we'd get out from under her feet.

But usually we played in Johnny's basement with its low-hung ceiling. We spent hours upon hours down there, including a good chunk of our winters. We established a league and kept statistics. Even then I enjoyed the decision making involved in managing and always maintained my cool in tight games. Now, Johnny—he was another story. Once he became so enraged at his starting pitcher that he took the player's card and stuck it under a faucet of running water. "I'm sending you to the showers!" he yelled. Johnny would get so furious after losing a hotly contested game that he'd fling the whole game off a table, sending pieces scattering across the basement floor. I'd just sit there and ask, "Are you through?" And then I'd pick up the pieces, place them back on the table, and quietly ask, "Are you ready for the next game?"

Even when I was as young as ten, I enjoyed the nuances of baseball more than anything, mostly because Frank had schooled me in the proper way to play the game. After a sandlot game I liked to talk to my friends about why we won or lost. They'd talk about a last-inning home run or a crucial error, but I'd always talk about little things—such as the way the outfielder threw to the wrong base, allowing a runner to advance to set up a run. That's one reason I enjoyed the 1996 World Series as much as I did, especially that classic ten-inning Game Four. Sitting in the trenches trying to run the other manager out of players, while at the same time trying to keep an ace in the hole yourself—that's the kind of game where a manager can really influence the outcome. There were so many twists and turns in that Series that had nothing to do with hitting home runs.

At an early age I was in love with the game and all its splendid intricacies, the way someone else might fall for a girl and love every single feature about her, right down to the way she laughs. In fact, I had little time for girls growing up. The combination of my devotion to baseball and my awkward shyness assured that I was one of a vanishing breed of Americans that stayed a virgin through all his teenage years. Frank found that out in 1956. I was fifteen when he invited me to join him in Milwaukee for two weeks. I took an airplane ride for the first time in my life. On the second leg of the trip, leaving from an airport in Indiana or Ohio or someplace, the airplane had engine trouble and had to turn back. I was scared as hell. When I finally got to Milwaukee, Frank introduced me to his roommate, Tommy Ferguson, who was the visiting clubhouse attendant at Milwaukee County Stadium and who, like Frank, was single. "Tommy says you can work in the clubhouse if you want," my brother said, "shining shoes and hanging up jocks." It sounded like paradise to me. Frank, though, was the kind of brother who wanted to cover every end of my life. He figured I was at an age when my hormones were kicking in. So he arranged to set me up with one of his old girlfriends in Milwaukee, a bombshell of a blonde. I told my brother I wasn't interested; I was too busy working for Tommy. That wasn't the only reason, of course. I was afraid I wouldn't know what to do with a woman. I was still so shy and embarrassed about myself, I didn't dare take my brother up on his offer. To this day Frank likes to say I was more interested in hanging up jocks than in getting together with a beautiful blonde. And he was right. I wasn't exactly proud of my physique in those days either. I wasn't too thrilled to let my buddies or Frank's teammates see my body, let alone one of his old girlfriends. I just didn't have the confidence. Besides, what could be better than being at a ballpark?

Seeing Frank at the ballpark was always a thrill for me. Our whole family was so proud when he phoned with the news that he had been called up to the big leagues in 1956. Sister Marguerite was semicloistered in a convent in Blue Point, Long Island, at the time. The place was run by a very strict humorless Mother Vicar, who was from Belgium and spoke English with a very thick accent. Sister Marguerite had warned me about her whenever our family would go to visit. She'd say, "Now, Joey, don't laugh when she says something, because she's going to think you're laughing at her."

So our family was visiting Sister Marguerite right after Frank had been called up by the Braves. We were chatting about it when the Mother Vicar came ambling over to us, the rosary beads rattling in her hands. "Oh, now the Torre family is all excited," she said. "What is going on?"

"Well, Mother Vicar," Sister Marguerite said, "we're excited because Frank was taken up into the major leagues."

"Oh, my dear," she said. "Does that mean he's going to be playing against Notre Dame?"

I would have broken out in hysterical laughter, except I remembered how my sister asked me not to laugh around the Mother Vicar. I nearly burst my spleen keeping that laugh inside me.

One of the great perks to having a brother in the big leagues, besides getting the chance to hang out with ballplayers before games, was having them actually visit the house. Frank made sure to bring teammates to our house to eat whenever the Braves played in New York. I remember guys like Johnny Logan and Chuck Cottier and Eddie Mathews coming over to our house. My mother would bring out a large antipasto platter, and the guys would dig in. Then she'd bring out the lasagna, and they'd all stuff themselves. And then she'd bring out the roast beef and chicken, and they'd look at each other like "What's this for?" They thought they were finished with the meal after the lasagna. Wrong. My mother would make a six-course meal and, naturally, insist that they eat most of it. Those guys would wind up lying uncomfortably all over the floor in our house, completely stuffed.

Little brothers are known to pester their older brothers and friends with all kinds of idiotic questions, especially if their older brother's friends are big leaguers. But it was just the opposite for me. I was afraid to open my mouth around them. I'd listen intently as they talked about everything from the pitchers they batted against to their favorite restaurants on the road. But I'd always be too embarrassed to ask any questions. I was the same way in school. There were many questions I wanted to ask, but I was afraid of asking one stupid question, so I kept my mouth shut. I always admired the kid who asked the stupid question that I wanted to ask because at least he had the courage to do it.

Like Frank, I brought friends home for meals too—friends from the sandlots and, later, the big leagues. My mother was a terrific cook who kept the place stocked with food, as if she had to be ready with the necessary provisions for a great flood or snowstorm that would keep everyone housebound for weeks. The house always was open to friends and always for a full meal. She'd never just say, "Here, fix yourself a sandwich." She kept at least a dozen or so steaks in a freezer in the basement. I'd bring some of my friends over to the house after playing a sandlot game, and Mom would dig out five or six steaks for us. After she cooked them in the basement over an old stove, she'd put the steaks on a hand rack and turn them over an open flame to give them a barbecued taste.

One day when I was about eighteen I brought home a chubby friend of mine from Manhattan named Tony. We both loved music and enjoyed talking about our favorite rock-and-roll singers of those days. Of course, my mom filled him with food every time he stopped by. A number of years later, when I was managing the Braves, I got a call in spring training from him, saying, "This is Tony Orlando. How come you never ask me over to the house anymore?" Until then I just never realized that that chubby kid from

Manhattan was the same Tony Orlando who became a big-time singer.

Playing baseball kept me out of serious trouble when I was a kid. I had great respect for my mom and never wanted to embarrass the family in any way. Moreover, Rocco was a police officer in Brooklyn, so I knew the importance of staying on the right side of the law. I still had Rae's streak of honesty in me to keep me in line. When I did find trouble, it was more mischievous than anything else. One time I was with Johnny and a few other guys when we stole one of those street barricades, the kind with a yellow flashing light atop a sawhorse. We tried hiding it under our jackets as we transported it as inconspicuously as possible to our block, wondering if we could actually divert traffic so we could play without being interrupted by cars. I don't remember what happened to the traffic flow, but I remember that we were such honest thieves that we felt obligated to return the barricade the next day, prompting us to stage a repeat of our charade: a bunch of kids trying to move around a big flashing light atop a sawhorse without anyone noticing.

That was about the extent of my delinquency, hardly the kind of material TV cop shows look for. I wasn't a drinker either. I'd have a beer now and then, although I never liked the taste. At home I drank some red wine mixed with cola. Other than that, I drank only on those rare momentous social occasions when you thought you were supposed to drink—like at the prom. I remember going to Johnny's prom for James Madison High. I attended with a girl named

Dorothy Bortko. Johnny took one of my former girlfriends, Elisa Castellon. In those days there was no Verrazano Bridge between Brooklyn and Staten Island; only ferry service. The real "in" thing to do on prom night was to ride the ferry in the early morning hours—drinking and, if you happened to be supremely confident and lucky, necking with your date—after spending the evening at a nightclub. After we hung out at the Copacabana, we headed to the ferry. Johnny and some of the other guys had the booze. I was entrusted with the shot glasses. As I jumped onto the ferry, one of the shot glasses escaped from under the cover of my jacket and broke apart on the deck with a resounding crash that I imagined matched the decibel output of the A-bomb. The ferry people, with a wink, let us on anyway. It wasn't long before Johnny was teetering along the edge of the ferry— not exactly a wise manuever in the middle of the night, especially for someone who couldn't swim. I advised him he'd better get his feet firmly back on the deck. That was typical of me. I had my moments of being irresponsible, but for the most part I was a pretty serious kid who was aware of what was dangerous and what wasn't.

Even though baseball helped me stay in line, we didn't have Little League when I was growing up, so I had to organize my own team. The most renowned sandlot team in Brooklyn was the Brooklyn Cadets, which began playing in 1944 and, with Frank's help, won a national tournament in 1949. The Cadets were like the Yankees in those days; they won the city title almost every year. I was ready to be a Cadet when I was twelve years old. The problem was, you weren't allowed to play until you were in high school. So I

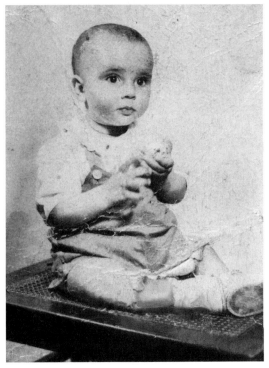

I was born Joseph Paul Torre on July 18, 1940, in Madison Park Hospital in Brooklyn, the first of my parents' five children to be born in a hospital.

One year old, on a pony in front of our house.

The front of our house at 3322 Avenue T in Brooklyn. The house has been in our family since 1935. My sister Rae still lives there.

Sister Marguerite, my sister, playing with me on our front stoop. She grew up with the name Josephine but changed it, as is the tradition, once she entered the convent.

Sitting between my two sisters, Sister Marguerite and Rae, who always doted on me.

Here I am, between my parents, at my brother Rocco's wedding in 1951. I remember this as my last skinny summer.

In Denver, Colorado, visiting with Frank. It would take me years and years of teasing before I lost the weight I gained in Denver.

I have always looked up to my brother Frank. This is Frank and me posing with some of his baseball trophies.

Frank, who was on his way to playing professional ball, ensured that I would start playing the game early. Rocco, who was in the Navy, was responsible for the Navy suit.

Thirteen years old, holding my nephew Robert in Rocco's apartment on Winthrop Street in Brooklyn. Robert had been at all the New York games during the 1996 World Series and at my house for the celebration after. He passed away suddenly in January 1997.

My eighth-grade graduation photo from P.S. 207.

The family out in Blue Point, Long Island, to visit Sister Marguerite at the convent. *From left to right:* Rae, Dad, Sister Marguerite, Rocco, Mom, and me.

My friends and I at the Copacabana the night of Johnny Parascandola's senior prom. Johnny is on my left.

This photograph ran in the New York papers on May 22, 1956, under the headline "Frank's Back With the Home Folks." Frank, already a hometown hero, was with the Braves, and they were in Brooklyn to play the Dodgers. *From left to right:* Rae, Rocco, Mom, me, and Frank. (INTERNATIONAL NEWS SOUND/PHOTO)

All my children came to celebrate Christmas 1996. *From left to right:* Michael's wife, Dayna, Lauren holding her daughter Kendra, Michael, me holding Andrea Rae, Lauren's husband, Gianni, and Cristina.

asked the coach, Dan Hill, if he had any old uniforms that my friends and I could wear so we could be just like the big kids. Hill said sure he did. So we'd get dressed up in these oversize Cadets uniforms and drum up some games, even though we weren't part of an official league.

Two years later, in 1954, I enrolled at St. Francis Prep, an all-boys parochial high school with about eleven hundred students in downtown Brooklyn. The rest of my family had attended public high school. When Frank paid the tuition, he said to me, "I want to make sure you really want to go there, and not just because your sister is a nun."

"Yeah, I want to go," I said. A good friend of mine from up the street, Bob Finelli, went to St. Francis, and it seemed like the fun thing to do.

It wasn't. I'm sure the education was great. But I quickly found out that the brothers who taught at the school thought nothing of whacking you with an open hand or a ruler. One of my teachers, Brother Charles, used to smack kids with a drumstick. I was so nervous around those teachers that I played hooky often, spending the day riding the trains. I just didn't want to go to school. Years later after the Prep went coed and moved to Flushing, Sister Marguerite wound up teaching at St. Francis. On one of her first days there she found herself in the bookstore talking with a brother who worked in the attendance office. When he found out who she was, he blurted out loud enough for the whole store to hear, "Ooooh, that brother of yours! Has he straightened himself out yet?" I wasn't exactly a bookish kind of kid in the first place, and once I missed a day of classes here and there, I was clueless. It was a dead-end

53

street. I look back on it now and realize how stupid I was to miss those classes and fall behind like that.

My high school years were not the best of times. The truth is that I had no confidence in myself. I didn't do anything, join any clubs or anything like that. I didn't even play baseball until my junior year. I think I tried out for baseball one time during my sophomore year but didn't feel confident enough to go ahead with it. I was a champion of self-defeat. I was this shy, overweight kid and didn't believe I had the skills or, especially, the confidence to play high school baseball. I didn't pull the ball—I hit naturally to center field and right field—and I thought that was a detriment. (It turned out to be a huge asset for me as a professional. It's much easier to hit when you can hit the ball to all fields.) Besides, when I was in high school my brother was on his way to the big leagues. I figured, how many families have *two* guys in the big leagues? I think back to the way I was, and it's too bad I didn't get involved more in high school.

In the summer after my freshman year, however, I did work up enough courage to join the Cadets, which really wasn't that hard to do because a bunch of my friends played with them. The Cadets played more than a hundred games each year over several different leagues. We played two or three nights during the week, doubleheaders on Saturdays and tripleheaders on Sundays, starting at nine-thirty in the morning. I remember I had to go to six-thirty mass on Sunday mornings, and I'd see people still dressed in Saturday night's clothes—staggering in sleepless from proms, weddings, or whatever.

That first season, playing in the freshman division for the Cadets, I was named the league's most valuable player while playing first base and pitcher, an honor I'd attain the next year as well. I also began to show further signs, that first year, of my future managerial skills. A couple of our players missed a practice right before one of our championship games, so our coach, Jim McElroy, suspended them. Many of the other guys got together and made some noise about not playing in the game unless the suspended players were reinstated. Here were fourteen- and fifteen-year-old kids discussing a strike of a championship game. I pulled the team together and said, "Listen, when we joined this team, we made a commitment to this team, and it's up to all of us to live up to it. It's our responsibility to play this game and for Coach McElroy to suspend those guys if he has to." I must have been persuasive—or maybe the guys were just chicken about going ahead with a strike—because we did play and the suspensions did stick. We wound up losing.

We played most of our games at the Parade Grounds in Brooklyn. The Parade Grounds included thirteen diamonds, only two of which had enclosed fences and stands. The rest were very ragged, dusty fields jammed together back to back. They had damn near flat mounds and clouds of dust with every step you took. With my shape in those days, I looked like a tumbleweed whenever I rambled around the bases. But the thirteen diamonds were almost always filled, especially during the weekends. The games at the enclosed fields drew large crowds, often with big league scouts included. In addition to Frank and me, other big leaguers who came out of the Parade Grounds included Sandy Koufax, Joe

Pepitone, Rusty Torres, Bob Aspromonte, Matt Galante, Frank Tepedino, and Don McMahon. I don't think they play as much ball there these days, but some of the more recent Parade Grounds graduates include Manny Ramirez of the Cleveland Indians and Frankie Rodriguez of the Minnesota Twins.

My mother came to some of my games, just as she had done with Rocco and Frank. She'd sit there in the stands clutching her rosary beads tightly in her hands, and she'd shoot the nastiest looks you could imagine to anyone who dared bring any kind of dishonor upon her sons, such as an opposing pitcher who threw a little too far inside. No one could give dirty looks like my mother. She didn't yell much during the game—she'd pretty much just be saying her rosary and throwing dirty looks. She was the same way when I got to the big leagues. Her support meant so much to me that I came up with a way to acknowledge her presence, whether she was at the game or watching on television. I told her that before every at bat I would take my helmet off and wipe my brow. That would be our little signal. And I did it every time I knew she was watching me at the plate. That was my way of saying hello and thanking her for all of her years of support and love.

During my second season with the Cadets, 1956, I stood about six foot one, weighed 240 pounds, and had a forty-inch waist. I turned sixteen that year. I was just about as wide as I was tall. Opposing teams took one look at me—this huge kid with a serious five o'clock shadow—and immediately complained to the umpire that I was way too old to be playing in that league. Jim McElroy took to traveling around with my birth certificate. Anytime we played someone who didn't know us, Jim would have to whip out that birth certificate and show it to the umpire.

After two MVP seasons with the Cadets, I finally convinced myself to play baseball at St. Francis Prep, starting in 1957. I did well playing first and third base, and I even pitched. I remember one home run I hit at Brooklyn Prep that cleared the fence and broke a window in the school. You don't forget those kinds of dingers. We had a left-handed pitcher who started calling me Joe Toots that year—I think because of all the chattering I did in the infield. I was always saying, "Come on, babe! Come on, toots!" Guys just started calling me Toots for short.

Sadly, that's something that's disappeared from baseball—all that infield chatter. It just doesn't happen anymore. Players today have less fun on the field than players of my generation did. The huge amounts of money involved have turned the game more into a business. In the big leagues I liked to talk on the field, especially when I was catching. I really enjoyed talking to hitters when they came up to the plate. I'd talk about baseball, restaurants, golf, whatever. I guess it drove some players nuts, like Tim McCarver. Timmy was wired a lot differently from me, when I first entered the league. He was a guy who fought himself, who thought he should get a hit every time up. Paul O'Neill and Tino Martinez are the same way. Later on Timmy and I would become not just teammates but really good friends. But one day in Atlanta in 1967, when he was playing with the Cardinals, he came up to me before a game and said, "Joe, look, I don't know what you're trying to do, but it really pisses me off when you talk to me in the batter's box. I'd really appreciate it if you didn't say anything to me." I just nodded to him.

The first time McCarver came up, I reminded him, "Now I won't say anything, just like you asked."

"Good," he growled.

I dropped into my crouch and put down a sign for Denny Lemaster, our pitcher that day. Everything was dead quiet, like McCarver wanted it. Just as Lemaster went into his windup to throw the ball, I broke the tense silence by blurting out, "I promise! I won't say a thing!" McCarver burst out in such a big laugh that there was no way he could swing the bat. The ball sailed past him for a strike. To this day he says he never laughed so hard and so sincerely during a baseball game.

I remember another game when I was catching for the Braves and Wade Blasingame was pitching against Houston. Blasingame hung a curveball to Rusty Staub so badly that as it was floating toward the plate, I said, "Oh, no!" Just as I feared he would, Rusty crushed it for a home run. As Rusty crossed home plate, he gave me a glance and said, "Oh, yes!"

At St. Francis Prep I turned out to be an even better hitter than I was a talker. Rocco's police assignments one summer were at Coney Island. He'd make sure the owners of the bat-a-way cages would allow me to hit for free. I'd hit until my hands broke open with blood. I'd hit the ball so far and hard that people would stop what they were doing and watch. The elevated subway train would pass by what would have been the outfield at those cages. I know I hit some balls over the train cars as they rumbled by, and they must have been three hundred feet away. Even one of the brothers at St. Francis Prep began to notice my hitting prowess. Brother Regis was the Latin teacher who gave students a healthy whack if they did something egregious like forgetting homework or missing class. But he would say to me, "When I come over to you and it looks like I'm going to do something, just yell, 'Baseball!' " The guy spared me a few licks.

Unfortunately, major league scouts didn't take as kindly to me. I never heard from any of them my senior year in high school, even though I hit about .500. Frank, though, did hear from at least one scout. I had pushed Frank to find out what the scouts thought of me, so he finally contacted somebody he knew with the Boston Red Sox. The scout sent back a telegram to Frank that said, "Not only is he not a major league prospect, he's not even a professional prospect." Everyone agreed: I was too fat and too slow to be a ballplayer. No one wanted me.

I later heard that Al Campanis, then a scout for the Dodgers, received a telephone call from someone that he should check out this certain first baseman–pitcher from St. Francis Prep. Campanis, who had signed Koufax out of Brooklyn under similar circumstances, decided to watch me play. He later summed up his report this way: "I couldn't believe it. The kid weighed about 245 pounds, and the other club knocked him out in the first inning. He went to first base and showed absolutely no coordination there. I turned the kid down flat."

Even my brother's team, the Braves, didn't want me.

Milwaukee farm director John Mullen called up Honey Russell, the same scout who signed Frank, to ask about me. Russell had been scouting me for a while. "Forget it," Russell told him. "He's a fat kid with no speed to play first base or third base." It didn't even help when I played great for the Cadets that year. I won the batting title at the 1958 All-American Amateur Baseball Association tournament in Johnstown, Pennsylvania, with a .647 average. (Frank had won the same batting title in 1949, making us the only two brothers to accomplish the feat.)

So instead of going off to play professional baseball somewhere, after I graduated from St. Francis I got a job working as a page on the American Stock Exchange. I earned thirty-three dollars a week. I still played baseball with the Cadets then. In fact, Frank had arranged through Jim McElroy to move me to the Brooklyn Royals, a team that played in a higher division than the Cadets. He figured the better competition would help me. However, I told them no thanks, that I'd prefer to continue to play with my friends. Jim always thought that showed a great deal of loyalty and humility. The truth was, it had more to do with my shyness. I wanted to stay around the people I knew.

I don't know what would have happened if I had stayed in the business of stocks and bonds. I liked the competitiveness of that arena. I liked the excitement on the floor—and the market was going crazy at the time. In fact, even after I made the big leagues, I would sell municipal bonds in the off-season. But as a high school graduate, I didn't know much and made my usual share of greenhorn mistakes, like the time I gave my family a tip to buy this great Cuban oil stock. Only Frank listened to me and bought some shares of United Cuban Oil. A short time later the government of Cuba was overthrown. Frank was none too happy about that. What I do know is that a tip from Frank that next year, 1959, changed my entire life.

Frank called up Jim McElroy before the start of the Cadets' season and said, "Jimmy, I want Joe to be a catcher. And as much as I want Joe to keep up the tradition and play for the Cadets, if you don't use him as a catcher, I'm going to put him on another team." Fortunately for me, the kid who had been catching for the Cadets was called into the service, so Jim agreed to switch me to catcher. Frank had a couple of reasons for wanting me to catch. First of all, I didn't have the body or the speed to play any other position as a professional. And second, he thought I was a candy-assed kid who needed to be toughened up. He hated the fact that I was the baby of the family whom my mother constantly coddled, calling me "my Joey" all the time. What better way to learn how to be tough than by taking foul tips off your body and getting run over by speeding base runners?

Actually, I liked catching right away, mostly because Frank sold me on the fact that it was the quickest way to the big leagues. I knew that not a lot of people wanted to catch, you didn't have to hit a great deal, and you didn't have to run fast. It sounded perfect to me.

Later that summer the Cadets were getting ready to go back to another All-American Amateur Baseball tournament in Johnstown. At the same time a firm on the American Exchange called Mann, Farrell, Jacoby and Green had plans for me: They wanted me to be a specialist clerk, which meant I would provide direct assistance to the broker on transactions. They would send me to school to be trained and would pay me if I was called into the service or the reserves. It was a full-time commitment. I'd have to give up baseball. I said, "Sorry, I'm going to the Johnstown tournament." I didn't tell the Exchange when I left for the tournament, so they fired me. I tried to collect unemployment, but they wouldn't allow it because they said I got myself fired, which was hard to argue. Big deal. How much unemployment was I going to get after making only thirty-three bucks a week?

I hit terribly at Johnstown, batting a buck-thirty or something. But by then the scouts were starting to see me in a whole new light. Suddenly, as a catcher, I had become a real prospect. Several clubs were interested in me, including the Giants, Cubs, and Braves. Honey Russell, in fact, called up John Mullen and said, "I want to give Joe Torre a five-figure bonus."

"What? What the hell happened?" Mullen said, remembering how Russell had flatly rejected me the previous year.

"He's catching now," Russell said, "and he looks great there."

St. John's University also wanted me and was prepared to give me a scholarship. I wanted no part of anything to do with books though. I decided what it would take a club to sign me: enough money to pay off the mortgage on my mother's house and to buy myself a brand-new Chevrolet Impala, which was *the* hot car at the time. For some reason Frank wanted me to sign with the Cubs. I guess he figured

Chicago had the most pressing need for a catcher. After all, his team, the Braves, had perennial all-star Del Crandall behind the plate. So the scout from the Cubs, Ralph DiLullo, presented his club's offer to my brother. Frank told him he was six thousand dollars short. DiLullo countered by saying he had reached his limit and wouldn't go back to his superviser to ask for more. The Giants offered even less than Chicago.

The Braves came through with what I wanted: $22,500 and a promise to send me to their Instructional League team in Florida that fall. As Frank likes to say, he had no choice but to let me sign with Milwaukee. So in August 1959 I signed my first contract. I was a professional baseball player. And I was a proud member of the same organization as my brother—not that my signing exactly sent squeals of delight through the Milwaukee front office.

The Braves' general manager, John McHale, called up Honey Russell and barked, "Why did you sign him? He looks like a boy bartender!"

Said Russell, "He'll be a better ballplayer than Frank."

I didn't know it at the time, but Frank had no problem telling other people the same thing. He'd say, "I'm nothing. Wait until you see my brother." Of course, he wouldn't lavish such praise on me when I was present. But the times I did get a small compliment from Frank—because he was so hard on me—meant more to me than any trophy or newspaper headline could.

With my bonus money I immediately paid off the mortgage on our house. I didn't get around to buying my car until the following year. By then I had cooled somewhat on the Impala, especially when Frank suggested I might get a good deal on a Ford through one of his many connections. Frank used to smoke cigars and play cards with a big car dealer in Milwaukee who gave special rates to Braves players. He put me in touch with the dealer's son, an eager young executive. I met him in the fall of 1960, when the 1961 models were coming out. He wanted to sell me a 1961 Thunderbird, but I explained how I preferred the look of the 1960 model, and we quickly worked out a deal. He was very easy to bargain with. He seemed very enthusiastic about selling a car to a ballplayer from New York. He explained that he was a big baseball fan who had grown up idolizing Joe DiMaggio. And that's how I wound up buying my first car, a 1960 T-Bird, from the future commissioner of baseball, Bud Selig.

CHAPTER 4

Destination: Milwaukee

I N SEPTEMBER 1959, ONE MONTH AF-
ter signing with Milwaukee at the age of nine-
teen, I telephoned Frank, who was playing
with the Braves. I was a little worried. "Frank,
I know the Instructional League is supposed to
be starting soon," I said, "and I haven't heard anything from
the Braves."

"Let me see what's going on," he said. My brother went
to the Milwaukee club offices to see John McHale, the general manager, and John Mullen, the farm director.

"What are you guys doing?" Frank said in his usual dip-
lomatic style. "My brother is supposed to be down in the
Instructional League, and he hasn't heard from anybody."

"Well," McHale said, "we feel he'd be overmatched down
there. The competition's too good for him. So we decided
against sending him there."

"Now you wait a minute," Frank said. "This organization

made a commitment to this kid. It was a promise. And I'm telling you, if I have to go right to the owner of this team, my brother is going to the Instructional League."

Frank, as usual, was persistent and persuasive. The Braves reluctantly agreed to send me to the Instructional League. I had lost some of my baby fat by then. I really had expected to be signed out of high school, so when it didn't happen, it snapped some sense into me. I knew I had to be more careful about my weight. However, I still weighed a robust 220 pounds when I entered the Instructional League in Florida. Mullen took one look at me and said, "You gotta get some of that fat off you." He came back three weeks later and said proudly, "See that? Now you look good." I didn't have the heart to tell him that I actually had *gained* five pounds since he saw me and was up to 225. But I think I looked in better shape just from the daily grind of catching. I was getting stronger. My body was getting firmer.

I started out catching only once every fourth day in the Instructional League, a league that included the top prospects of every organization. By the time the league ended, I was catching every other day and playing the outfield on the other days. I think it's safe to say I proved to the Braves that I was not overmatched. I wound up leading the whole damned league in hitting with a .364 batting average. My confidence soared. I knew heading into that league that I had above-average ability. I knew I had quick hands at the plate, and I had always been the best player on my block in Brooklyn. But now I knew that I belonged as a professional ballplayer. I still wasn't nearly as confident off the field—

I was still shy and chubby—but I felt at ease on the diamond.

A few months later, in February 1960, I unofficially reported to the Braves' spring training camp in Bradenton, Florida.

It was a little strange being there. I knew many of the Braves from my summer vacations visiting Frank in Milwaukee or from working out with them before games at Ebbets Field. But now I was a professional myself, and I had to go out and perform. At least I was in better shape since the last time most of the Braves had seen me. Warren Spahn took one look at me and said, "This can't be the same fat kid!" After a week or two, the Braves assigned me to a training complex in Waycross, Georgia. This kid who had grown up on the asphalt streets of Brooklyn amid sewers and stoops found himself amid swampy fields and snakes. You had to be careful while shagging balls into the outfield during batting practice. If you chased a ball deep into that murky field, you would come across some of those healthy-sized creatures. I wasn't much of a naturalist, but I guess I did show them something with the bat. My teammates found themselves tiptoeing through the high grass to retrieve my home run balls almost daily.

The Braves decided to assign me to one of their two Class C teams, which I figured was better than going to Class D, the lowest rung on the pro baseball ladder. The C teams were in Boise, Idaho, and Eau Claire, Wisconsin. The Braves sent me to Eau Claire, in the Northern League, because its manager, Bill Steinecke, was a former catcher and would be able to tutor me. He taught me mostly the old-school stuff about blocking the plate and, if you got banged up, just to spit on it and keep playing. Steinecke was a grizzled, gruff, tobacco-spitting old goat. I remember after games we'd take showers in this tiny room—no bigger than a closet—with three nozzles. You'd be taking a shower, and all of a sudden you'd feel something warm on your leg. It was Steinecke pissing on you. Steinecke's lessons were straight from the school of hard knocks. Those lessons actually underscored some of the same things I had heard from Frank, who wanted me to be more assertive. It was Frank who ingrained in me how important it is to have the people who play alongside you respect you. And the only way for that to happen is to go out there and play hard every day.

Eau Claire was a complete joy for me. You hear a lot of horror stories about players adjusting to their first minor league season—guys getting homesick, putting up with terrible living conditions and long bus rides—but I thoroughly enjoyed my time in Eau Claire. I lived with two other players in the house of an elderly couple. The three of us shared a room. The couple charged each of us five dollars per week, which was very reasonable for a guy pulling down four hundred a month to play ball. The wife was nicknamed Strawberry because of her strawberry blond hair. She used to make us coffee and breakfast in the morning and come to every one of our home games, yelling in her deep strong voice and clanging a cowbell. She called all of the players PT-ers, for pants tearers, because she thought we were all girl crazy and couldn't wait to tear the pants off the local beauties. "Go out and get all the girls, you PT-ers," she'd say. Strawberry was great. She was like having a mom away from home.

Eau Claire was a pretty suburban city with a pretty ballpark. Our team traveled in shiny red Chevrolet station wagons with the Braves' Indian logo painted on the side door. We all took turns driving, covering many miles, mostly at night. The worst trip of all was to Minot, North Dakota—an expedition of about six hundred miles. We stuffed all the baseball gear into a trailer and hooked it up to one of the wagons, which made driving that vehicle particularly difficult. You'd find yourself dozing off at the wheel sometimes. When you snapped yourself awake, you inevitably caused the wagon to swerve, and you'd look in the rearview mirror and see the trailer swaying back and forth like a fish, threatening to go crashing off the road with all the bats, balls, and equipment.

When we played in Fargo, North Dakota, we actually stayed across the state line in Moorhead, Minnesota, which was weird because Moorhead time was an hour ahead of Fargo. More than a few guys were confused when we tried to figure out what time we were supposed to be at the ballpark. The worst part was coming back to the motel after the game, because we lost an hour just on the ride back; we couldn't get anything to eat. Talk about bad eating habits— we hit more hamburger stands than doubles that season.

We played in other places such as Winnipeg, Manitoba; Aberdeen, South Dakota; and St. Cloud, Minnesota. The games could get heated because everyone from the players to the umpires was fighting his way to the big leagues. I had several up-close-and-personal confrontations in that league with future National League umpire Bruce Froemming. He threw me out of games six times that summer. I hated him, and he hated me. We both were young and had quick tempers. I'd complain about a pitch when I was catching, and he would scream back at me. Being the spoiled kid that I was, I'd scream back at him. Of course, he would always get the last word; he'd run me from the game. Usually he'd follow up on that by tossing Steinecke out of the game too. The Braves wanted to punish me for being so hot-headed by sending me to D ball. When Steinecke, who saw me crushing the ball all summer, heard about that, he said, "Why don't you send the kid to Triple-A instead?" He thought I belonged in a higher league, but I stayed in Eau Claire. Some people might have a hard time believing that I had such a short fuse then. Actually, I still have a temper now. The difference is I have more patience. It's just been a matter of growing up. And believe me, I took a long time to grow up.

As for Mr. Froemming, I guess his job is not as conducive to mellowing as mine. He's still a good umpire who likes to scream, and he's actually become a good friend as well. One day in the late 1970s, when I was managing the Mets through the course of yet another hopelessly lost game, I decided I'd try to fire up the club by getting myself thrown out. I don't even remember what the argument was about, but I ran out there to Froemming between second base and third base and was getting started with my expletive-filled act. But Bruce was too smart. "I know why you're out here," he said. "You're out here to get thrown out of the game.

And you know what? I'm not going to do it. No matter what you say."

"Well," I said, "I might as well take the opportunity to do this," after which I proceeded to call him every name in the book, especially those magic words that otherwise earn you an automatic expulsion. By the time I gave it up and left the field—still in the game, of course—I was laughing.

My first professional season, Froemming notwithstanding, was a huge success. I won the Northern League batting title by hitting .344. I banged out six hits in a doubleheader on the final day of the season to edge Max Alvis. I also finished with 16 home runs and 74 runs batted in over 117 games, made the all-star team, and was named the league's rookie of the year. I even stole seven bases, a modest total that I'd never again duplicate on any level. The worst part of that year was when the Braves demoted Frank to Louisville, one of their Triple-A teams. I was shocked. Frank was twenty-nine years old, had been in the big leagues for four and a half years, and had played on two pennant winners, and the next thing you know he's back in the minors. Looking back, that wasn't so unusual in those days—not with only sixteen teams in all of major league baseball. Competition for jobs was fierce, nothing like what you have today, where guys can easily hang on. Back then you had fewer major league teams and more levels of minor league clubs.

When my season ended, I headed to Milwaukee, where Frank maintained a home, to wait for him to come back from Louisville when his season ended. When I arrived in Milwaukee, I received a message to go see John McHale. I had no idea what it was about. I was stunned when he gave me the news: They were calling me up to the big leagues. It was a thrill just to be in that clubhouse and be getting dressed with all those great players. It really helped me that I knew most of the Braves players already; I wasn't as much in awe of the situation as I might have been otherwise.

My only regret was that Frank wasn't there with the Braves when I broke in. My timing, never one of my better traits, was the slightest bit off. We had missed each other by about three months, with Frank going down to the minors while I was on my way up. We played against each other later, in 1962 and 1963 when Frank was with Philadelphia, but we never played on the same team, except in spring training. Frank had had more to do with getting me to the big leagues than anybody else, so I would have loved to share the experience with him.

My promotion happened so fast and so unexpectedly that no one in my family saw my big league debut. People just didn't hop on a plane then as they do now. On September 25, 1960, I was sitting on the bench in Milwaukee, and left-hander Harvey Haddix of the Pirates was beating us 3–1 in the ninth inning. All of a sudden our manager, Charlie Dressen, yelled out, "Torre!" He wanted me to hit for Warren Spahn. I grabbed a bat and stepped in the batter's box. My legs were actually shaking. I figured I might as well just look for a fastball and hope to get some wood on it. The first pitch was a ball. Then Haddix threw me a fastball away, and I hit it up the middle for a base hit. When I got to first base, I was feeling on top of the world—until I looked over and saw they were sending out a pinch runner for me, Lee Maye.

I didn't even get the ball as a souvenir. I didn't even think about it at the time. Now rookies and veterans alike routinely stop games to claim the baseball from every milestone hit they get.

A few days later in Pittsburgh, Dressen used me as a pinch hitter again. This time Bob Friend, a right-handed pitcher, threw me a slider and two curveballs. That was it. I was soup, striking out on three pitches. My batting average went from 1.000 to .500, which is where it stayed for the rest of the season as I had no more at bats. When I came home to Avenue T, I was the hero of the neighborhood. It was only the previous summer that I had been playing for a sandlot team and catching for the first time in my life, and now here I was, a real big league player with a real big league hit to my credit. The best part was thinking about all those games of APBA baseball I played with Johnny Parascandola in his basement—all those big league ballplayers we pretended to be, through the magic of cards and dice. Now I was one of those guys. Even now, twenty years after my playing career has ended, every once in a while somebody writing to me for an autograph will enclose my own APBA card. Whenever I see one, it's like opening an old photo album.

After the 1960 season the Braves sent me back to the Instructional League to continue to work on my catching skills. I had the worst luck there. I developed a stiff throwing shoulder that kept me out of action for a few days. I wrote a letter to Johnny Parascandola telling him about it but asked that he not tell my mother. I didn't want her to worry about me getting hurt, because I knew she still thought of me as her baby. But really I was embarrassed about how it happened. I had been wading in a swimming pool, then come home and taken a nap with no shirt on in front of an air conditioner. (I've worn a shirt to bed ever since.) I also came down with tonsillitis and the flu there, which turned out to be a blessing in disguise. I lost about twenty pounds, dropping to 195. But when I went home to Mom's cooking, I quickly put the weight back on.

After one year of professional baseball, I was a training-camp holdout the next spring. There were no player agents in those days. I was getting my advice from Frank. The Braves offered to pay me six hundred dollars a month. I wanted a thousand. After my brief holdout of a few days, I agreed to play for eight hundred. Best of all, Milwaukee invited me to my first big league camp. It was the only time Frank and I played together, not including the stickball games on Avenue T. It meant so much to me to have the opportunity to play with him. In those days teams played a lot of split squad games, known as B games, and usually those games were on the road. The Braves would throw together a B squad consisting mostly of guys the club didn't have to find out about or didn't care to find out about. That's how I wound up playing a lot that spring with guys like Frank, Wes Covington, Johnny Logan, Billy Martin, and Warren Spahn.

One day Frank and I were driving to the Braves' training complex in my new T-Bird. I had had it out of Bud Selig's showroom for only a few months. I was approaching an intersection in the right lane as the light turned green. I passed a large truck that was stopped in the left lane. All of a sudden Frank yelled, "Watch out!" A man was driving through the red light on the other side of the truck. He struck my T-Bird on the front side. The car was totaled. We had no serious injuries, though Frank did suffer some nagging shoulder and back injuries that shortened his career.

Frank and I talked all the time that spring—we'd sit together on the team bus, and he would correct me during games. I'd come back to the dugout after an at bat, and he'd say something like "Did you know with two strikes that you move closer to the plate?" And I'd say, "Yeah. I did know that." That's Frank. He would be so aware of everything I did, no matter how subtle.

One day we were playing the Washington Senators in Pompano Beach. I was catching, Frank was playing first, and Spahn, whom everybody called Hooks, was pitching. Spahn kept shaking off my signs that day. Finally, after somebody smacked a curveball for a hit, I walked out to the mound. Naturally, Frank had to be there too.

"Curveball was not the pitch," Frank said to me. "We call him Hooks because of his nose, not because of his curveball."

Another time, during an intrasquad game, I blocked the plate against Frank and tagged him out. Frank got up from his slide cursing. It was tremendous fun playing that spring with him. I even had fun in later years playing against him when he was with the Phillies. Gene Mauch was the Phillies' manager then. He would hold clubhouse meetings before games to review how to pitch to the opposing hitters. Whenever the Phillies played the Braves, Mauch would ask Frank, "How should we pitch to your brother?" And Frank would lay out his plan of attack to get me out. Then, after Frank went out on the field for batting practice, Mauch would call the pitchers and catchers back for a clandestine meeting. Mauch had convinced himself that Frank was setting him up, so he'd change the way they pitched me. The kicker is that I absolutely destroyed Philadelphia pitching in the years Mauch managed the team.

Despite the joy of spending so much time with Frank during that 1961 training camp, one of my most vivid memories from that time doesn't include my brother at all. I remember playing the Yankees in Bradenton. It was the first inning, and Mickey Mantle stepped into the batter's box. He wore a rubber jacket beneath his uniform to sweat off some of the pounds he'd gained over the winter. To me, this twenty-year-old kid squatting behind the plate, he looked absolutely enormous. He appeared, as he did to many people in those glory days, larger than life. Mickey Mantle, right there next to me. I got goose bumps. I don't remember what he did that day, but I'll never forget what I did. I nailed a pitch from Whitey Ford toward center field. I hit it pretty well, but I think the wind helped it a little. Mantle chased after it, but the ball carried over the wall. Some moments just stay with you in life; the images never lose their sharpness of focus or richness of color. This was one of them: a home run off Whitey Ford, with Mickey Mantle, his powerful legs giving up the chase, looking up at the baseball that I had hit as it flew away against the blue Florida sky. I've always wished I had a picture of that moment. But I guess I do.

That happened to be the first spring camp in which the

Milwaukee Braves wanted every player on the team to stay together—black and white players alike. The South was very much still a segregated place then. In fact, the exclusive hotel in Bradenton where the team planned to stay wouldn't have us under those conditions, so we had to move out to the Twilight Motel in Palmetto, a neighboring town. And even there they had to feed us in a private room where no one else could see blacks and whites eating together. The whole thing just struck me as very, very strange. In Brooklyn there were blacks and whites and there were Jews and Italians—we were aware of our differences—but there never was any segregation. I just couldn't understand what was happening in the South. Segregation first struck me back in 1954, when I visited Frank while he was playing in Atlanta during his minor league days. I was a fourteen-year-old kid walking through the stands of Ponce de Leon Park when I saw a sign that said "Colored Water Fountain." And then I saw one that said "Colored Rest Rooms." I just didn't understand it. When the game started, I noticed that all the blacks were sitting in the outfield bleachers. They weren't allowed to sit in the stands with the whites. I said to myself, This doesn't make any sense. I had black kids in my high school, and they were treated the same as anybody else. I couldn't fathom why it would be so different in the South. It was like another planet.

I had a great spring in 1961: nine hits in 15 at bats, with four home runs and 11 runs batted in. I didn't expect to make the big club. After all, the Braves were set behind the plate with Del Crandall, an all-star who was only thirty years old. I wasn't surprised when they assigned me to Triple-A Louisville. The Braves also sent Frank to Triple-A. Unfortunately, they sent him to their team in Vancouver, where the roster was filled more with older players than with prospects. It felt kind of odd, because I think we both knew at that juncture that my career was in its ascension and that it was about to eclipse his. Frank was great about that, though. He continued to support me and encourage me—in his brusque manner—through our frequent telephone conversations. Frank was a very good hitter who could pull anybody's fastball. He talked to me a lot about the mechanics and strategies of hitting.

When the Braves sent me to Triple-A, Dressen, the manager, told some reporters, "We don't have to worry as much about a replacement for Crandall anymore. If anything happens to him, we'll send for Torre." Even Crandall was gracious, calling me "the best young catcher they've brought up to this club since I've been here." It was in Louisville where I first met another catcher in the Braves' system who would become a lifelong friend and source of many moments of hilarity on and off the field: Bob Uecker. Bob had been my brother's roommate at Louisville the previous season, and now he was my backup. Uke was a real sweetheart who always kept things loose around the team.

One time Bob got his hands on some rocket fireworks. He buried them in a canister near the back wall of the bullpen, where he sat during games. When one of our players, Neil Chrisley, hit a home run, Bob lit the fuse. The fireworks left the ground when Chrisley touched second base and soared so high that they didn't explode until he hit third base. Streams of brightly colored lights fell to the field. Chrisley was so shocked he almost forgot to touch home plate. Uke proceeded to make his fireworks salute a Louisville tradition. The crowd loved it every time—but not everyone else did. Uke's pyrotechnics violated a local ordinance that prohibited loud noises after 10 P.M. John McHale traveled from Milwaukee to Louisville specifically to tell Uke to knock it off. Uke was a great guy to have on your club. Over our several years together in Louisville, Milwaukee, and Atlanta, Uke and I must have shared a million laughs.

Meanwhile, in spite of Uecker's distractions, I continued my hot hitting, especially during one road trip in May when I was getting hits all over the place. By May 19 I was hitting .342 and had knocked in twenty-four runs in twenty-seven games. That night after a game in Omaha, my manager at Louisville, Ben Geraghty, tried to reach me in my hotel room. Trouble was, I was in someone else's room playing cards. Geraghty finally tracked me down at about two in the morning in my room after I had been in bed for an hour.

"Get your things packed," Geraghty said. "You're catching a three thirty plane to Cincinnati."

I knew what that meant. I was going to the big leagues. Crandall had been bothered by a lingering problem in his throwing shoulder. His backup, Charlie Lau, who became a famous hitting coach, had been filling in, but now it looked as if Crandall would be out longer than the Braves first thought. I rushed off to the airport, only to find that my flight was delayed until 4:50 A.M. Because of that delay, I missed my 7:25 connection in Chicago by five minutes. The next plane left at ten o'clock. I arrived in Cincinnati forty-five minutes before the Braves' game against the Reds, so they didn't play me. They gave me uniform number 15. I was twenty years old and had only 144 games of minor league experience. As it turned out, I'd never play another game in the minors.

Warren Spahn was the starting pitcher for the first big league game I ever caught. He had been pitching in the big leagues for as long as I had lived. The old left-hander called me over before the game and said, "Call your own game. If I don't agree with the pitch you call, I'll shake you off."

There was one thing I felt most nervous about: pop-ups. I had had trouble with them in the minors. The pop-ups would go above the height of the lights in those minor league parks, and I'd lose them for a moment. When they came down, too often they did so on the ground behind me. Thankfully, this was a day game. Sure enough, a pop-up went up behind the plate in the first inning. I saw it right away and caught it easily. There—that was what I needed. I was relaxed now. I had a great doubleheader: a home run off Joey Jay, a double, a single, and a circus catch of another foul pop-up with two runners on. I also threw out Frank Robinson, Vada Pinson, and Eddie Kasko trying to steal and, with a one-run lead in the ninth inning of the second game, saved the win by tagging out Pinson in a big collision at the plate.

Spahn, even though we lost the first game, shook off my signs only three times. I thought that was great—until I deduced later on that if Spahn didn't like the signal, he'd just throw the pitch for a ball. That's how good his control was. He was remarkable. Later that season I had the great honor of catching his three hundredth career win. The sad part about Spahn's pitching was that when he had his pin-point control, the umpires would give him pitches a little bit off the plate, but later in his career when he started losing that precise control, they stopped giving him those calls. And then it got ugly; he was hit hard.

Lew Burdette pitched the second game of that doubleheader. That was an experience, too, because Burdette was rumored to be a spitball pitcher. He told me before the game that he threw a "mystery pitch," and we worked out a sign for it. Burdette said I had to give him that sign quickly so that he had time to "prepare" to throw the pitch. A spitball breaks down so sharply that if you don't know it's coming, it's very difficult to catch. I found that out four years later, when I was catching Don Drysdale in the all-star game at Shea Stadium in New York. I knew Drysdale had a reputation for throwing a spitter, so I asked him before the game what sign I should use for it. He told me he didn't want me to use a sign; he'd just throw it sometimes when I called for a fastball. That didn't work so well. I wound up chasing it to the backstop three times. Burdette never told me or anybody else on the team what substance he used or where he stashed it when he threw his illegal pitch. He knew if he told a teammate about his secret and that person was traded, the word would be all over the league.

Unfortunately, I was hitless in my next ten at bats after that doubleheader. I lived in constant fear that at any moment I was going to be sent back to the minors. But six days after my first start, I had a home run, a double, and a single against the Dodgers, with my dinger coming off Drysdale. Then on Memorial Day my family came to see me play in the big leagues for the first time. It was a doubleheader in Philadelphia. My mother, Rae, an uncle, an aunt, and my girlfriend at the time, Joan Zock from New Jersey, came to see me at Shibe Park. I had another good day, with four hits in the doubleheader.

Another time at Shibe Park that year, Johnny Parascandola came down to watch me play. It was another doubleheader. I didn't play the second game, so I watched from the bullpen. I invited Johnny to come watch with me. In the back of the visiting team's bullpen, in a small storage area where the ground crew kept the bases and equipment, there was a door that opened to the street. I told Johnny to meet me there, and I let him in. Rumor had it that some players would duck out that door during games, sit at a bar in uniform, and drink a beer while watching the game on television. I do know that the visiting bullpen used to be the home team's bullpen. But the Phillies' front office switched bullpens after they found out their players were smuggling women through that door and into the bullpen.

Though many of my friends and family watched me play that year, Sister Marguerite was not allowed to leave the convent. That really bothered me. I wanted everyone in my family to come see me. I wrote a letter on Braves stationery to Cardinal Spellman, the archbishop of New York, asking that he contact the Mother Vicar and allow my sister to come to the ballpark. But they refused to excuse her. The Mother Vicar told her, "Just as you have rules in baseball, so we have rules in the convent." My letter, though, did convince them to allow Sister Marguerite to watch my games on television. The rest of the convent would be at church or a novena or something, and the Mother Vicar would tell her, "Your brother is on. You can stay and watch."

One of the first times I remember Sister Marguerite coming to watch me play was at a doubleheader at Shea Stadium in New York against the Mets on Mother's Day in 1965. She had been assigned to a convent in Connecticut, and her Mother there was much more lenient than before. My mom was at the game too. Before the first game Sister Marguerite gave me a St. Joseph's medal. I pinned it to the inside of the left sleeve of my uniform shirt. Sure enough, I hit a home run and a single. In the second game I popped out my first time up. I looked for the medal and it wasn't there. Suddenly I realized that between games I had changed shirts. I sent the batboy into the clubhouse for the medal and pinned it on the new shirt. I promptly banged out four straight hits, including two more home runs. On each one of my homers I waved to my mother and family in the stands as I ran between second and third base. They stood up and waved back. After the game, instead of traveling with the club to Pittsburgh, I went back to Brooklyn and spent the night at home. When I caught up with the club the next day, I read in the newspapers that the Mets had tried to obtain me from the Braves—for half a million dollars. Nothing ever came of it, except that it was great for my ego.

My early success in my rookie season put me at ease right away. I wasn't intimidated facing great pitchers like Drysdale and Koufax—not that the National League pitchers didn't try to shake me. I remember facing the Giants for the first time. Jack Sanford threw his first pitch right at my head. I had never met the guy before in my life. The game was different then. At that time they were going to see how you responded. You were being tested. If they found out you were afraid, you might as well have gone home. My thinking—and I felt this way throughout my career—was that I'd rather get hurt than be embarrassed. That was the way the game was played; there was an unwritten but understood code about throwing at hitters, a code that has disappeared partly because the union and frequent player movement have diluted the adversarial nature of the game. Players seem too friendly with their opponents now. I especially hate to see pitchers laughing it up with opponents before games. They should have an air of mystery about them when they're facing a hitter.

Those Braves of the early 1960s, the team I grew up with, were a bunch of rough, tough, hard-bitten veterans. It was a team with swagger. It was easy for me to fit in there because I knew most of those guys. If I had to start out cold with another group of guys, it would have been a lot harder on me.

Frank also had prepared me for the big leagues by teaching me how to be a professional. For instance, he taught me at an early age that you never touch anybody else's equipment. If I saw Crandall's shin guards with his number on them, I wouldn't touch them. But if his number was crossed out, then I could use them. Knowing how to act made it easier for me to be accepted as a rookie. Spahn and Burdette were especially helpful to me. They were like older brothers. They used to take me to the movies with them in the afternoon and to restaurants at night. Dressen, however, wasn't too hot about me striking up a friendship with them. "Don't hang around Spahn and Burdette," he'd say. "They're like the Katzenjammer Kids."

Spahn and Burdette used to make Dressen's life miserable. Dressen liked to be a disciplinarian, always making sure we made curfew, for instance, which was a big deal in those days. In Chicago, where we always played day games, Dressen would give a baseball to the hotel elevator operator, who came on duty at midnight, and tell him to get every player to autograph it. That way Dressen knew who was late getting in. Guys like Spahn and Burdette, though, caught on to the trick and started signing wrong names on the ball. Spahn and Burdette were also the kind of guys who were always the last ones on the bus. One time Dressen got so fed up with them that he flat-out left them at the airport. Just when they got to the door of the bus, Dressen made the driver close the door and take off without them. Another time Dressen was hiding in the bushes of the Ambassador Hotel in Los Angeles, spying on the players as we would come and go from our cabanas around the main lawn in front. While Dressen was in the bushes keeping an eye on us, Burdette tossed a firecracker in there, scaring the hell out of him.

Dressen always was keeping tabs on us. One day in Pittsburgh he sent a house detective to check on Eddie Mathews and Bob Buhl, a pitcher who had arms like a blacksmith. Neither one of those guys had gone out that night, but Dressen didn't know that. He thought they were still out carousing somewhere. So the house detective knocked on the door to their hotel room. I happened to be in the room across the hall. All of a sudden I heard some yelling and screaming. I ran to my door and peeked out. There was Buhl holding this guy up by his collar with one hand—the detective's feet were dangling about a foot off the ground—and Mathews was standing right over Buhl's shoulder yelling, "Don't you ever pull this shit again, or else we'll knock the crap out of you!"

Mathews was the embodiment of those Braves teams. He was a man's man, a guy who needed a shave every time you saw him, who played the game hard, and who worked to make himself a better player. Eddie had started his career as a bad defensive player but became a pretty good one through sheer hard work—much the way Wade Boggs, my third baseman with the Yankees, worked hard to become a gold glove defensive player. Mathews was one of my idols growing up, and so it was a real thrill to have him as my teammate.

Hank Aaron was one of the quietest players on the team. He would dress immediately after games and go home, just slide out of there without anyone noticing. That was unusual, because in those days players hung out together in the clubhouse after games. I don't know why, but players scatter from the clubhouse much more quickly today. But I never saw Hank off the field. Of course, I realize now that when I played, black players were careful about not going places where they would be embarrassed. There were still many public places where they were not welcome. Hank was a quiet guy anyway, and I think that's why he never got the recognition he truly deserved. I know later in his career he resented not getting proper credit for his extraordinary skills and career. Willie Mays would get much more attention, mostly because he had a much flashier style and played in New York. But Henry was a better hitter than Willie; he had fewer holes. Willie had a knack for rising to the occasion, but Henry would do everything to win a game, including stealing bases when he had to. Willie played center field, a more glamorous position, while Henry played right field. Willie would sometimes fire the baseball to the catcher on the fly, while Henry would always throw the textbook one-hopper to the catcher or hit the cutoff man. That was Hank's style. He didn't call a lot of attention to himself.

I didn't dream at the time, in the early 1960s, that Henry would become baseball's all-time home run king. He wasn't a home run hitter. While Willie would hit those long high flies with his big hard swing, Henry would just smash line drives all over the field with those quick strong wrists of his. Believe me, no one better appreciates his amazing hitting talents than me—I hit behind him in the batting order for eight years. I used to stand there on deck and watch him just devour pitchers, especially young ones. They'd get two strikes on him and figure they could waste a fastball inside and then go away with something off speed—except they'd never get to that second part of their plan. Henry would just eat up fastballs. Never in my life have I seen a better fastball hitter than Henry Aaron.

The one guy who Henry could not hit was Curt Simmons of the St. Louis Cardinals. Simmons once said, "Sneaking a fastball past Henry Aaron is like trying to sneak the sun past a rooster." So Simmons would throw Henry one big, slow sloppy curveball after another, and Henry never hit them. Henry would manage some measly twelve-foot pop-up and have to laugh himself at how easily Simmons could get him out. Then one day in September 1965 Henry decided he'd run up in the batter's box to try to hit that big slow hook before it even reached the plate. He tried it his next to last time up and popped out to shortstop Dal Maxvill. The home plate umpire, Chris Pelokoudas, said to Tim McCarver, who was catching at the time for the Cardinals, "If Maxie drops that ball, I'd have to call him out." In the ninth inning, with the Cardinals ahead by a run, Aaron tried the same thing. This time he blasted the damned pitch on the right-field roof. As soon as Henry made contact, though, Pelokoudas yelled, "You're out!" Well, just about our entire ballclub went nuts. Pelokoudas wound up ejecting several of our guys. I was on deck but managed to stay in the game with a more restrained argument. I asked Pelokoudas, "Would you have made that call if a hitter of lesser stature was up?" He always called his games by the book. It seemed to me that Pelokoudas delighted in making that call. If he hadn't, the magical number atop the all-time home run list would be 756, not 755.

I had three managers in my first three seasons in the big leagues: Dressen, the J. Edgar Hoover of managers; Birdie Tebbetts, who replaced Dressen midway through the 1961 season; and Bobby Bragan, who actually lasted three and a half years before he too was fired. I had a tough time playing for the Braves in 1962. Crandall was back playing, and I became a cold weather catcher. If Tebbetts thought it was too cold to risk Crandall's cranky shoulder, he'd start me instead. I hit .282 that year with only 220 at bats, about half as many as the previous season. Every day when I came to the park, I didn't know if I'd be playing or not. I hated that. But I'll always remember that Birdie Tebbetts used to say something about himself that applies to me as a manager now: He was easier to get along with when his team was losing than when it was winning. As long as players are giving you their best effort when they're losing, what can you do? If you start yelling and screaming at them, you'll only make them more uptight. I've always felt more compassion for players when my teams were losing. But if we were making mistakes while we were winning, it would aggravate me, because over the long haul you're not going to get away with mental mistakes. Don Zimmer, my bench coach with the Yankees, found out that I'm more of a stickler when we're winning. Somebody would miss a sign or a cutoff man, and I'd get angry in the dugout. Zim would say, "Relax, what are you getting excited about?" That's what was so great about having him around. He gave me energy when I needed it and calm when I needed that.

By 1963 I had wrested the starting catching job away from Crandall. That was the year I made the all-star team for the first of five straight seasons, a year I hit .293 with 14 home runs. My career was taking off, and the Braves knew it. They traded Crandall to San Francisco after the 1963 season. The job was mine, though I'll always be grateful to Crandall for being a true professional and being so quick to help me during my first few years in the big leagues. Beginning with that difficult 1962 season, my home run total improved four straight years, from five to 14 to 20 to 27 to

36. In 1965, only my sixth year of catching, I won a Gold Glove as the finest defensive catcher in the National League. My star was shining—so brightly, in fact, that it even blinded some people. In 1964 my manager at the time, Bobby Bragan, said, "There is no doubt in my mind that he will become one of the truly great players of baseball. I wouldn't trade him for anybody you could name, and that includes Willie Mays, Sandy Koufax, and all the rest."

I had become one of the elite players in the game. But the eight seasons I played with the Braves—five in Milwaukee and three in Atlanta—were far from gratifying. Not only did we not win anything over those years, but we never even managed to play our way into a pennant race. Once again my timing was terrible. Before I arrived in 1960, Milwaukee very nearly had won four straight pennants. It finished a close second in 1956 (losing out to the Dodgers on the last day of the season), finished first in 1957 and 1958, and lost a best-of-three playoff to the Dodgers in 1959 after the two clubs finished the regular season tied. (The Braves lost both playoff games by one run.) Frank was lucky enough to play on all of those great Milwaukee teams. My years with the Braves included not a whiff of such greatness. We were never terrible but almost always barely a notch above mediocre. From 1960 through 1968 my Braves teams won between 81 and 88 games every year but one, 1967, when we managed only 77 wins.

We were a club that could pound the ball as well as anyone. In 1965 we set a National League record with six players hitting at least twenty home runs—and finished fifth. Our problem was that we couldn't hold down the other teams. We never had enough pitching. I joined the Braves just as the golden years of pitchers—Spahn, Burdette, and Buhl—were running out. The pitchers who followed them, such as Tony Cloninger, Hank Fischer, Wade Blasingame, and Denny Lemaster, never developed into the same kind of consistent winners.

I hungered for more than just playing decent baseball. I wanted desperately to reach my dream of playing in the World Series. Through Frank I had seen what it was like to play for a winner. And in 1960, when I was a wide-eyed kid in the big leagues for the first time, I saw the excitement in Pittsburgh as the Pirates prepared for the World Series. We played a series there at the end of the year that meant nothing as far as the standings were concerned. The Pirates had already clinched the pennant. But I could feel the electricity in the air. It was invigorating. It was what I wanted. It reminded me of being in the clubhouse in 1957 in Milwaukee with Frank. For the next thirty-five years I hated to watch the celebrations after the World Series or championship football or basketball games ended. It was like watching somebody else eat a hot fudge sundae. I wanted one too.

CHAPTER 5

Growing Up Again

I LOVED THE MAJOR LEAGUE LIFE—
the hotels, the travel, the restaurants, the
nightlife, and all the trappings that come
with being recognized wherever you go. People considered ballplayers heroes in those
days, not as millionaire celebrities as they do now. I was
earning $17,500, a decent amount of money for 1963. I was
young, and I was single. But not for long. In the early
1960s Frank and I used to go to Miami every January to
begin working out for the season. We'd stay at a motel,
work out with some other big league players at Flamingo
Park, go to the racetrack, and then hit the nightclubs, including the Playboy Club in Miami. One night, in January
1963, I met a twenty-one-year-old Playboy bunny named
Jackie. I married her nine months later.

Looking back, I was much too immature and irresponsible at the time to get married. I'm embarrassed to think of

how I acted then. I didn't listen to my family's constant warnings that I wasn't ready to get married. I felt I had reached a level of independence from my family where I didn't need to listen to them. The first time I brought my fiancée to meet Sister Marguerite, we went to her convent on Long Island. Sitting next to me in the company of a nun, my sister, Jackie started stroking my thigh with her hand. I did nothing to stop her. Sister Marguerite's eyes grew wide as they lowered to watch what was happening. She knew right then we had no business being married.

The spring after I met Jackie was the first time the Braves trained in West Palm Beach after all those years on the west coast of Florida. I got to see Jackie often. We rushed through our engagement, and then, on October 21, 1963, we were married without anyone in my family in attendance. I didn't bother inviting them because I knew they all disapproved of the marriage. I'm sure I hurt them very much, especially my mother. It didn't take very long for us to find out our marriage wasn't working. It seemed like we were talking about a divorce almost immediately. And then, two months after we were married, Jackie became pregnant. We put our divorce plans on hold until after the baby was born.

We never really set up a traditional home but moved from one apartment to another. It was a very disjointed relationship. I can never say, though, that my first marriage was a big mistake or that I regret it. That's because out of that marriage my son Michael was born. He's always been the kind of son that makes a father proud, even if this father may not have devoted as much time as he should have to raising him. I was having too much fun in those days. I was like a kid in a candy store, thinking I should have anything that I wanted without attaching any responsibility to it. Sadly, sometimes I applied that attitude to my family.

Because of my experiences at that age, I have a keen understanding of how and why young players get swept away with themselves when they get to the big leagues. Two of my players with the Yankees, Dwight Gooden and Darryl Strawberry, are prime examples of that. I'm patient with the attitude of some young players because I was a rebel myself. But there's a big difference between being selfish off the field and being selfish on the field. I'm very proud to have been an unselfish player throughout my career. I have little tolerance for a player who puts his personal goals ahead of winning.

After the 1964 season ended, and seven weeks after Michael was born, Jackie and I started divorce proceedings. I ended up retaining custody of Michael, who basically was raised by my mother and Rae, until my mother's death, when Sister Marguerite got permission from her superiors to live at home with them in Brooklyn. He grew up in Frank's and my bedroom at our house on Avenue T.

At the age of twenty-three, after batting .293 in 1963, I held out of Milwaukee's training camp because of a salary dispute. I stayed out of camp for three weeks until they came up with a number I liked: $28,000. And then I went out and had a breakthrough season in 1964. I batted .321, with 20 home runs and 109 runs batted in. The Braves rewarded me with a raise to $39,500.

It was in that 1964 season that the Braves announced

plans to move the franchise to Atlanta. The people of Milwaukee tried to muster enough support to keep the team there. We drew almost one million people that season while finishing in fifth place, only five games behind the league champion Dodgers in a tightly packed race. Still, that was not an overwhelming show of support for a franchise that had drawn more than twice that many fans (2.2 million) only seven years earlier. We were bound for Atlanta. The city of Milwaukee, though, kept us there for one more season by obtaining a restraining order in court to postpone the move. It was a terrible decision because it created a lame duck status for us. In 1965 we drew only 555,584 fans. Every night at County Stadium, it was like playing in front of your closest friends.

I didn't shed a single tear about leaving Milwaukee, even though I had great memories of the place during the years my brother Frank and I were there. I was at a selfish stage in my life where I wanted a more exciting city. Milwaukee had some nice restaurants and would have been fine if I were older, but it had very little nightlife. I couldn't wait to get to Atlanta and Peachtree Street, where all the bars and clubs were. I remembered visiting the city in 1954 when Frank played there in the minor leagues. It was a dynamic, vibrant town. I recalled a minor league all-star game there in 1954 that drew so many people that they put the overflow part of the crowd in the outfield and rigged up a rope fence in front of them. I knew Atlanta would be more excited about having a baseball team than Milwaukee.

I thought I was hot stuff then. In 1965, in discussing my $39,500 salary with a reporter, I joked that "I don't keep much of it anyway. Between taxes and my love for clothes, it all goes." That wasn't far from the truth, though I was also great at picking up tabs at restaurants and bars. I owned eight suits at that time, for which I paid about $150 each—a princely sum in those days. I bought them from Gene Oliver, one of my Braves teammates who worked in the off-season at a Rock Island, Illinois, clothing shop. I also bragged to the reporter that I owned about forty-five shirts, fifty ties, and seven pairs of shoes. I still enjoy nice clothes and shopping for them.

I became so full of myself that around that time Frank scolded me for forgetting about Mom. "Damn it, Joe," he said to me on the telephone one day. "You know she was your mother before you became a big leaguer, and she doesn't love you because you're in the big leagues. She loves you as a person, and you've got to treat her accordingly." I can't say the message hit home immediately. I spent too much of those years in the mid-1960s acting like a jerk. Frank, in fact, became so ashamed of my irresponsibility that he stopped talking to me for a year or so.

Atlanta suited me fine in every way. In addition to christening the ballpark there with its first home run, I went on to hit thirty-six home runs that season, a record for a Braves catcher that still stands. Balls fly out of Atlanta County Stadium because of the warm air and lack of troublesome winds. It got to the point where the ballpark was referred to as "the Launching Pad." I also batted .315, knocked in 101 runs, and established myself as one of the true clubhouse cutups. One day I flopped around the clubhouse wearing a complete outfit of scuba gear that belonged to Felipe Alou, my teammate. My defense, though, worsened. My work habits behind the plate were getting sloppy. After winning a Gold Glove the previous season, I made 11 errors and was charged with 13 passed balls in 1965. My manager, Billy Hitchcock, told me after the season that I needed to lose weight; I probably weighed about 220 pounds at the time. "I'd hate to see Torre remembered as simply a good hitting catcher," Hitchcock told the press, "because he has the talent—and has shown it—to be one of the best defensive catchers around. He could wind up as the greatest all-round catcher of all time."

I did briefly lose a little weight, with the help of three weeks of military life and cutting back on the food on a goodwill baseball tour of Vietnam after the 1966 season. After a sendoff from President Johnson in Washington, I traveled there with five others: Mel Allen, Brooks Robinson, Harmon Killebrew, Hank Aaron, and Stan Musial. In other words, everyone in our party except me wound up in the Hall of Fame. In January 1997 I failed on my fifteenth and final try to be voted into the Hall of Fame by the baseball writers. If only I had managed seventeen more hits while I was playing—just one extra hit each season—I would have finished with a lifetime .300 batting average instead of .297. That would have improved my candidacy, though I never had the great power numbers or postseason exposure that catches voters' attention. I am, however, a proud member of the Parade Grounds Hall of Fame and the Italian American Hall of Fame.

My trip to Vietnam had its scary moments, but I guess it helped me that I still was young and a little wild at the time. I didn't have enough sense to be afraid. We spent one afternoon in Da Nang having lunch at the home of a General Walt. The next day, after we had left, it was mortared. The planes we traveled in would get fired at by the Vietcong, though not enough to cause serious damage. I did, however, see many bullet holes in the wings. Because that was a strange war where there were no lines drawn, it was difficult to tell who was the enemy. But whenever we were flying, we could tell the Vietcong from the Vietnamese: the Vietcong were the ones diving for cover into the rice paddies.

Most of our time during the day was spent shaking hands and talking baseball with the troops. But one night they asked Stan Musial and me to visit a small unit in a cemetery. They gave us both pistols. We drove in a jeep with the headlights off for camouflage; the driver had to point a flashlight straight down the narrow pathway to see where we were going. Stan was sitting in the front, afraid to say a word. He didn't like it one bit. I sat in the back. As I said, I was young and stupid, and I was having a good time on the trip being with these great baseball players. It was like an extension of the season for me. When we got to the place where the unit was stationed, we discovered about twenty troops bunkered in a tiny hut made out of ammunition boxes. Stan decided he was going to stay in the jeep. I joined the unit and said hello to the guys. Then at nine o'clock the unit started harassment fire, in which they expel rounds just so the Vietcong wouldn't get comfortable. They happened to be firing right over the top of Stan and the jeep. He couldn't wait to get the hell out of there.

I'll always remember how happy the troops were to see us. Those guys were great and, no matter what their condition, loved talking baseball with us. I recall visiting this one soldier and staring at his helmet. It had one hole in the front and another on the side. A bullet had gone through the front, grazed his head, and gone out the side. He was lucky. I left with enormous respect for those fighting men. And they made me feel lucky too. As a ballplayer, I was required only to join the reserves. I was fortunate not to be in harm's way like them.

The next season, 1967, had to be the height of my irresponsibility. We had an awful team that year, the first losing season for the Braves since 1952. We finished in seventh place, twenty-four and a half games out of first place, but we led the league in drinking and hospitality. That was also the year Clete Boyer and Bob Uecker joined the Braves and became my partners in crime. Boyer and I bought a bar in Atlanta called Pig Alley. Players from other clubs used to come to our place to drink, and we never charged them anything. It was a hell of a place. I don't know how we did it, but I think we ended up losing only about five dollars apiece on that investment. Pig Alley was one of the big reasons why the newspapers used to call that Braves team "the playboys of Peachtree."

On June 6, 1967, the Braves made a trade with the Phillies to get my buddy Uecker. Uke has made a second career for himself by making fun of his baseball abilities, but he was a good defensive catcher with a strong arm who was particularly adept at catching knuckleball pitchers. Atlanta figured he would be perfect for Phil Niekro, our ace knuckleballer. That was fine with me. I knew how difficult it was to catch that pitch. I had a standard line when people asked me how to catch the knuckler: "Use a big glove and a pair of rosary beads." On the first day Uke joined our team, I laid out a white carpet of towels from the door to his locker, where I hung a sign: "Thank You Very Much. God Bless You. And Lots of Luck. Your Buddy, Phil Niekro."

I was so happy to see Uke again that I invited him to be my roommate in Atlanta. We stayed in an apartment complex that loosely was arranged in two sections, one for families and one for singles. Somehow I was in the family section when Uecker joined me. We threw great loud parties in that place, always inviting players from visiting teams to drop in. Unfortunately, drinking was an accepted and sometimes encouraged form of behavior around baseball in those days. I'm glad we've come a long way since then.

The people who ran that apartment complex finally got so fed up with our parties that they kicked us out into the singles section. The apartments there had the exact same floor plan as the ones on the family side, only they were reversed—like a mirror image. On our first night after moving to the new apartment, Uke and I went out and partied long and hard. I made it home first. A while later I heard Uke come through the door. Then I heard him stumbling down the hallway, bouncing off the walls in the dark. He reached for the door of what he thought was the bathroom, took a step inside, and threw up. When we awoke, we found out that Uke actually had thrown up in a closet; he was accustomed to the old apartment and wasn't sober enough to remember the reversed floor plan.

Uke wound up catching a lot after joining us because I had a strained ligament in my ankle. I wore a cast for a while and couldn't play. That happened to be during the middle of the summer, while we had a grueling stretch of doubleheaders. Uke used to kid with me every day about my injury. "How long are you going to nurse that thing?" he'd say. "What's the big deal about a cast? You can play with a cast. Just tape it up and get out there. I'm wasting away here. My hat size has already shrunk from a seven and a quarter to a five while you're milking that injury. I figure the more I play, the closer I am to going back to the minors."

One day during that 1967 season, we were taking batting practice before a game against the New York Mets at Shea Stadium when I noticed a great-looking blonde sitting in the stands. A New York photographer I knew, Louie Requena, came up to me and asked if he could take a picture of me.

"Sure," I told him, "on one condition."

"What's that?" Louie said.

I pointed to the woman. "If you get her phone number for me, I'll let you take the picture."

"Get out of here; you're too ugly," he said.

"No picture then," I replied.

Louie reluctantly walked over to the railing and explained to the woman that I would like her phone number. She agreed to give it to him. I called her later, and we arranged to see each other the next time I came to New York with the Braves. Six months after that, in January 1968, Dani and I were married in the house of friends of mine, Charlie and

Mary Helen Luke from Atlanta. Again, I didn't bother inviting anyone from my family because I knew they approved of this whirlwind courtship about as much as my first one.

My luck with marriage didn't get any better, and my baseball career hit some bumps too. Early in that 1968 season, on April 18, we were facing the Cubs in Atlanta, and I was batting against a small right-handed relief pitcher named Chuck Hartenstein. The count was one ball and two strikes. Hank Aaron was on first base with two outs. I knew Henry had a habit of stealing when the count worked against the hitter. As Hartenstein swung his arm back to deliver the ball, I took a peek at Henry to see if he was going to run. I saw him take off. And when I refocused my vision to pick up the ball coming out of Hartenstein's hand, I couldn't find it. I never saw it. It smashed against my cheek. It split my palate, broke my cheek and my nose. It's a wonder I didn't lose any teeth. My teammates had to carry me off the field and into the clubhouse. I was in shock. The trainer held a finger up and asked me to follow it, but I couldn't. I couldn't see. They took me to a hospital where I spent the next three or four days. It took almost that long for the bleeding in my nose to stop.

Although there was no permanent damage, I couldn't play for five or six weeks. I watched the games from the press box. It wasn't like now, where guys on the disabled list stay in uniform and watch games from the bench. The way we do it now is much better because it keeps players more involved in what's happening with the club. After one of those games while I was hurt, I went out to dinner with a friend of mine from Pittsburgh, Joel Aranson, who was in

Atlanta on business. I had my usual share of cocktails and wine with the meal. Driving home in the early morning hours, I decided to straighten out some of the curves on Peachtree Street. All of a sudden I saw police lights in my rearview mirror. I pulled over, and the officer asked if I had been drinking. "Yeah," I said. "I had some wine." He took my license and recognized me. Unlike Frank's run-in with the law after the 1958 World Series, I wasn't let off the hook. He put me in the paddy wagon and hauled me back to the station—but not before stopping twice to have me sign autographs for his friends. They arrested me for driving under the influence. I called up a friend of mine who was a policeman, Buddy Whalen, and told him I was in jail. He thought I was kidding, but then he arranged for me to be released on my own recognizance.

"Don't worry," he said. "Nobody's going to know about this."

Later that day, as I got a ride back to the station to pick up my car, news of my drunk driving arrest was on the radio about every fifteen minutes. The fans got on me pretty good about that. I blamed the cop for not letting me go; I hadn't been driving that fast anyway. But looking back, I realize I was so spoiled that I easily placed blame on other people but never on myself. I wish I had had the same kind of mature attitude that John Wetteland had with the Yankees in 1996. He was unhappy that the front office fought him during the year over a clause in his contract that permitted him to be a free agent after the season. He also was angry that they discouraged him from Rollerblading around the stadium, one of his favorite pastimes. But John never let that affect him. He went about his business like a professional and was one of the best closers in baseball last season.

We managed to play .500 ball that 1968 season, a year noteworthy in retrospect only because our team featured three future managers (myself, Alou, and Dusty Baker) and a sixty-two-year-old pitcher, Satchel Paige. Actually, Bill Bartholomay, the Braves' president, signed Satchel as a trainer because he heard that Satchel was short the necessary service time to qualify for a pension. Satchel wasn't on the active roster, but he would put a uniform on and be on the field before games. In the clubhouse he'd sit in his chair and tell stories, and we'd gather around him, like a family clustered around the potbellied stove. He told us how his control had been so good that he could throw a baseball over a resin bag. He told us about the great players of the Negro League, like Cool Papa Bell, who he said was so fast, he could turn out the light and be in bed before the room got dark. And he told us he personally didn't believe in running. "You might step in a hole," he explained.

I played in only 115 games in 1968 because of getting hit in the face with the pitch. I batted .271, a career low at that point, with 10 home runs and 55 runs batted in. I had a hard time getting my confidence back after being beaned. It wasn't until the next year that I convinced myself I had to either get over it or quit. Paul Richards, the Braves' general manager, wanted to cut my salary from $65,000 to $52,000—the maximum twenty percent pay cut allowed. I guess Richards figured it was my fault that my face got in the way of a baseball and I should pay for it. I think he also disliked me because I served as our team's player representative to the union, which was gaining increased strength under the strong and wise leadership of Marvin Miller. Richards hated Marvin intensely.

What bothered me even more than the proposed pay cut was that Richards made statements in the press that I hadn't done very much for the club over the previous two seasons and that as far as he was concerned I could hold out until Thanksgiving. I decided there was no way I was signing anything unless Richards offered me a public apology. I was a spring training holdout again. It wasn't just about money anymore. I knew I had to take a stand to regain the respect of my teammates. I could not allow myself to be publicly insulted like that and just walk into the clubhouse as if nothing had happened. Besides, it wasn't as if I still was a young player who needed to sign quickly because I needed the money. Those days were over for me. I was working in the off-season selling municipal bonds for a firm called Valeriano & Craig on Wall Street. A lot of players took off-season jobs in those days. Warren Spahn, for instance, worked on his cattle ranch. Besides, the way I was spending money, I needed a second job. Valeriano & Craig paid me $1,000 a month over the calendar year. The firm told me I could keep working for them as long as I wanted. They even gave me my own business cards.

Bill Bartholomay called me up at my home in New Jersey and said, "There must be some way we can work this out between you and Paul Richards. Why don't you come down to Florida, and you two guys can talk about it? He's ready to make you another offer, but it's not going to be a raise."

"I'll come down," I said, "on one condition: You buy me a round-trip ticket."

"Fine," Bartholomay said. "We'll see you in West Palm Beach."

I flew down the next day or so. I figured Richards would offer me the same salary I had the year before. I walked into Richards's office at the ballpark in West Palm Beach, where the Braves trained.

"Well, what did you want to see me about?" I said to Richards.

"I didn't want to see you," he said.

"Bill Bartholomay said you were ready to make another offer," I said.

"The same deal stands—not one cent different," Richards said.

"What about an apology for what you said about me?"

"I don't see the need for an apology. I don't consider those remarks I made personal. This is a business."

"I'm sorry, but I consider them very personal to me."

Then I reached into my wallet for one of my Valeriano & Craig business cards. I threw it on Richards's desk. "Well," I said, "if you ever need me, here's how to reach me."

Richards took my card and threw it in a trash can. And that was it. I walked out. I knew my ten years of service to the Braves organization were over.

The New York papers were full of rumors about me being traded to the Mets. I thought I wanted to go—playing at home and all that—but deep down I wasn't sure. Sometimes playing at home can be distracting, what with all the ticket requests and the pressure to do well in front of family and friends.

I later found out that Richards did try to trade me to the Mets. He was prepared to trade Bob Aspromonte and me in exchange for pitcher Nolan Ryan, catcher J. C. Martin, first baseman Ed Kranepool, and third baseman/outfielder Amos Otis. The Mets agreed on the entire package except Otis. Richards knew Otis was untouchable. The Mets countered by saying they would replace Otis in the deal with infielder Bobby Heise. Richards turned them down.

Then on St. Patrick's Day, 1969, Richards traded me to the St. Louis Cardinals for first baseman Orlando Cepeda, a former most valuable player who had been a colorful, popular figure in St. Louis. The Cardinals had won the two previous National League pennants and had been the 1967 world champions. I told my mother the news, and she said, "Now go to church and thank God." When Bing Devine, the Cardinals' general manager, called me up with news of the trade, we negotiated a contract in about one minute over the phone. Bing asked me what I wanted. I told him I wanted the same contract I had with Atlanta the previous year: $65,000 and the use of a car. He told me the Cardinals did not include the use of free cars in their contracts, but that he'd give me $70,000. I took it. Not quite the same process that goes on today. Bing was such a classy guy that when I flew to Florida to join the Cardinals in St. Petersburg, he was at the airport to greet me.

That was the first season of divisional play, and I remember talking in spring training about how the West Division teams would be fighting it out for the right to play against us in the playoffs. I should have known better. My timing, as usual, was awful. After two straight World Series appearances, the Cardinals slipped to fourth place in the East Division as soon as I got there. We finished 87–75, thirteen games out of first place.

And what about my former club, the Braves? They won the West Division, of course. And who did they play in the National League Championship Series? The Mets, naturally. The team that I *wasn't* traded to. I started to think I was the black cloud, and so did some of my more humorous Cardinal teammates. Bob Gibson used to say to me, "You know, we used to win before you got here." When the Mets clinched their East Division title that year, they did so by beating us at Shea Stadium. And who took care of the final outs by grounding into a double play? Yours truly. The Mets went on to win the World Series, with the series MVP award going to Donn Clendenon, the first baseman whom the Mets had acquired after failing to get me. If that wasn't enough, Dani insisted that we go to Shea Stadium to watch the World Series in person. I had to go there and watch her root for the Mets. Now that was torture. I saw Game Four, the one in which Ron Swoboda made that diving catch in right field. That definitely was not the way I wanted to get to the World Series.

I had a good year for the Cardinals in 1969—knocking in 101 runs and batting .289 while playing mostly first base because Tim McCarver still was the regular catcher in St. Louis. I felt a lot of pressure trying to replace Cepeda but found myself surrounded by a great bunch of teammates. The Cardinals were coming off two straight pennants. They knew how to win, and they had this professional, cool personality that contrasted with the rough-and-tough style of the Braves teams I had known. Red Schoendienst was the perfect manager for those Cardinals. As a manager, sometimes you assume a lot—that your players know what they are supposed to do and that they understand your moves. Red was able to take that approach because he had such a smart seasoned bunch. And luckily, so did I with the Yankees. It was the first year that kind of approach worked for me. The Yankees' professionalism really made me think back to those classy Cardinal teams.

The first guy who welcomed me to the team was Bob Gibson. The team was on a trip when I joined them in spring training, and right away Gibson made a joke of trying to get me to steal McCarver's number, 15, which had been my number with the Braves. He took the number 15 that hung above McCarver's locker and tacked it up over mine. (The Cardinals gave me number 9, which I thought was great because it had belonged to Roger Maris, a player I much admired.) Like most people, I was a little intimidated by Gibson at first. He was notorious for knocking down hitters and never talking to opponents. The first time I met him was actually at the 1965 all-star game. Gibby was pitching, and I was catching. He worked ahead of Tony Oliva, the leadoff hitter, no balls and two strikes. I knew Gibson hated catchers coming out to the mound under any circumstance; he figured he knew more about pitching than they did. But I knew that Oliva liked to hit pitches down and in, and I wanted to make certain Gibby knew that.

"This guy's a good hitter who likes the ball down and in," I told Gibson. "Let's keep it up and in." He basically just snarled at me in response.

Oliva hit the first pitch Gibson threw—it was down and in—for a double. It turned out to be harmless because an obviously perturbed Gibby retired the next three batters, striking out Joe Pepitone, on three blazing, high fastballs. Afterward I happened to be in the shower room with Gibson. We were standing under adjacent nozzles. "Nice game," I said. Gibby never even turned his head to acknowledge me. I think I detected a grunt out of him—that was it. He wouldn't talk to me. I had no idea at the time that Gibby would turn out to be one of my very best friends in life—and not just among the baseball people I know. We're so close that he's become like another brother to me. Gibby is also the one guy I'd pick for my pitcher if I had to win one game. Nobody I know has ever been better at pitching the big game. Maybe a couple of guys could be his equal at it, but no one's been better.

I didn't become close with McCarver right away. In fact, I remember there was some unspoken tension between us my first year in St. Louis. We had been rivals as catchers—always in a duel, for instance, at balloting time for the all-star game—and now we were on the same club, even though the Cardinals got me to play first base. After the 1969 season St. Louis traded Timmy to Philadelphia, in the same deal that prompted Curt Flood to challenge baseball's reserve clause. I got a lot closer to Timmy when he returned to the Cardinals in 1974. We had a lot in common: a love of food, wine, and the nuances of baseball, to begin with.

Timmy and I talked a lot about managing in those days. We actually kicked around the idea of some day becoming co-managers of a team. During that 1969 season Timmy, Gibson, Dal Maxvill, and myself formed what we called "the Dinner Club." Every time we played a day game on the road, we'd get together for dinner. We'd spend most of the night talking about the strategies and intricacies of baseball. On any given night, there would be six to nine players joining us. I've never seen such a large group of players consistently going out together.

We used to love to drink expensive wine with good dinners. And we always split the tab equally, whether any one of us ate much or not. In other words, you had to pay for the privilege of eating with us.

Timmy and I were almost always the first ones at the ballpark. One of our coaches, George Kissell, always was there early too. The three of us would spend hours talking about baseball. Looking back on it, that's when I started to get the foundation for my managing career. I learned more baseball from George Kissell than from anyone else in my life. He used to have a great saying: The most important word in the baseball dictionary is *why.* And that's pretty much what Timmy, George, and I would do. We'd constantly ask ourselves why things had happened in games. Sometimes Gibby and Maxie would sit in too. They were very stimulating and enlightening sessions.

With the Cardinals, a team that didn't score runs nearly as readily as the Braves, George showed me how to create runs by stealing bases and moving runners. He taught me that while running to first base, you should run *through* the bag and not *to* it. He taught me that outfielders should reposition themselves according to the count on the hitter, and not just plant themselves in the same spot. And he taught me an unorthodox defense with a runner on third when it's time to bring the infield in: With a right-handed hitter, and with the count in his favor, you leave your third baseman back at normal depth. That puts pressure on the runner and third-base coach in whether to decide to break for home on a ground ball. It's good thinking, and I've used a number of George's defensive inventions throughout my career. But as I found out in Game One of the 1996 World Series, it's not guaranteed to work. I kept my shortstop, Derek Jeter, back at normal depth with runners on second and third, one out, and Chipper Jones batting right-handed. We were down 2–0 in the third inning and wanted to avoid a big Atlanta rally. When my pitcher, Andy Pettitte, worked the count to one ball, two strikes, I brought Jeter in, figuring Jones would have a more defensive swing with the count against him. He promptly grounded a single past Jeter, driving in two runs.

Surrounded by those intelligent, dedicated professionals in St. Louis, I finally began to grow up and mature. Timmy and Maxie, in particular, taught me a lot about being very positive all the time. Maxie would tell me things about myself I didn't know: that I was a team player and a guy who could handle pressure. I thought that until you went to the World Series, you hadn't proved you could handle pressure. That was my mindset.

Steve Carlton was another guy who loved to have fun, talk baseball, and enjoy wine. He was my roommate for a while.

He pitched one of the most amazing games I ever saw. In 1969 I was playing first base when Lefty struck out nineteen batters—and lost. Swoboda hit two two-run home runs to beat him, 4–3. The next season, 1970, Carlton had even worse luck and wound up losing nineteen games. One time that year we were playing the Reds in Cincinnati on a Saturday afternoon. Lefty always had trouble with Johnny Bench. He couldn't get Johnny out if it was midnight and no lights were turned on. That day Johnny hit three home runs off Lefty: one to left field, one to center field, and one to right field. After the game Lefty and I commiserated over dinner and a little wine. I guess we had more than a little wine. When we got back to our hotel suite, I think we broke every stick of furniture in the room. When we awoke in the morning and realized what we had done, we tried to glue everything back together. It wasn't very well-made stuff. We bought glue and delicately put the tables and chairs back together. When we left the suite, we had to make sure we didn't close the door too hard because we were afraid the noise would cause everything to fall apart.

Lefty was a mess that year. He began pitching very defensively. He fell in love with his breaking ball and wouldn't use his fastball. Once in a while I'd ask Red Schoendienst if I could catch Lefty. One time in Los Angeles every single pitch I called was a fastball. He shook me off one time, and it was a two-run home run. Lefty beat the Dodgers 3–2.

In contrast to Lefty, I had a great year in 1970. I finished second in the batting race, with a .325 average, and knocked in a hundred runs. I really felt comfortable in St. Louis. I had somehow come over to the Cardinals with a reputation as a troublemaker with management. I was there for two years when somebody in the front office told me, "You know what? You're not a troublemaker." I'd tell people, "I had trouble with Paul Richards. That was it." But I did settle down as a more mature person. As a sign of my newfound responsibility, in spring training of that season I finally took off my excess poundage for good. I had played most of my career in the range of 220 to 230 pounds. With McCarver traded and with his heir apparent, Ted Simmons, scheduled to miss the first two months in the service, I knew I'd have to open the season behind the plate. I had to get in better shape. Also, I was a little concerned about turning thirty that season. I knew you had to work harder to stay in shape once you hit that mark. My brother Frank told me about Dr. Stillman's water diet. You drink eighty ounces of water a day and eat a ton of protein—eggs, steaks, things like that. I had a refrigerator full of hardboiled eggs. Every time you eat a hardboiled egg and then have two or three glasses of water, it's like swallowing a sponge and filling it up. That's the idea; you're full.

The diet worked. I lost twenty pounds in spring training, dropping from 228 to 208. During the season I actually went all the way down to 195, and my waist shrank so much—to about thirty-two inches—that I briefly had to wear the batboy's pants. The diet also made me aware of everything I put in my mouth. I was the kind of guy who thought nothing of eating candy, soft drinks, banana cream pies, and junk like that. But I really watched what I ate after the diet and learned to reduce my portions. That's the way I am to this day: I love to eat good food—and sometimes the

115

table in front of me will be filled with different dishes—but I enjoy it in small quantities.

Jack Buck, the Cardinals' broadcaster, thought I got too skinny in the early 1970s and had lost some of my power. I didn't think that was true. But I didn't have the heart to tell people the real reason I kept losing weight: I was a nervous wreck because of my family life. Dani and I just were not meant for each other. I couldn't relax in my own home because we weren't communicating well. On top of that, my daughter Tina, who was born in 1968 without a hip socket, seemed always to be in a hospital or seeing specialists. It wasn't until Tina was six years old that she underwent surgery at the Children's Hospital in Toronto, in which Dr. Robert Salter split her pelvis to form a hip out of it. Later on, when I was managing, I'd take the money from the fines I collected from my players over the course of a year and send it to Dr. Salter for his research.

Dani had been married at nineteen to one of the band members of Jay Black and the Americans. She had danced on Broadway a little bit. We were just a bad combination. I'm sure she must have been unhappy too. The atmosphere in our house was chilly. I'll never forget when one of my friends came to visit us, and as he left he whispered to me, "Is it always like this here?" "Yes," I told him. So I poured myself into my work, and as a result I played well, but our marriage suffered even more.

It's sad to say, but 1970 and 1971, when I really kind of shut off my family life and concentrated on my job, turned out to be the two best years of my career. Baseball was mine. It was my accomplishment. Dani couldn't mess with that.

Looking back, I was wrong to think that way, but at the time I felt like that was the only way that I could do my job. When Dani brought it to my attention, I tried to change. I admitted I *was* selfish, and that I wasn't very good at being a family man and a ballplayer at the same time. So I tried to change. And this is what happened: I couldn't do either one well. I wasn't very good at home, and I went to the ballpark worrying about that, and so I wasn't very good there either. My career was never the same afterward.

That 1971 season, though, turned out to be my career year, my MVP season. Sadly, my father wasn't alive to see it. In January of that year, my father left for his usual winter getaway. On the very first day he got there, he suffered a stroke and died. He was sixty-eight years old. Frank and I arranged to have the body returned to New York for burial.

George Kissell turned me into a third baseman in spring training in 1971. We'd worked out together every morning from eight-thirty to nine, just doing all kinds of drills. For instance, he'd stand behind me and throw a ball off a concrete wall, and I'd have to react to its bounce and catch it. The more we did it, the closer I moved to the wall, and the closer I moved to the wall, the more my reaction time quickened. On the first day of the drills, George said to me, "Take your stance." He didn't like it—he thought I had my feet spread too wide. He didn't come right out and say it, though. Instead, he asked me, "You know Bob Cousy, the basketball player?"

"Sure," I said.

"If he had the basketball right now in front of you, how would you guard him?"

I immediately shortened up my stance. That's what George wanted to see.

"Why'd you do that?" he said.

"So he can't drive by me to the right and he can't drive by me to the left," I said.

"Good," he said. "Look at your feet. From now on that's where they'll be playing third base."

I learned one of my many lessons from George that day. As a manager, you have to find a way to communicate with people—to correct and suggest things—without having them resent you for it. That's what I try to do: get a message across to the player by getting him to sort of agree with me, rather than scolding and lecturing.

I led the National League third basemen in errors that year, but in time I made myself into a good defensive player and took pride in my glovework, especially since all those who scouted me as a teenager had said I could never play the infield. Of course, I was red hot at the plate all season. I was so consistent, it was scary. My monthly batting averages, starting with April, went like this: .366, .355, .393, .324, .368, and .368. I batted .363 against right-handers and .362 against left-handers.

I was locked in all year. I used to go home and know what pitches I was going to hit off the pitcher the next day. It was weird. I had such a feeling of concentration, of being able to block everything out. And the more hits you get, the more confident you are. The key is your confidence level.

I had a ton of hits to right field that year, even more than I usually did. My philosophy on hitting was pretty simple: Dare 'em to jam you. For some reason, hitters are embarrassed to get jammed. I think there are a lot more hits on the handle than on the end of the bat. Normally, if you hit the ball on the end of the bat, it means your head is coming off the ball—leaning back and away from it. I like to tell kids and even big league players that the front shoulder is the key to good hitting. You have to keep that shoulder pointed toward the pitcher. Once it opens up away from the ball, your head follows, and it shortens the area of the plate you can cover with your bat. You wind up hitting the ball off the end of the bat. Frank had taught me all about this and more. He always served me as something of a personal hitting coach. Even in 1971, when I was pounding the ball, Frank would talk to me three times a week, reminding me in his usual no-nonsense manner that I wasn't a home run hitter and that I should hit the ball up the middle.

Just about the only team I didn't wear out that year was the Dodgers. I hit .271 against Los Angeles. There were two reasons for that. Number one, they always had a great pitching staff. And number two, Milton Berle would distract me. Uncle Miltie was a big baseball fan whom I met at Dodger Stadium. He would sit in his box seats next to the dugout eating sandwiches he'd brought from home. We developed a friendship. Whenever I'd bat at Dodger Stadium, Milton would call out my name, blow kisses, and sing, "I love you, Joey!" He used to invite me and some teammates over to his house for breakfast when we played in Los Angeles. Milton's been a great friend. He came to my fiftieth birthday party, and I went to his eightieth. He also was one of the many people who called me up looking for World Series tickets. He was in the stands when we won the Series in Game Six.

The 1971 Cardinals were the only team I ever played for that won 90 games. Still, we finished a distant second behind the Pirates. Even though we led the league in batting and stolen bases, we had little thunder in our lineup. While I hit 24 home runs and had a league-high 137 runs batted in, no one else hit more than 16 home runs or drove in more than 77 runs. I guess my MVP season also caused a lot more people to notice the success I had had with my water diet. All kinds of people, and not just baseball fans, were inspired by the fact that I had solved a lifelong weight problem and was able to keep the fat off. So many people wrote to the Cardinals and me that year asking how I did it, that the front office began mailing out copies of my diet. I must have been the only MVP in history who received more requests for a diet program than for an autograph.

I kept the weight off that winter, even though I was on the banquet circuit with my most valuable player award. Then I held out of training camp—again. It seemed like an annual event for me. But it did have a great benefit. I hated going to the start of spring training when all those young, wild-armed prospects would be trying to impress the coaching staff. In those days the hitting backgrounds were terrible in the Florida ballparks. It was dangerous, especially for a guy like me, who liked to crowd the plate. So I'd hold out until those young bucks were sent to the minor league camp. That year I wanted $150,000, a $35,000 raise after a MVP season. Bing Devine told me, "Anything under $150,000 is acceptable." That was the ceiling that Stan Musial and Bob Gibson had once established. I wound up signing a two-year contract worth $280,000.

I was hitting the ball great in spring training when Maxvill and I left for a players association meeting in Dallas with other player reps and alternate player reps. We were prepared to take a strike vote. Some of the players wanted to wait until the all-star break to strike. Marvin Miller told us, "At that time, four teams will be in first place. Are the players on those teams going to want to strike then? We have to be unanimous about this. If you want to strike, do it now or don't do it." Marvin painted a scenario that led us to believe it would not be a long strike. This wasn't about money, it was about benefits—the pension plan in particular. He said the owners were making too much money to let the strike go on. And so we voted to strike.

I returned to St. Petersburg with Maxie—I was his alternate—to tell our owner, Gussie Busch, that we were striking. That was horrible. Gussie was another owner who hated Marvin. We sat across from him in a tiny office at Al Lang Field in St. Pete. His son, August Busch III, was standing behind us near the door. Gussie pounded his fist on the desk and roared, "Goddammit! That man is leading you down a path to ruin! And he's getting paid and you're not." I said, "Excuse me, but Mr. Miller is not getting paid during the strike." That pissed Gussie off even more.

Marvin was right—the strike didn't last long. It was settled one week into the regular season. I was in New York for the settlement—that was when someone stole Frank's 1958 World Series ring out of my hotel room. As part of the settlement, the owners decided they were not going to make up the games that were lost, even though it could easily have been arranged with doubleheaders. Maxie turned to me

121

and said, "Did we win or lose this thing?" The owners wanted to hurt us. They didn't want to pay us. We all were docked about five percent of our salaries for the missed games.

Our club stood to lose more than most teams with the settlement. That's because the Cardinals had a history of treating their players better than other clubs. For instance, they used to give everyone a single room on the road—that was unheard of then. But after the strike was settled, the Cardinals took away that perk and doubled up on rooms like everyone else. It just so happened that they put Maxie and me, the two union guys, in the same room. We used to joke about sending someone else up to our room to turn the key, thinking the room might be booby-trapped or something.

My union activity did not sit well with the fans. On opening day of the 1972 season, I was introduced in St. Louis for the first time as the most valuable player of the National League. They booed me. The decline of my career had officially begun.

CHAPTER 6

Three Outs

I WAS SITTING AT A BAR WITH BOB Gibson one night on the road with the Cardinals early in the 1972 season. He was drinking wine. I was drinking vodka. He could tell that I was beating myself up inside about not hitting as well as I had the previous year, when I won the MVP award.

"Joe," he said, "I've got a question for you. Do you really think of yourself as a .363 hitter?"

"Well, I . . . ." I started to say.

"Tell me, what's your lifetime average?" Gibby asked.

".305," I said.

"And what are you hitting now?"

".310."

"So what's your problem?"

Gibby knew me too well. We had become so close over the last season that I couldn't hide anything from him. I was trying too hard to duplicate a once-in-a-lifetime season. It's difficult to be productive when you fight yourself like that, a problem I knew Tim McCarver experienced early in his career. I had other problems too. I couldn't relax because of my personal problems. I was trying to be a better husband and father to relieve my guilty conscience about the years of being too selfish about my career—and it just wasn't working out. My marriage to Dani was coming apart. She didn't like living in St. Louis very much, so we moved back to New York while I was playing for the Cardinals. That only made matters worse. The secret to playing baseball consistently well is to be relaxed enough so that you just react to things, as opposed to trying to force things to happen. I could no longer do that because I was too distracted and unhappy. I'd have a game here or there where I'd be able to get locked in and block everything else out, but for the most part I had too many negative thoughts creeping into my game. My numbers turned out to be decent but not up to the standards I expected. From 1972 through 1974 I batted between .282 and .289 for St. Louis without hitting more than 13 home runs or driving in more than 81 runs.

Ironically, as my career declined, I came as close to the World Series as I ever would as a player. In August 1973 we were in first place in the East Division, with a four-game lead. But then Gibson tore ligaments in his knee while running the bases against the Mets at Shea Stadium. He fell so suddenly that my mother, who never missed a game when I played in New York, said it looked like he'd been shot. Gibby was such a fierce competitor that he insisted on trying to pitch the next inning. He threw one pitch that didn't even reach home plate, then collapsed on the mound. He pitched only once the rest of the season. We finished in second place, one and a half games behind the Mets.

I don't blame losing that season on Bob's injury, and I don't bother wondering what might have happened if he hadn't been hurt. I've always been the kind of person to deal with reality, not conjecture—a trait that has served me well as a manager. With the Yankees, for instance, I never brooded about not having my ace pitcher, David Cone, for three months. First of all, I was very concerned about his personal health after doctors discovered an aneurysm in his right shoulder. And secondly, there's nothing you can do about it once somebody goes down with an injury. Whatever players you have available make for the best team you could possibly have at that time. The worst thing you can do when someone gets hurt is to say, "If we had had that guy, we would have won this game." That has a negative effect on your team. That's why as a player or manager, I've never wasted time wishing for things that were not possible.

As painful as that 1973 season was, the next year was worse. I had been asleep in a hotel room in Montreal on May 12, 1974, when the telephone rang at three o'clock in the morning. It's weird, but I knew exactly what it was about even before I picked up the phone: My mother was dead. She was sixty-nine years old and had died at a hospital on Long Island. Doctors listed the cause of death only as "heart failure," and we never ordered an autopsy.

My mom's death brought our family closer together. I realized that I had not been talking with my family as much as I did in the past. I knew they weren't crazy about my marriage to Dani, so I had drifted away from them a little bit. My mother's death brought on heavy feelings of guilt for me.

Four months later it was in that same hotel in Montreal that our pennant hopes ended. On the last day of the season, we were rained out of a game against the Expos. The first-place Pirates, who had a one-game lead on us, were playing the Cubs. We checked out of our rooms and were sitting around the hotel lobby while one of our announcers made telephone calls to get updates on Pittsburgh's game. If the Cubs beat the Pirates, we would play Montreal the next day in a makeup game, and if we won that, we'd play a one-game playoff in Pittsburgh. The Cubs looked like they were on the verge of victory, but then Chicago catcher Steve Swisher dropped a third strike, helping the Pirates to a winning rally that clinched the division for them.

I felt terrible. It was dark and wet in Montreal. The bus we took to the airport was quiet and sad. I had one more reason to feel awful: I knew I wasn't going to be back with the Cardinals. They had brought up a young first baseman from the minor leagues named Keith Hernandez and made him eligible for the playoffs if we won the East. I was right—a few weeks later St. Louis traded me to the Mets for Ray Sadecki. I quickly forgot about getting to the World Series. I was going to a team whose season had just ended with ninety-one losses.

That was a very fragile time for me. On top of being unhappy with my marriage, I hit rock bottom in the big leagues with a losing team. And to make matters worse, I became a part-time player. I hated it, and it showed. I had the worst season of my life in 1975 with the Mets, batting .247. The only good that came out of that season was that it eventually made me a better manager. I think that, because I was an MVP and because I struggled as a part-time player, I can relate to anybody on my roster. That's probably my biggest asset as a manager. I experienced a huge range of emotions, including humiliation, as a player.

On one especially humiliating night that awful year, on July 25 in a 6–2 loss to the Houston Astros, I tied a major league record by grounding into four double plays, all of them against pitcher Ken Forsch. In every case Felix Millan had preceded one of my grounders with a base hit. I've always tried to be a standup guy with the media, and that night was no different. I figure eventually you're going to have to face them, so why prolong the agony? I even tried a little dark humor. First I thanked Millan. "I couldn't have done it without him," I said. And then I said, "When I retire, I'm going to buy a shortstop. At night, when I'm lonely, I'm going to hit grounders to him."

From my days as a shy kid growing up in Brooklyn, the only thing I ever wanted to be was a ballplayer. I was happiest when I was on a ballfield, especially when it allowed me to escape problems at home with my dad or, later, with my marriages. But in 1975 for the first time in my life, I dreaded going to the ballpark. Baseball felt like work. I thought maybe it was time to quit. After the season, in which we actually finished two games over .500 in third place, Mets general manager Joe McDonald said I could manage one of the Mets' minor league teams the next season. Even though my thoughts of managing had turned serious, I didn't want to retire on such a bad year.

I worked hard that winter at the Downtown Athletic Club in Manhattan with a trainer, Paul Mastropasqua, to strengthen the muscles in my shoulder and back. I also did a better job of accepting my part-time role, even if I still didn't like it. I hit the ball very well that year, finishing at .306. In August McDonald came up to me and said, "How would you like to go to the Yankees? They want you, and I can work out a trade."

I thought, Hell, yeah. The Yankees were in first place and looked like they were headed to the World Series. One of my old teammates with the Braves, Billy Martin, was the manager. It sounded great. But I didn't trust McDonald's question. I thought perhaps he was trying to get me out of the way because he knew I wanted to manage and I represented a threat to the job security of Joe Frazier, his hand-picked manager at the time.

"I don't know," I said. "I don't want to go if it keeps me from coming back here and managing the team someday. I'd like to talk to Mr. Grant."

M. Donald Grant was running the Mets in those days. I met with him in the manager's office. I told him, "Look, you don't need my permission to trade me to the Yankees, but if it's going to keep me from being considered here as a manager, I'd rather not go." Grant thanked me, and they didn't trade me.

In May of the next season, 1977, we were playing an exhibition game against our Triple-A team, Tidewater, in

Virginia. I didn't play, and was shaving in the clubhouse before the end of the game to expedite our quick getaway. In the mirror I saw McDonald walking up behind me. Oh, shit, I thought. He's going to get on me about shaving during the game. Instead McDonald said, "How would you like to manage this team?"

"Yeah, I would," I said.

"Tomorrow meet Mr. Grant at his apartment in Manhattan at nine o'clock in the morning."

After McDonald left, Tom Seaver walked out from a bathroom stall. He had heard the whole conversation. He didn't say a word to me. He just raised his eyebrows as if to say, "Wow," and never mentioned it again. The Mets traveled to Philadelphia after that game, whereupon I rented a car and drove home to New Jersey so that I could meet Grant in the morning. Grant made it clear to me at the meeting that he wanted me to replace Frazier, though he had not decided on the timing of the move. I drove back to Philadelphia and had lunch with my friend McCarver, who was playing for the Phillies. I told him about the managing offer. He was very happy for me. I really liked Frazier as a person, but I had trouble playing for him because he didn't have a lot of confidence in my ability. When I got to the ballpark that night, Frazier called me into his office.

"We checked for curfew last night, Joe," he said. "You weren't in your room."

I felt terribly uncomfortable. Here was a guy who was going to lose his job to me, and I knew it and he didn't. It was horrible.

"I had to go home," I told Frazier.

"Why didn't you ask me?" he said.

"Well, if I asked you and you said no, I had to go home anyway," I said. "And then it would have been insubordination. So I took my chances. I'll pay whatever fine you think is right."

"No, there's no fine," Frazier said. "Just don't do it again."

One week later, on May 31, 1977, the Mets named me manager. I remained on the active playing roster for about three weeks before I decided to devote all my time to managing. My energy and my outlook were completely rejuvenated by becoming a manager. The best job in baseball is playing every day. The next best job in baseball is managing—it easily beats playing part time. I wasn't nervous at all about managing, even though I had never done it before (although Gibson used to accuse me of doing it all the time with the Cardinals). My excitement was equal to being called up to the big leagues for the first time. I won my first game and eleven of my first sixteen, but again my timing was terrible. Sixteen days into my first managing job, the Mets shook up the team with what became known as the Midnight Massacre, the symbolic beginning of one of the Mets' most inept eras. Just before the June 15 trading deadline, they traded Seaver, who had been feuding with Grant over his contract, to the Reds; Dave Kingman, our best power hitter, to the Padres; and infielder Mike Phillips to the Cardinals. We finished 64-98, the first of four straight seasons in which we lost at least 95 games—a streak broken only by the 1981 players' strike.

The World Series? That was as far away as the moon. In

those years I set my sights on much smaller goals. Winning two out of three games against the Dodgers practically made our season. My bad timing was easy to rationalize in this case: If the Mets had been more committed to winning, they would have hired a more experienced manager. They needed a popular figure in New York and someone who was adept at handling the media during that time of transition.

We may have been an awful club, but we had our share of fun. I had some colorful characters on those teams, such as Willie Montanez. One day he got upset when I sent Joel Youngblood to pinch-run for him. He was so mad, he challenged Youngblood to a race in the outfield after the game. They ran a dead heat. Montanez couldn't wait to tell me about it. "Great," I said. "If you ran hard like that all the time, I wouldn't have to pinch-run for you."

In 1979 we had Richie Hebner at third base. Richie used to tell us stories about his off-season job: He worked for his father digging graves in Massachuetts. One time his father complained that Richie wasn't digging the graves deep enough. Richie told him, "Ain't none of them crawled out yet."

We also had a confident kid from Brooklyn named Lee Mazzilli. After the 1979 season the Mets gave him a three-year contract, even though he wasn't close to being a free agent. He came up to me and said, "Listen, Joe, if there's anything I can do for you, with the front office or whatever about a contract extension, just let me know." When players felt so secure, because of their contracts, that they were giving advice to managers, that's when I knew that big money was starting to make a mess out of the traditional order of the game. When I first joined the union, our big concerns had been things like getting better shower nozzles and squeezing another couple of bucks of meal money out of the owners. The union eventually grew so powerful that it created a monster.

In 1980 Fred Wilpon and Nelson Doubleday bought the Mets and hired Frank Cashen to be their general manager. That June they held the first pick of the amateur draft. Darryl Strawberry looked like the most talented player available. The Mets briefly toyed with the idea of not drafting him. They were a little afraid of stories that Darryl had gotten into some trouble in high school, like missing practices. They had another player in mind, Billy Beane, and asked my opinion. "You've got to take the best player available and worry about the other stuff later," I said. They drafted Darryl and wound up getting Beane in the second round. I met Darryl at Dodger Stadium in Los Angeles soon after the draft, and we joked about him playing for me someday soon. It took sixteen years and a lifetime of trouble for Darryl, but we finally found ourselves on the same team with the Yankees, in 1996.

I had two astute pitching coaches with the Mets, Rube Walker and Bob Gibson. Rube taught me that you can't win without good pitching—baseball is the only sport where you can't run out the clock by freezing the ball. You need twenty-seven outs and the pitcher's involved in every one of them. Gibby had tremendous knowledge to give pitchers but was willing to share it only with people who sincerely wanted to listen. A lot of pitchers don't think they need help, and Bob was turned off by those types and wouldn't hesitate to show them his gruff side.

Cashen thought I was too soft as a manager. That was a rap that followed me for a long time: that I was too much of a "player's manager." But I wasn't any different as manager of the world champion Yankees than I had been with the last place Mets. In fact, I was probably more of a player's manager with the Yankees. I was always hanging out in the clubhouse before and after games. That's what made 1996 so sweet for me. It's nice to know you can be all those things people thought of as negative and still win. I've always believed you can make your point without throwing food across the room or embarrassing people in the newspapers. I'm very proud that I never tried to make myself look good by blaming somebody else.

Though Cashen considered me too laid back, the biggest disagreement I had with him happened over an episode when he thought I was too tough on my players. When I took over as manager of the Mets, I permitted the players to drink at the hotel bars on the road. Too many players took that as a mandate. My coaches and I practically had to drag guys out of the bars at closing time, so we changed the rule and prohibited players from hotel bars. That's always been my approach: I give players privileges, and if they abuse them, I take them away. One late night in Montreal in 1981, I walked into the hotel bar as I came back from dinner with my coaches. I saw Ron Hodges, a catcher, and Dyar Miller, a pitcher, drinking beer in there. I sent one of my coaches, Chuck Cottier, to tell them to drink up and get out. They refused. I did all I could to keep Gibby from pulverizing those guys right there.

That was one of the toughest nights I've ever had as a manager. I had to decide how to punish them. They were guilty of insubordination. The next day I decided to suspend them and sent them back to New York, while the rest of the team traveled to Philadelphia for a series against the Phillies. It wasn't long before I got a call from Cashen.

"Don't you realize that this whole incident is over just one beer?" he said.

"Yep, I sure do," I told him.

"Well," Frank said, "if you reconsider and lift the suspension, I can have them in Philadelphia in time for the game tonight."

"Frank," I said, "if we do that, we might as well take all the rules and shove them up your ass."

As a manager, you can have all the rules you want, but you have to have the right people to make them work. That's one of the reasons why we won with the Yankees. We didn't have players who wanted to test me. They understood the team concept. John Wetteland was the most honest guy I've ever managed. He would fine himself over infractions I knew nothing about. He would walk into my office every once in a while and throw money on my desk. "What's that for?" I'd ask. He'd say something like "I was late for stretching exercises." Jimmy Leyritz would push the envelope with me—he liked to be thirty seconds late a lot—but it was nothing close to insubordination. And every once in a while I'd have to chew out the players hanging out in the clubhouse during games. Some guys liked to go back there to stretch or hit into a net, but every once in a while it was ridiculously crowded back there. I'd be into the game and all of a sudden I'd look at the bench, and there would be only two guys there. I'd tell them later, "If we ever had a fight on the field, we'd get our asses kicked. At least assign yourselves numbers so you can go back during different innings."

Cashen fired me after that 1981 season, though it wasn't because of that disciplinary incident. Doubleday, Wilpon, and Cashen had given me a two-year contract going into that year, but I considered it more of a nice gesture, like a golden parachute, than a firm commitment, because new owners and new general managers don't like inheriting somebody else's manager. I wasn't bitter about being fired. Look at my record: 286-420. The fact that I lasted five seasons in New York with that record may have been my greatest accomplishment in baseball.

The 1981 season was a miserable one. Not only did I get fired, but a strike by the players wiped out almost one-third of the season, and my marriage to Dani got so bad that I finally moved out. I'm not sure why I stuck it out so long with her. Maybe it was because divorce meant another failure. And for a long time I believed I could make things right. I tried to open up more and pay more attention to her, but she seemed to think it was too late. That was when I felt like we had hit a brick wall. But there was one night in that otherwise awful season that turned my life around. Gibby, myself, and some of my other coaches were sitting in a hotel bar in Cincinnati after dinner on August 23. It was a Sunday. The place was dead, and I nearly was too. I was in no mood to meet anybody. I was sipping a glass of sparkling water. And then I saw this tall slender waitress. She was reading a book—that's how slow the place was. She was striking. I said out loud, "Wow. Would you look at her."

"Go over and introduce yourself, Joe," Gibby said.

"Nah," I said. I really wasn't in the mood for it.

"Then I'll go talk to her for you," said Gibby, and he walked over and told her that I wanted to meet her.

She came over to our table, and we hit it off right away. I learned that her name was Alice and that she was a few days away from her twenty-fourth birthday. I was forty-one. Gibby said, "Why don't you ask her to lunch tomorrow?" So I did. She accepted. The next time August 23 fell on a Sunday—six years later—we were married. I fell in love pretty quickly with Ali. She was very easy to talk with right from the start, probably because she grew up with fifteen brothers and sisters. I was relaxed around her. That was so important for me, because up until I met Ali, home was never a comfortable place. Home to me had been a place of fear, because of my father, and then a place of tension, because of my two failed marriages.

When the Mets fired me, they also fired Gibson. He took it much harder than I did. Gibby had played with one club, the Cardinals, his whole career and was a Hall of Famer. The rejection devastated him. He was so burned by the experience that when I later asked him to coach for me with the Braves, he said he wouldn't come unless they gave him the security of a two-year deal, an unusual contract for a coach. He got it.

Unlike Bob, I had been traded twice before, so I was

somewhat accustomed to that empty feeling of rejection. It didn't last long, though, because two weeks later I interviewed for the managing jobs in San Diego (the Padres hired Dick Williams) and Atlanta. John Mullen, the Braves' general manager, interviewed me in Atlanta. We agreed on a three-year contract with an attendance clause. A few days later I was awakened by a telephone call from Ted Turner, the America's Cup yachtsman, CNN founder, and colorful Braves' owner whom the press liked to call "the Mouth of the South."

"You drive a hard bargain," Ted said.

"Yeah," I said. "Is it a deal?"

"Yeah," Ted said.

A little while later John Mullen told me, "You weren't my choice, but let's work together the best we can." I didn't like the sound of that. I also found out later from Ted that Mullen hadn't told Turner about the attendance clause. Ted said later he would not have agreed if he'd known about it, so he wouldn't put it into my contract. My tenure in Atlanta began on shaky footing. But when the 1982 season opened, I was as happy as I could be: I had a three-year contract, I was in love with a beautiful woman, and my team had started with thirteen straight wins. It was after our first five that we went to Cincinnati and I called Ali's parents, Lucille and Ed Wolterman for the first time. I asked them if they wanted tickets to the game. They said no. I heard a lot of mistrust in their voices. Ali told me later that when she first told them she was dating the manager of the Braves, Ed, who was pretending to be sleeping on a couch, jumped up and said, "How the hell old is this guy?" I eventually won them over though. When I called them to ask for their daughter's hand in marriage, Ali's mother told her she had worn out three pairs of rosary beads praying for that day to come.

The first time I met Ali's parents was on the Braves' second trip to Cincinnati in 1982. I was more nervous about that than I was for the 1996 World Series. My palms were sweaty. I wanted to be so agreeable around her father that I said yes to everything he asked. "Do you want a sandwich?" Sure. "Do you want a beer?" Sure, though I never drank on the day of a game. "Do you want spaghetti and meatballs?" Sure. "Another beer?" Sure. "Another beer?" Sure. By the time I left for the ballpark, I was both stuffed and tipsy.

That 13-0 start was incredible. We had so many come-back wins that during one game, which we were losing 5–0, Dale Murphy, our great center fielder, said to me, "Well, they got us where we want them." We had thin starting pitching that year, but we did have good arms in the bull-pen and a lot of thunder in our lineup with Murphy, Chris Chambliss, who became my hitting coach with the Cardinals and Yankees, and Bob Horner. Bob had awesome talent, enough to hit .320 with 30 to 40 home runs every season. But he never got in very good shape, which caused him to get hurt. He'd always be looking to find reasons to come out of games. I knew about Horner's reputation, and I knew how important he was to us. So one of the first things I did as manager of the Braves was to name him captain of the team. Murph and Chambliss, both of whom were leaders, were much better suited for that role. So before I told Horner about it, I explained to Murph and Chambliss why I was doing it: I needed Bob to be more responsible. Being true professionals, they understood and never beefed. Bob had a good year for me, batting .261 with 32 home runs and 97 runs batted in, despite missing twenty-two games with an injury.

I never seriously considered naming a captain on the Yankees. One of the big stories in spring training regarded how we were going to replace Don Mattingly, the former captain, and his leadership. If I had picked a new captain, I might as well have drawn a bull's-eye on his back—that person would have been inundated with questions about replacing Mattingly. I told reporters that people like Joe Girardi, David Cone, Paul O'Neill, and Wade Boggs all had leadership qualities. Some people in the front office, though, insisted that we at least needed to select someone who would lead the team on the field at the start of every game, a responsibility that belonged to Mattingly. That's something I never would have thought about or considered important, but I was told we had to have someone do it. So I said it might as well be Boggs, an everyday player with the most experience.

After Captain Horner and the rest of my Braves posted our twelfth straight win, which set a modern major league record at the start of a season, the fans ran on the field as if we had won the pennant. We won again the next night. In our fourteenth game we had a thousand different ways to win, but we lost. We lost four more in a row after that. We were up and down all year. After that 13-0 start we went 76-73 the rest of the season, including one stretch where we were 2-19. We took a one-game lead over the Dodgers into the last day. We were playing the Padres in San Diego, and the Dodgers were playing in San Francisco against the Giants. Before our game Turner walked into the clubhouse.

After some friendly greetings I said to Ted, "You know, Ted, I was just telling Gibby that I wish I could give him the ball to pitch this game."

Turner looked at Gibson and said, "You think you could?" He was ready to sign my forty-six-year-old pitching coach to a contract. As it turned out, maybe I should have started Gibby. We got our ass kicked. The Padres jumped out to a big lead. As our game wore on, we knew we needed help from the Giants. If they beat the Dodgers, we would be West Division champions. If the Dodgers won, we would have to play them in a one-game playoff the next day. Toward the end of the game one of my players, Jerry Royster, grounded out and then came running back to the dugout at full speed with a smile on his face.

"Joe Morgan just hit a three-run home run!" he said. Jerry was talking about the game in San Francisco. The Giants were winning. He explained that the Padres' catcher, Terry Kennedy, had told him about it while he was batting. Kennedy got the information from the Padres' dugout, where one of the San Diego coaches, Whitey Wietelman, had a radio. We hurried through the rest of our game in time to watch the last inning of the Dodgers' loss on television. We were West Division champions. It would have been much more fun to win our game and celebrate on the field, but no one in our clubhouse was complaining. The Braves had not been to the postseason since 1969. We'd take it any way we could get it.

That was my best shot at the World Series until 1996. We needed three wins against St. Louis in the National League Championship Series to get there. We started off with a 1–0 lead in Game One with my ace pitcher, Phil Niekro, on the mound. And then it rained and the game was called off. We lost three straight games after that. The Cardinals simply were a better team than us. We were over-matched.

I lasted only two more years with the Braves, even though we finished in second place both times. Ted and I just never had a relationship built on trust. After we won our division title, for instance, I was still so angry about Ted's refusal to honor the attendance clause that I tried to stop the release of our television movie, because they weren't paying me. Turner's TV people had hooked me up to a microphone for every game that season to record all my dugout conversations, arguments with umpires, and meetings with pitchers on the mound. The recordings became the centerpiece to the movie. Another time, in 1983, Ted second-guessed me about some moves I had made in a losing game the previous night. He was screaming wildly at me in a conference room adjacent to his office in front of other people from the Braves' front office. I was humiliated. We won the game that afternoon, and Ted came into the clubhouse with a big smile. I asked him to come into my office and I closed the door behind him.

"Ted," I said, "you can fire me or do anything you want with me. I respect you. You're the owner. And if I worried about being second-guessed, we never would have won last year. But don't you ever, ever yell at me in front of a bunch of people again. You can yell at me all you want—just come in this office and scream. Don't do it in front of an audience."

Ted got the message. Steinbrenner gets a lot of notoriety for aggravating his managers, but George isn't nearly as meddlesome as Ted was in those days. Working for Steinbrenner has been a walk in the park compared with working for Turner. Once the 1996 season started, I didn't hear from Steinbrenner until four weeks into the regular season—and that was only because I called him up to ask about one of his horses that was running in the Kentucky Derby. I called him April 29 as our team bus was driving to Baltimore for a series against the Orioles. "George," I told him, "I've heard all these horror stories about you bugging your manager, and I had to call you." George laughed. At least he doesn't like to hang out in the clubhouse the way Turner did. Ted wanted to be loved by the players more than anything. The players came first, and then his staff. He had a habit after the last out of jumping over the wall of the stands and running through our dugout to the clubhouse. One night he ran from the stands into the dugout, and I had to tell him, "Uh, Ted, that's only two outs." And he ran all the way back and jumped back into his seat.

I liked Ted. We just never hit it off. He took me to his plantation in South Carolina after the 1983 season to talk to me about my contract. (He actually added two seasons to it, extending it through 1986.) He gave me a rifle and made sure I was in front of him when I was carrying it. After a long walk through the woods, he sent me up a tree to shoot deer. I saw one deer but didn't dare pull the trigger. The next day we got up at four in the morning to go duck hunting. All I could think about was getting back to sleep. I was a kid from Brooklyn. About the closest I had ever been to that kind of country life was chasing batting-practice balls on the swampy field of Waycross, Georgia. What did I know or care about that stuff?

Toward the end of the 1984 season I started picking up signals that the Braves were going to fire me. If you hang around baseball long enough, you can see it coming. I was making phone calls to the front office, and nobody was returning them. Nobody from upstairs was coming down to the clubhouse. It was like I had a contagious disease. Some people in the front office were quietly pushing Ted to hire Eddie Haas, a southern man who had been in the Atlanta organization for years. Finally I called Ted on the day after the season and said, "I want to come see you." I had a feeling I was going to be fired, and I wanted to make it easy for him. He invited me to his office. Sure enough, he told me I was fired. Ted looked a little uncomfortable doing it. He appeared relaxed whenever he was dealing with people in a large group. But in a one-on-one setting, he looked ill at ease. Being fired by him hurt me much more than being fired by the Mets. In New York the team had changed owners. I understood and expected that move. But in Atlanta it was political. It really bothered me.

A few weeks later I was watching television with Ali. Some celebrity was being interview. The person was asked, "How would you like to be remembered?" Ali turned to me and said, "That's a great question. What would you say, Joe?"

"I don't know," I said. "Just a guy who never realized his dream."

I was really down in the dumps. This time after I was fired, nobody called. So I picked up the phone and called the California Angels, when I heard from a New York sportswriter, Phil Pepe, about an opening there for a broadcaster. I sent them a tape of color commentary I had done for CBS radio with Jack Buck during the 1981 Division Series between Philadelphia and Montreal. Gene Autry, the old cowboy and Angels owner, hired me. I worked for five years with Bob Starr and then, in 1990, with Joe Garagiola and Reggie Jackson. I enjoyed the work, but I missed managing. I received slight interest about managerial openings with Houston and Pittsburgh in 1985, Minnesota in 1986, and Boston in 1988. Those jobs went to Hal Lanier, Jim Leyland, Tom Kelly, and Joe Morgan, respectively.

After about three years of broadcasting, I began to think, This is it. I'm finished with managing. I'll never get to the World Series. I heard rumors that people were afraid to hire me because I wanted more control over running a team than most managers. I heard rumors that teams were afraid of having Gibson as a pitching coach—people assumed we were a package—because of his intimidating personality. I don't know what it was, but I do know that to be hired as a manager, you need connections. And I had none. Actually, I did have one connection. My friend Dal Maxvill was the general manager of the Cardinals. But that didn't do me any good because his manager, Whitey Herzog, was a fixture in St. Louis. Then one day in July 1990 Maxvill called me. Herzog had tired of managing and quit. Maxvill needed a manager. He wanted to talk to me. I was on my way to Las Vegas to celebrate my fiftieth birthday. Maxie told me he'd meet me there at the Sands Hotel.

We sat for two and half hours in a back booth at the Sands coffee shop. I let Maxie know I was very interested. Ali encouraged me to do it. I had a comfortable job in the broadcast booth, and we liked living in California, but she knew how much my World Series dream meant to me. Maxie wanted me to manage right away, but the Angels were just about to start a three-city trip, and I didn't want to leave them short in the broadcast booth. Maxie and I agreed I would begin managing the Cardinals August 1. We also agreed that my contract would include the same roll-over provision the Cardinals gave Herzog. The club would extend my contract before the close of each season so that I would never go into the next season as a lame duck manager. I was excited. I hadn't managed in six years. It was like getting my first job all over again.

It turned out that the Cardinals were entering a transitional period. Gussie Busch had died in 1989, leaving his son, August, in charge. August was a terrific businessman with the Anheuser-Busch brewery, but he had no passion for baseball. If something didn't fit into his bottom line, then it didn't make sense to him. He wasn't going to spend the necessary money on the baseball team to make it a contender. I think Whitey had seen that change coming when he quit. We had some decent teams in St. Louis when I was there, but we never made the necessary player acquisitions in the off-season or down the stretch to get us over the hump.

The Cardinals posted winning records in my first three full seasons managing. George Kissell was a tremendous help to me as my spring training coordinator. He held a yellow pad during the games and jotted down things he noticed about our club that needed attention. Then we would review his list of our mistakes. He'd give me advice on strategy and then say, "I'm just giving you the aspirin, Joe. You decide whether to swallow it or spit it out." Just as in my playing days with the Cardinals, he questioned everything. He had a favorite line: "Joe, who wrote the book?" And I'd say, "Nobody, George. Nobody wrote the book." That was George's way of reminding me that I could make any move I wanted as a manager as long as I had the right reasons for it—whether it was unpopular or unorthodox. That style helped me in the 1996 World Series. I surprised some people with moves like benching Wade Boggs against a right-handed pitcher, letting my pitcher bat in the ninth inning, and putting the potential winning run on base intentionally. But that's the way I've always managed. I'm more concerned about winning the game than trying to cover my butt.

When you don't get results with that kind of managing style, you look like a dummy. I looked real dumb in 1994, especially in a game in Houston on my birthday. July 18 has become a dreaded date for me. I can hardly remember ever getting a hit as a player on my birthday or a win as a manager. Ali had flown in to be with me on my birthday, but I wasn't such great company that night. The game in Houston was a catastrophe. We blew an 11–0 lead and lost 15–12. On top of that, I got up in the middle of the night to go to the bathroom and broke my toe on the end of the bed. The next day Stuart Meyer, the president of the club, gave me a public vote of confidence. I appreciated the sentiment, but the timing wasn't great after such a bad loss that had the radio talk shows in St. Louis calling for my head.

Two days later I was called by August Busch to a meeting at a building at a soccer park on the west side of the city, where Anheuser-Busch likes to hold corporate meetings. Stuart Meyer and Maxvill also were there. Maxie and I sat down and thought we were going to talk about the club's game plan for the next year. August started the meeting by saying to me, "There is not going to be any extension of your contract."

Maxie jumped in right away, saying, "I can't do this to this man. When he came over here, I told him he would never go into a season on the last year of a contract."

"Well, we're changing that around here," August said. Apparently the public humiliation of that loss in Houston and the odd timing of Meyer's backing of me reflected poorly on the brewery. August hated to see even a hint of embarrassment come to the family business.

I looked at Maxie, and I could see the veins bulging in his neck. He stood up.

"This is all about that fucking 11-0 game, isn't it?" Maxie yelled. "Why don't you just sell the club?"

Then August stood up and his veins started to bulge. "Don't you tell me what to do," he screamed.

The meeting lasted about fifteen minutes. When we left, Maxie and I had to check if we still had our clothes on—that's how badly we were undressed. On our way home we stopped for breakfast. Maxie said, "Joe, I think I got myself fired this morning." I said, "Well, you did what you think is right. That's most important."

About a week later the major league players walked out on strike. We happened to be in Florida at the time, one of fourteen clubs on the road. All of the thirteen other clubs flew their players back on charter flights to their home cities. The Cardinals told their players to find their own way home. My players were rightfully pissed about it. August Busch then replaced Meyer, who resigned, with Mark Lamping. One day Maxvill was supposed to fly to St. Petersburg to watch some of our minor leaguers play. Lamping asked him to change his flight to sometime later that day. He was just stringing him along; Lamping fired Maxvill before he ever made that later flight. I felt badly about that because Maxie had sealed his fate when he stuck his neck out for me at that meeting with August. He's a loyal guy, and I've always appreciated that quality in a person. Lamping never bothered to pick up the phone and call me after he was hired. He started calling some of the players instead. Finally I called him and told him I wanted to meet with him and Jerry Ritter, one of August Busch's top executives. "How can you talk to the players before you even talk to the manager?" I said at the meeting. "You might as well make it easy on the next general manager coming in here and fire me; give him a clean slate." I went to the ballpark and started cleaning out some of my stuff. Lamping saw me. "What are you doing?" he said. "You don't have to do that." I knew that in interviewing possible general managers—he eventually hired Walt Jocketty after also talking with Lee

The year is 1962, and I am with Stan Musial in the old Busch Stadium.

On the field with my son Michael and Willie Mays.

Sitting with a friend in my first car, a 1960 Thunderbird that I bought from an unassuming Milwaukee car salesman named Bud Selig.

Frank and I at the Milwaukee Writers' Dinner in 1962 celebrating my rookie of the year award with the Braves.

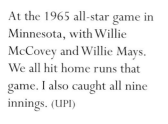

At the 1965 all-star game in Minnesota, with Willie McCovey and Willie Mays. We all hit home runs that game. I also caught all nine innings. (UPI)

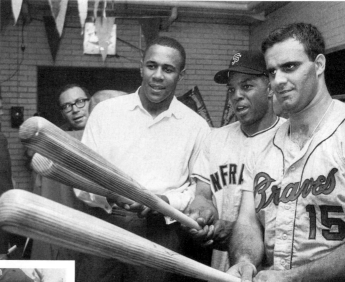

At the all-star game in St. Louis in 1966. The signature says: "To Joe, a great hitter. Best always, Ted Williams." (NEWS DEMOCRAT)

Accepting the 1971 MVP award and batting championship award in 1972 from National League President Chub Feeney.

Honored in February 1972 for the MVP award alongside Sandy Koufax, who won the Cy Young award that year.

Spring training, 1972, in St. Petersburg, Florida. Behind me, doing sit-ups, is Stan Musial, who liked to work out with the club even after he retired.

The most courageous ballplayer I've ever known—Bob Gibson. Shea Stadium, 1973: Gibson had blown his knee out the top half of the inning before, running the bases, but he still tried to pitch. He collapsed after releasing the ball. After his recovery he came back to pitch again.

Me, Gibson, and Tim McCarver in 1974. Because Gibson was pitching that day and wore his trademark game-face scowl, he refused to have his picture taken. We convinced him his back would do, so he agreed.

July 16, 1977, one of my favorite photographs: in the dugout at Shea Stadium for an Old-Timers' Day Game with Mickey Mantle, Ralph Kiner, and Joe DiMaggio. (LOUIS REQUENA)

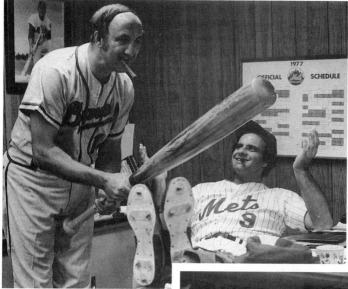

With my brother Frank in
my office as the Mets
manager in 1977.
(AP/WIDE WORLD PHOTOS)

At another Old-Timers' Day
game with Frank.

My fiftieth birthday party, July 18,
1990, with Rocco and Frank. That
day I had a conversation with the
St. Louis Cardinals about the
possibility of managing them.

October 1982: in the dugout talking to the press as the manager for the Braves in the playoffs against St. Louis. (HERREN)

With George Kissell and Mike Shannon in San Diego. I learned more about the game of baseball from Kissell than from anyone else.

Interviewing Roger Clemens. I was an announcer for six years, from 1985 to 1990.

December 14, 1995: in the hospital, holding Andrea Rae for the first time.

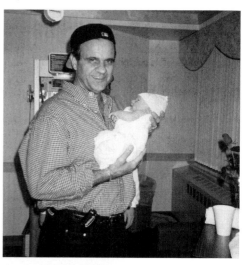

Making a point with President Bush at Dodger Stadium.

Thomas and Doug Melvin—Lamping spoke with Chris Chambliss about managing and also tried to get Jim Leyland from the Pirates. Once Jocketty was aboard, I'm sure he made a run at getting Tony LaRussa. I was treated with no respect, and it bothered the hell out of me.

As the strike lingered on, the owners made plans to bring in replacement players. I wasn't around for the Black Sox scandal in 1919, but the travesty of replacement baseball in the spring of 1995 was the darkest time in the history of baseball, as far as I'm concerned. No baseball would have been much better than trying to force that inferior product on the public. I hated being around it, but I had signed a contract to manage the St. Louis Cardinals, no matter what players wore the uniform. As an old union man, I thought the players overreacted to the replacement player charade. Those guys weren't a threat to their jobs. If anything, the replacements reminded the whole world how talented and special the major leaguers are.

The owners were way off base in thinking the replacement idea would fly. One day in spring training I was in the restaurant at the Don Cesar hotel with Jocketty, Lamping, and Jerry Ritter. Our wives accompanied us. Jerry asked me, "What class of baseball do you think the replacements are equivalent to?" I said, "Low A ball." He looked at me in disbelief. He thought it was close to Triple-A baseball.

Then Lamping said, "It doesn't matter. By July the fans aren't going to really care who the players are on the field because all they want to do is come out to the ballpark, drink beer, and have fun with each other."

I looked at my wife, and she had to bite her lip. I was

shocked myself. Here I was trying my whole life to win a championship, and this guy didn't even care who he sent out there in the uniform of the St. Louis Cardinals. I felt ashamed even to be associated with baseball management. August Busch also held a meeting with my staff and me about presenting a positive image to the press about replacement ball. Before the meeting I asked to talk with him privately. He was about to learn about the streak of honesty I shared with Rae. "I just want to tell you something," I said. "I will do anything you need me to do, but there's one thing I won't do: I won't lie. I can't lie and say I'm enjoying this or looking forward to this or whatever we're going to do. I can't do that. I'm telling you that now one-on-one so that you understand."

Then I told Busch that I had attended a union meeting in Orlando the previous night. I had gone there with some other managers, including Jim Fregosi, Gene Lamont, and Jim Leyland, to fight for my coaches because I heard the players were considering taking coaches off the list of people who get a cut of their licensing revenue. Busch was furious about me going there. I didn't give a shit if he fired me on the spot. He started talking again about the need to sell replacement baseball.

"I can't do that," I told him, "because eventually the major league players are going to be back."

"How do you know they'll be back?" he said.

Right then I really knew how screwed up the owners were. They actually believed that they could permanently replace the best players in the world with truck drivers, softball players, and a collection of has-been players. With the help of a court injunction, the major leaguers did come back in April—a lot quicker than August had thought. My relationship with them was irreparably damaged. I could tell they resented me for managing the replacement players. By June 16 we were in fourth place with a 20-27 record. Early in the morning we traded Todd Zeile to the Chicago Cubs. The deal wasn't supposed to be announced until one P.M., but I heard about it on the radio at about ten A.M. as I was driving home from getting a haircut. I called Walt Jocketty to tell him about it when I got home. He said, "Where are you?" I said, "I'm home." And he said, "I'll be right over." I hung up the phone and told Ali, "I think we're getting fired here." It was a strange feeling. I had never been fired during the season.

Walt came over, and he started crying. "We have to make a change," he said. "Don't worry about it, Walt," I said. I was the one getting fired, and there I was cheering *him* up. We talked for a while, then I gave him a bottle of wine and sent him on his way. I was sort of thankful he did fire me. It was bound to happen. It was like going to the dentist: Just get it over with. My first reaction was to want to curl up and hide. But then I told Ali, "Let's go out." She said, "You want to go out to dinner?" I said, "Yeah, let's do it."

I wasn't ashamed of anything. There was no reason to hide. I had had a good run as a manager, and I planned to go back to broadcasting. The politics and players' attitudes in St. Louis had left a sour taste in my mouth anyway. I thought I was treated shabbily by the Cardinals, though I never said anything to embarrass the organization even when I was fired. I talked with Frank, and I could tell he was happy that I was finished with managing. He told me I didn't need the aggravation anymore. I couldn't argue with him.

I knew my window to getting to the World Series was not just closed, it had been slammed shut. I had been lucky enough to get managing jobs with all three of the teams I had played for—and been fired by every one of them. I had no more former teams left to come calling. Who would want a fifty-five-year-old manager who had been fired three times, had never been to the World Series, and had a lifetime record of more losses (1,003) than wins (894)? Nobody, I figured. By George, was I wrong.

CHAPTER 7

Season of a Lifetime

**A**FTER I WAS FIRED ALI AND I MOVED to Cincinnati to be close to her family. In October, just before the Braves and Indians began the 1995 World Series, I took a trip to Las Vegas with one of my friends from Atlanta, Ed Maull. One day when I called home to talk to Ali, she said, "Joe Molloy and Gene Michael are trying to get in touch with you." Joe Molloy is George Steinbrenner's son-in-law and the Yankees' general partner. Gene Michael was the general manager of the Yankees, who I had heard was stepping down. I told Ed, "It's probably about the general manager's job." My instincts were right. I flew to Tampa to meet with them. I decided down there it wasn't the job I was interested in. Ali was almost eight months pregnant, and with a baby on the way, I wasn't looking to work twenty-five hours a day, thirteen months a year, which is what being general manager for Steinbrenner requires.

A few days later, on October 23, I heard the Yankees had hired Bob Watson to be GM. Bob had played for me in Atlanta, when I managed the Braves. He was a very energetic person who had served me unofficially as a hitting coach. He loved to work with other players in the batting cage. Now he was leaving his job as general manager of the Astros to come to New York. While in Houston, he had overcome prostate cancer. With gallows humor I called him up to congratulate him on his new job.

"Have you gotten yourself checked lately by the doctors?" I said. "Did the doctors tell you you had six months to live? Is that why you took this crazy job?"

I wrote a note to George Steinbrenner thanking him for the interview. "Maybe someday down the road we'll work together," I wrote. I licked the envelope shut and put a stamp on it. That night, before I mailed it, one of my very good friends, Arthur Richman, called me. Arthur had worked as the Mets' public relations director and later traveling secretary while I played and managed there. He works with the Yankees as a senior adviser to Steinbrenner.

"Joe, would you be interested in managing the Yankees?" he said.

"Sure I would," I said. I knew that managing did not require the around-the-clock work hours that being general manager for Steinbrenner required. The manager is responsible only for what happens on the field, while the general manager oversees every facet of the organization.

"It looks like Buck Showalter is leaving," Arthur said, referring to the Yankees' manager, whose contract expired

October 31. "George asked me to come up with a list of candidates, and I recommended you. He didn't even know that you're a New Yorker. When I told him that, he got excited. Sit tight. George is going to call you."

I put the note in the mail. About a week later George called me at home.

"You're my man," he said. "We're not doing anything yet and the final say will be up to the general manager, but you're my man. You can pick your own coaches, but I'd like Willie Randolph and Tony Cloninger to stay on, and we're considering Mel Stottlemyre as pitching coach. And if anybody asks you, you can't say you talked to me." George didn't want anyone to think he had started looking for another manager until Showalter officially was gone. We talked for about fifteen minutes. George stressed the importance of loyalty to himself and the organization, and I assured him that that was never going to be a problem with me. We didn't talk about a salary or length of contract. We didn't even talk about a timetable for when I would be hired. A couple of days later, on November 1, Watson called me and told me a prepaid ticket was waiting for me at the Cincinnati airport for a trip to Tampa. George wanted to meet with me that day and introduce me the next day at a press conference in New York as the new manager of the Yankees.

I telephoned Frank from the airplane on my trip to Tampa. Frank didn't want me to manage at all—I think he was even more bitter about the St. Louis situation than I was.

"You don't need this crap anymore," he said.

"But Frank," I said, "it's too good an opportunity to get to the World Series."

Frank heard the excitement in my voice. He, more than anyone, was aware of my dream. He didn't try to talk me out of it.

"I can tell you want to do this," Frank said. "Go ahead and do it. That's all that counts—you have to do what you want to do. And as long as you're going to manage, this is the perfect job for you."

George told me about the contract: two years, $1.05 million. That was nonnegotiable because that was his offer to Showalter. It was a pay cut for me—I'd earned $550,000 with St. Louis—but I understood. He was taking a lot of heat for losing Showalter, so it wouldn't look good for him to give someone else more money. He also gave me a piece of advice for the press conference. "Just be upbeat." He didn't have to worry about that. I was thrilled. Like everyone else, I had heard all the horror stories about working for George. But I didn't care because of one thing: I knew George was willing to spend the money to win a world championship. It wasn't like St. Louis, where sometimes I had felt as if I were in a fight with my fists while the other guy had a gun. I didn't see any downside. I called up my wife, brothers, sisters, and some friends late that night to let everyone know I was the manager of the Yankees.

The press conference the next day, November 2, was more like an indoor grilling. Showalter had been a popular young manager, and the press looked at my record and figured I was a retread. The line of questioning focused on my losing record. The next day one of the writers referred to me as Clueless Joe. None of it bothered me. I didn't feel that I had to qualify myself to anyone. I told them, "Let's wait and see."

Bob and I flew back to Tampa to meet again with George, this time about my coaching staff. I noticed some people in the Yankee front office called him Mr. Steinbrenner. Not me. I called him George or Boss right from the beginning. That's important to me, because that way I'm talking to him on the same level. I had heard all the stories about how intimidating George can be, but I have never felt pressure being around him. Maybe that was because I didn't expect to get a job like this again. It was a bonus for me.

I liked the idea of trying to get Mel Stottlemyre to be the pitching coach. That was fine. I admired the way he had pitched—he was a no-nonsense guy who wasn't afraid to knock a hitter on his ass—and he had won a world championship as pitching coach for the Mets. George and I agreed that Chris Chambliss would be the hitting coach. I added that I wanted Jose Cardenal as my outfield coach. Jose is a class person, and I think it's important to have a Latin coach on your staff. A manager needs someone to help communicate with his Latin players. It's a bad idea to use a player as your translator because if you have to criticize someone, it should not be done with other players in earshot.

"You've got one more coach," George said. I needed a bench coach. I asked Arthur to give me a list of candidates. I drew up my list. Both lists included Don Zimmer. Though I had often chatted with Zim, we weren't real close friends. I liked the fact that he had managed in four places with an aggressive style, had coached in New York for Steinbrenner, and was very loyal. I called up the sixty-five-year-old Zimmer and said, "So, are you enjoying retirement?"

"Just cashed my first Social Security check," he said.

"I've got a question for you," I said. "How would you like to be my bench coach?"

There was silence on the line. Finally I said, "Well, what do you think?"

"Did George ask you to make this call?"

"No, this is my decision."

"I'll have to think about it."

Zimmer hung up and dialed Billy Connors, the Yankees' organizational pitching coach, and asked him if George had put me up to hiring him. Zim knew no manager wants to have a bench coach forced upon him. He would take the job only if he knew I sincerely wanted him next to me. When Billy assured him it was my decision, he called me back and accepted the job. I got to him just in time, because Buddy Bell, the new Tigers' manager, wanted Zimmer too.

Zim turned out to be the perfect bench coach. I talked more in the dugout than I ever had before, and that's because I ran everything past Zim. When one of my moves didn't work out and I was hard on myself, Don would say, "I should have said this to you . . . ," or, "No, you did the right thing. You'll be fine." We had a great rapport and a lot of fun. We acted silly in the dugout sometimes. He would call me a goof, and I would call him a goof back. So we started a Goof Club. I was Goof I, and he was Goof II. We'd joke about oddball moves during the game—"Hey, Goof I, how about having Cecil Fielder steal a base here," he'd say—and break up laughing. The combination of Zim and me worked so well that it made me think back to how Tim McCarver and I used to talk, when we were Cardinals teammates, about being co-managers someday. It was as stimulating and as fun as Timmy and I had envisioned. Zim and I made such a good team that in one of my telephone conversations with Steinbrenner during the season, I said, "George, how about after you fire me, you put Zim and me in the broadcast booth?" George roared with laughter and said, "No way!"

Five weeks after the Yankees hired me, Ali gave birth to our daughter, Andrea Rae, who is a miracle in herself. Ali and I had tried for years to have a baby. A few years ago she lost a baby during pregnancy. We talked about adoption. And then all of a sudden along came little Andrea. I was thrilled. People would kid me about having a baby at my age. I'd tell them, "Hey, I'm a fifty-five-year-old man. I have to get up in the middle of the night all the time. She's on *my* schedule."

Ali has been unbelievably supportive. When spring training began, she told me, "You're going to win the World Series this year. This is the year." In August she was telling my daughters from my second marriage, Tina, who lives in England, and Lauren, who lives in Italy, to make plans to be in New York for the World Series. "Would you be quiet?" I said. "It's only August." She'd fire back, "You guys are going to do it. You'll be fine."

Ali and I are such a perfect match that Steinbrenner likes to get on me about being henpecked. I tell him, "You know what? You're right. I can't help it." I have no problem pleading guilty to that charge. It's nice to feel that you want to do something for someone. Ali will tell me, "Don't do it because of me." And I'll tell her, "Why not? Who else am I going to do it for?" The truth is, Ali already has done so much for me. She's made me into a better, happier person—and a much less guarded one. About a month after the World Series, something was bothering me, and I said something to her that nearly caused her to faint right on the spot. I turned one of her favorite lines on her: "Ali, we've got to talk." After a few seconds to recover from the shock, she burst out laughing.

Ali knew how important the World Series dream was to me. And in my first meeting of spring training, I made sure my players understood too.

"Men," I said, "every single one of my coaches has been to the World Series. I haven't. I plan to rectify that this year. I'm determined as hell to get there. One thing you can count on is that I won't manage through the media. If there's something you should know, you're going to hear it from me first. I'm going to do everything I can to eliminate tension on this team. I'll put it in simple terms for you: The one thing I'm interested in is the way we perform on the field, and I'm going to make it as tension-free as possible so that we can devote all of our energy to that."

I thought the meeting went well. As I scanned the room while I talked, I saw the eyes of every player. Nobody was flipping through mail or trying on spikes. I had their attention and I thought this group was serious about winning. I knew we had the potential to win the pennant, especially because of pitchers like David Cone, Jimmy Key, Andy

Pettitte, Kenny Rogers, Dwight Gooden, and John Wetteland. It was easily the best pitching staff I ever had as a manager.

On our first day of full workouts in Tampa, outfielders Tim Raines and Gerald Williams showed up on the field after the entire team had run a warm-up lap. I told them, "I don't want to take your money, so you owe me a lap. You can run it at the end of stretching exercises." And they did. I wanted them to know everyone would be treated equally.

That was the most difficult spring training I've ever had because I didn't know very much about my players. I had never played or managed in the American League. I relied a lot on my coaches and Mark Newman, the assistant farm director who did an amazingly efficient job of running a crowded camp of about sixty players at our new facility in Tampa. Stottlemyre, for instance, was the one who convinced me to be confident about Dwight Gooden, even though he was hit hard in spring training. "He's got good pop on the ball," Mel told me. The New York writers were convinced that I believed in Gooden because he was Steinbrenner's personal project. One of them wrote that I rigged an intrasquad game to have Gooden pitch against our reserve and minor league players, instead of our starters, just to make him look good. Not only was that a lie, it was absurd to suggest I would do such a thing.

My six years in the broadcast booth gave me a better understanding of the media and made me more patient with them. But that day forced me to make a decision: either I could stop reading the New York papers and just be as clear and concise as possible with reporters, or I could read the papers and continue to get agitated and overreact enough to distract me from my job. The answer was easy: I would live in a vacuum and not pay any attention to the stuff in the papers, because it doesn't mean anything.

I had more serious problems in spring training anyway. Tim Raines, Tony Fernandez, whom I expected to be my starting second baseman, Pat Kelly, Melido Perez, and Scott Kamieniecki all were hurt in spring training. David Cone concerned me more than Gooden—he had no snap on the ball. And Mariano Rivera, who I had heard had a live arm, showed me an average fastball that was very straight. I knew other teams wanted Rivera, and I told the front office to listen to any deals for him. I don't think they paid attention to me on that suggestion. Rivera started the year as the long man in my bullpen. Jeff Nelson was my setup guy in front of John Wetteland.

I learned very quickly about the mental toughness of my team. After an April Fool's Day opener was snowed out in Cleveland, we beat the defending league champion Indians twice in their own park. By the end of the season and post-season, we would be 18-0 on the road against the Indians, Orioles, and Braves, three of the best teams in baseball.

We didn't fare nearly as well on my nostalgic returns to Milwaukee County Stadium, scene of Frank's magical 1957 World Series home run and my major league debut. The Brewers battered us there in April and in another series in July—including a typical 16–4 rout on my birthday. We were 1-5 in Milwaukee while being outscored 42–22. The way the Brewers smacked us around reminded me of how we used to steal the opposing catcher's signs when I played at

County Stadium with the Braves. Our relief pitchers could see the signs from a hut in the outfield bullpen. Only one of them would keep a hat on during a game—he would be the one to relay the signs to the hitter. The pitcher would look straight ahead for a fastball, to the right for a curveball, to the left for a slider, and would put his hand on his head for a change-up.

I don't know for sure if teams still steal signs that way, but the Brewers hit us like they knew what was coming. When teams play you much better in their park than in yours—the Brewers and the Texas Rangers come to mind—it makes you think maybe something is going on. There are a few players who don't like to know what pitch is coming. I found that out when I was catching Lew Burdette with the Braves. He had so much trouble getting Orlando Cepeda out that he resorted to telling him what pitch was coming. He'd say, "Here comes a fastball," and all of a sudden Cepeda couldn't touch him. When he threw his infamous "mystery pitch," he would just mouth the words "wet one." Cepeda was so thrown by Burdette's ploy that he once stepped out of the batter's box and said to the umpire, "Make him stop doing that!" The umpire just shook his head and said, "Nothing I can do."

I don't know how we survived that first month of the season. Jimmy Key, who was coming off major rotator cuff surgery, had no command of his pitches. Cone couldn't spot the ball either because of occasional numbness in his fingers. Gooden was being pelted. Bob Wickman, whom I counted on for important innings out of the bullpen, was a disappointment. The one bright spot was Rivera, whose fastball came alive. As late as April 19 he still was so buried in my bullpen that he pitched three innings of mop-up work in a 7–1 loss in Minnesota. But he threw so well that I decided to try him as a setup man. Three days later he and Wetteland combined for four shutout innings in a 6–2 win over the Royals. All of a sudden my job was a hell of a lot easier. The Formula was born. With Rivera for two innings and Wetteland for one, I knew we could shut down teams after the sixth inning.

During our game the next night, a 5–2 loss to Kansas City, a flyball fell between Bernie Williams and Paul O'Neill in the outfield. I thought O'Neill should have caught the ball, and I told him so. After I removed O'Neill late in the next game, Michael Kay, one of our radio and TV broadcasters, asked me if I was punishing O'Neill. I answered the question, but I didn't like his accustory manner. When I saw Kay the following night in the middle of our clubhouse, I jumped on his ass.

"Don't fuck with me," I told him. "I don't appreciate you trying to stir up something in the clubhouse. We've got a pretty good chemistry going, and I don't need you to create things to mess it up." I was really angry. If I had seen Kay in a hallway or my office, I would have done it in those places. I happened to see him in the clubhouse. But I admit I didn't mind the players hearing me. It was good for them to know that I do get pissed sometimes.

While I was working out in our exercise room that night, O'Neill came up to me and said, "I read in the papers I'm miffed at you." I said, "I don't read the papers, so you'll have to tell me what they said. Besides, are you miffed?" And he said, "No." So I said, "So it doesn't really matter." I'm proud that I was able to accomplish one of my major goals with the Yankees: to remove the tension in the clubhouse that often is created in New York. Pressure is part of the game, but you shouldn't have tension.

It was shortly after that, on that bus ride to Baltimore April 29, that I called George just to screw around with him. We were 12-10 and tied with the Orioles for first place. "Let's see if we can open up a lead on Baltimore," George said. With my starting pitching problems, I was thinking, let's not get too far behind Baltimore. It turned out to be a landmark series for us. That's where we established our identity as a gritty, determined club with a lot of heart—the mentally toughest team I've ever been around. We fell behind in the first game, 9–4, but came back to win 13–10 in the longest nine-inning game in major league history (four hours, twenty-one minutes). We beat the Orioles again the next night in fifteen innings, 11–6.

Andy Pettitte, who had been knocked out of the previous game in the second inning, showed me a lot of character as he pitched three scoreless innings of relief for the victory. Andy demands so much out of himself that my only concern about him going into the season was that he would get off to a slow start and then make it worse by pressing. Fortunately, we scored a lot of runs for him early when he wasn't pitching well and then he went on a roll. He had a Cy Young award kind of season, but so did Pat Hentgen of the Toronto Blue Jays. When I called Andy after he finished second to Hentgen in the balloting, I heard real disappointment in his voice. He spoke glowingly of Hentgen, but admitted he'd wanted to win it. A lot of guys will tell you, "Oh, it doesn't matter." But I liked hearing Andy say he was disappointed. He is an earnest, hardworking kid who sets high standards for himself.

After our two-game sweep in Baltimore, David Cone kept us on the winning track when he pitched a brilliant five-hitter to beat Chicago 5–1. But his circulatory problem would not go away. When doctors discovered an aneurysm two days after that start, I figured he was gone for the season. Fortunately, just as Cone went down, the old Doc Gooden came back. On May 8, the day we put Coney on the disabled list, Gooden won his first game in almost two years, having spent almost all of that time on baseball's suspended list for drug use.

On May 14, Gooden's next start, Bill Cosby called our public relations department asking for tickets to that game against Seattle. I met Bill through Bob Gibson while I was playing for the Cardinals. Bill has become a good friend who is such a kind person that he once did seventy-five minutes of comedy at a charity dinner Ali and I helped organize in St. Louis, then refused to accept a fee. Bill planned to stop by the clubhouse before the game to visit the players. He canceled at the last minute. Cos missed a hell of a game. Gooden had a no-hitter and a 2–0 lead with runners at second and third in the ninth inning and one out. He struck out Jay Buhner. The next batter was a left-handed hitter, Paul Sorrento, with a right-hander, Dan Wilson, on deck.

"Who's the next hitter?" Zimmer asked me. I've learned

that when Zim says that, it's his key to suggest a strategic move.

"Wilson," I said.

"Want to put this guy on?" Zimmer said to me.

"Don't bother messing around with me now," I told him. "He's walked six guys already. I can't do that. I may be sorry later if this guy whacks one, but I can't do that. The last thing I want to do is load the bases where he has to throw a strike."

We got lucky. Gooden threw Sorrento a high breaking ball but got away with it. Sorrento popped it up. Dwight had his no-hitter. I never was fortunate enough to catch a no-hitter, though I did play third base when Bob Gibson no-hit the Pittsburgh Pirates in 1971. I'm not superstitious enough to avoid saying "no-hitter" when a guy is throwing one—that's supposed to be the ultimate jinx—though as Dwight rolled on I didn't move from my seat after the fifth inning, even though I felt a pressing need to go to the bathroom. The most amazing part of the night was that he no-hit probably the greatest offensive machine I've ever seen. The Mariners could beat you by belting home runs and manufacturing runs. It was tremendous to watch Dwight leave the field on his teammates' shoulders, pumping his arms and screaming with joy. It seemed like he had been walking on eggshells after his suspension from the game for drug abuse, and a lot of emotions came pouring out. The victory kept us two and a half games ahead of Baltimore, with a 22-14 record. Dwight really gave us a lift while Cone was out. He pitched well until his arm grew weary late in the season. He wasn't equipped to pitch a lot of innings after being out of baseball that long. And when Gooden did falter, Cone came back just in time to replace him.

We hit our first stretch of poor play on a West Coast trip in May, losing four of the first six games. Some guys were getting careless in their work habits. Base runners and batters were missing signs. When we opened a series in Oakland May 31, I decided we needed what I call a red ass meeting. I'm not a screamer and I don't throw things in the clubhouse, but I do have a temper. I get real worked up when I'm angry. I'm very forceful with my words. And I made sure I let my team know I was angry.

"This is the best chance I've ever had to get to the World Series," I told them. "I'm determined to work hard to do it. And if it takes making your life miserable, that's what I'm going to do. If I didn't think we had the team to do it, then it wouldn't bother me. But I sure as hell know we do have the team to do it. And when you're not doing all the things you need to do to win, that's when this shit has to stop. I'm an easy manager to play for. But when you're making mistakes that you shouldn't make—and it has nothing to do with striking out or making errors—then I can make your life miserable."

I remember in that meeting I singled out a few players, such as Ruben Sierra and Bernie Williams, for making too many mental mistakes. After the meeting was over I walked around the clubhouse, kind of taking inventory. I could tell something wasn't right with Bernie.

"You all right?" I said. "What's the matter?"

"You didn't get on Boggs," he said.

Bernie's a smart guy who doesn't miss too much. He knew that during a recent game Wade Boggs had made a mistake on the bases by not knowing how many outs there were at the time. I pulled out my notes for the meeting and showed Bernie I had written down Wade Boggs's name, too, but had forgotten to get on him.

"I thought you didn't get on him just because he's a future Hall of Famer," Bernie said.

"No, I just forgot," I told him.

I made sure that I got on Boggs in the dugout in front of everybody. I did it in a different kind of way—more light-hearted than my mood in the meeting—about not keeping track of the number of outs. I wanted everyone, including Bernie, to know that in my quest to get to the World Series, everybody would be treated equally.

It was during that series that Sierra called me a liar, claiming I had reneged on a promise to play him in the outfield instead of as the designated hitter. I didn't worry about it too much. I just considered the source. Ruben was the toughest guy I ever had to manage. As much as I tried to talk to him about the team concept of baseball, he just never did get it. I guess a long time ago somebody must have decided, "He has a great deal of ability. Just leave him alone," because Ruben has no clue what baseball is about. That was evident when he came back to New York after we traded him to Detroit. He thought he was ripping the Yankees when he said, "All they care about over there is winning." That told you everything you needed to know about Ruben Sierra. He announced to the world that he cared only about his statistics, regardless of whether his team won or not. The day after Ruben said that, Tigers' manager Buddy Bell came up to me and said, "He's going to find out we want to win too." Ruben doesn't play for Detroit anymore. He's now with Cincinnati, his fifth team in six years.

It took time for me to understand what Sierra was all about. We made him our project in spring training. He came in heavy, and we worked to get some weight off him. We had Chris Chambliss work with him on his hitting, Jose Cardenal on his outfield play, and Reggie Jackson on all aspects of his game, including his mental approach. He did okay in the outfield. His feet got quicker as we worked with him. But Ruben is like a spoiled kid. He wants everything his way. He always thought he should have been playing right field instead of Paul O'Neill. He always thought he should be wearing number 21, his old number, instead of O'Neill.

When Tim Raines started the season on the disabled list, I told Ruben, "You can't play the outfield. Gerald Williams is playing left field. I can't put you in left field and DH Gerald Williams. He is a better defensive player. I can't do that." But Ruben would never acknowledge that he understood what I was talking about or that it was the right thing to do. I'd talk to him, I'd put my arms around him, I'd be positive around him—it was a lot of work. And he still didn't get it.

Every time he didn't play, he was moping. I'd explain to him why he wouldn't be playing against a certain pitcher, and he never understood. When he called me a liar, I told him, "Look, when I say something, I mean it. But when things change, like Raines getting hurt, my thoughts change."

Finally I went to Bob Watson and told him, "Get rid of Sierra." Somehow, someway, Bob made a deal for Cecil Fielder on July 31, in which he convinced the Tigers to take Sierra. He should have been named executive of the year right on the spot.

The only other guy who really gave me some grief was Jimmy Leyritz, and that was only because Jimmy's a proud guy who objected to me pulling him for a pinch hitter. I took him out in a situation where I wanted a left-handed batter facing a right-handed pitcher. I didn't think it was such a big deal. After all, I wasn't afraid to hit for former batting champions like Wade Boggs and Paul O'Neill to get what I thought to be better matchups. But Jimmy made a scene in the dugout about it. I felt he was showing me up. The next day I met privately with him and told him I didn't appreciate the way he acted. Jimmy told me, "I'm a better hitter the bigger the situation. I rise to the occasion"— words I would recall distinctly when he hit a huge home run in Game Four of the World Series. I told Jimmy, "I'm glad you're a better hitter in big situations. But if I'm going to pinch-hit for you or anybody, I'm going to pinch-hit. I'm going to do what I can to win the game."

We played better after I chewed out the team in Oakland, winning all three games there. But I had something else to worry about: My brother Frank was sick at his home in Florida, and the doctors could not pinpoint what was wrong. I talked with him every day, and he sounded worse with each conversation. Frank's friends would call me up—

as many as six of them a day—and say, "Have you talked to Frank lately? He doesn't sound good. You've got to do something." Those guys were driving me nuts.

Frank said his stomach hurt, and he felt so lethargic that he didn't even feel like getting out of bed and walking across the room. Doctors removed his gallbladder, which they called the worst-diseased gallbladder they had ever seen. Frank felt a little better after having it removed, but he quickly deteriorated again. The doctors couldn't pinpoint the problem. I noticed something terrible in his voice. The world's greatest needler, the guy who would battle you with all his might at everything from cards to golf, and the guy who toughened me up, wanted to quit. He was ready to die. Now it was my turn to return the favor. I pushed Frank to keep fighting. My first order of business was to get him into a better hospital in New York. He refused, saying he didn't feel up to the trip.

While I was worried about Frank, George called me and Stottlemyre up to his office on June 18. George called Watson frequently during the season to complain about players if they weren't producing. He's very reactionary. Every once in a while he would suggest I bench someone, take a pitcher out of the rotation, or send someone to the minors. Never did I make any decision like that because he suggested it. Anytime I did make a personnel decision, it was for one reason: I thought it was best for the team.

He also loved to blame my coaching staff when things went wrong, which I can understand because it's part of his football mindset. If a guy wasn't hitting, it was the fault of Chris Chambliss, my hitting coach. If the bullpen was struggling, it was the fault of Tony Cloninger, my bullpen coach. One my outfielders, Gerald Williams, had a bad habit of trying to pick up a rolling ball with his bare hand. Every once in a while he would drop the ball, and whenever he did, George would complain to me that Jose Cardenal, my outfield coach, wasn't doing his job. But I knew Cardenal worked with Gerald constantly to get him to field the ball with his glove. My coaching staff worked long and hard, so they shouldn't be blamed for players' mistakes.

George would second-guess me sometimes about game decisions too. That didn't bother me. I was harder on myself than anyone else when things didn't work out. But George never second-guessed me on the same decisions on which I beat myself up. He never hit on the same nerve, so his second-guessing never rattled me.

Steinbrenner wasn't second-guessing when he called Mel and me up to his office that day in June. He was worried about a day-night doubleheader we were scheduled to play in Cleveland in two days. I planned to pitch two rookies against the Indians, Brian Boehringer and Ramiro Mendoza. George was afraid we were going to get embarrassed by a powerful Indians team in his hometown.

"We can't go into Cleveland with these two kids," he told us. "What else can we do? Can we call up somebody from the minors with more experience? What about Wally Whitehurst?"

Maybe it's because everything else seemed small compared with Frank's problems, but I told George, "Don't worry about it, Boss. We'll win. And if we lose, it's not going to be because of our starting pitchers. Besides, Mel already told Mendoza he's starting. Do you want to circumvent my pitching coach's authority and just negate his credibility?"

Eventually George said, "Fine, but it's your ass that's on the line."

We fell behind Cleveland in the opener of that Friday doubleheader 5–1, then staged one of our patented rallies to win in ten innings 8–7. One of the most important elements in our ability to come from behind was our bullpen. I knew we had enough good arms there to hold the team down to enable us to come back. I also hammered home the importance of thinking small, of chipping away at deficits rather than trying to make them up in one giant chunk—a philosophy that would never be more important than in Game Four of the World Series. I like my team to play the first six innings of a game as if the score is 0–0. Even if we're down by four or five runs, for instance, I'll continue to steal bases up until the seventh or eighth inning, when the urgency of the situation forces you to be more conservative. We did a terrific job of doing whatever we could to get one run at a time, no matter how much we trailed.

It was a huge win, coming back like that on the road against a team like Cleveland. I walked back to the visiting manager's office at Jacobs Field feeling great. We had about two hours to kill before the second game, so we ate dinner in the clubhouse. And then about thirty minutes before the second game, the telephone rang. It was Ali.

"Are you sitting down?" she said. I immediately thought that Frank, who was in a hospital in Florida, had died.

"Rocco died," she said.

I was in shock. I couldn't believe it. Ali started crying.

"What are you going to do?" she said between sobs.

"Let me think for a minute," I said. "I'll call you back." I told Arthur Richman, who was in the room with me, what had happened. He started crying. Then I called Rocco's wife, Rose. She told me Rocco had been watching our game on television. We were losing in the ninth inning, and Rocco said, "They haven't won one of these games all year." Rose said, "There's always a first time." And we did come back to win. Then Rose said to him, "What would you like for dinner? Would you like to go out, or do you want to cook something here?" Rocco didn't answer. He just reached up and grabbed both sides of his head and fell over. He was dead from a heart attack.

I called Ali back. I said, "He's gone. There's nothing I can do. My responsibility is here. I'll come home Sunday."

Word spread through the clubhouse about Rocco. John Wetteland walked into my office and expressed his sympathy.

"What's your sister-in-law's name?" he asked.

"Rose," I said. "Why?"

"I want to pray for her," he said.

I went right back to work. We won the second game 9–3, behind Mendoza. We won again on Saturday 11–9, with another big comeback after being down 5–0 to Dennis Martinez. Then on Sunday, in a game we would win 6–5, I left in the second inning to fly home. I said good-bye to Rocco that night, and we buried him the next morning. Before the casket was closed, I placed in it my lineup card from the first game of the Friday doubleheader, the last game Rocco ever

175

saw. I also put my cap in the casket and a baseball auto-graphed by all my players.

Rocco was sixty-eight when he died. My father was sixty-eight when he died. My mother was sixty-nine when she died. Frank was two months away from his sixty-fifth birth-day when he received his new heart. I am very aware of my own mortality and the prevalence of heart disease in my family history. I undergo an extensive, high-tech stress test at least every two years, including as recently as January 1997. My friend and cardiologist, Dr. Joe Platania, tells me my heart is functioning normally. With my beloved Rocco gone, I wonder if his fancy machines can tell that it is also a little bit broken.

About a week before the all-star game, Indians' manager Mike Hargrove called me to say he wanted me to be one of his all-star coaches. I gratefully accepted. Three days later I called him back and said, "Mike, I hope you don't mind if I back out. I have a new baby and I haven't been able to spend a lot of time at home. Plus, I'm exhausted." Mike said he understood and wished me luck. He had sent me a very nice note after Rocco died, and later, after we won the World Series, he sent me another sensitive letter congratulating me.

At the same time, George signed Darryl Strawberry from the independent Northern League. He sent him to Triple-A Columbus to get some at bats. I was reluctant to have Darryl. I hadn't heard too much that was good about the guy, especially concerning his past problems with alcohol, drugs, women, and the IRS. When reporters asked me if signing Darryl was my idea, I told them, "It's an organizational decision." George was ready to bring him up right away to the Yankees. He kept asking me, "Do you want him for this game?" And I'd say, "No, let's just wait." Finally I decided to bring up Darryl on the day before the all-star break. I knew his arrival would create a genuine New York circus, and I didn't want that to distract us from a big four-game series right after the break in Baltimore. I preferred to sacrifice our last home game before the break (and we did lose, 4–1) than mess with that Baltimore series.

Darryl told me on his first day in New York, "I'll do whatever you want me to do."

"I only judge people from the day I meet them," I said, "and see how they play for me. I only deal with effort. I know you can't always perform like you want to, but you can always try."

I never had a bit of a problem with Darryl. He played very well for us and, by stealing some bases and playing hard, gave us some energy in addition to some big home runs.

George called me at my office in Baltimore before we opened the series against the Orioles. We had a six-game lead. "You have to split these four games," he said.

"It depends what happens early," I said. "If we win the first game, a split may not be enough. If we win the first two, a split will definitely not be enough. And if we win the first three, we'll want a sweep. We'll be fine, George."

We won the first game 4–2, with a rally in the eighth inning. We won the second game 3–2, with a rally in the ninth inning. And after we won the third game 7–5, I knew we would win the fourth. The Orioles were a dead club at that point. You can't lose so many close games at home without being demoralized. We finished the sweep behind Pettitte, 4–1, to take a ten-game lead. By July 28 our lead was up to twelve games. I felt good, but I knew the race wasn't over, not after the whole world watched the California Angels blow a big lead the previous season.

Meanwhile I kept badgering Frank to come to New York for better medical help. A friend of ours, Sy Berger, had recommended Columbia-Presbyterian Medical Center in Manhattan. I told Frank about it, and he seemed ready to make the trip, but then he said, "I can't stand to go through any more tests. I'm worn out." But the next day, Saturday, August 3, he finally gave in.

"I made up my mind," he said. "I'm coming up Tuesday."

"Great. I'll be there to pick you up," I said.

I hadn't seen Frank since spring training. He hadn't been feeling great then, but he was walking around and looked fine. Frank is a tall man—six foot four—and has always had a strong constitution. When he came off the plane, being pushed in a wheelchair, I hardly recognized him. He was a frail, crooked old man, a shadow of his former self. As we waited at the baggage claim, I couldn't believe this was my brother. He sat slumped in the chair, rubbing his eyes and not having enough strength to lift his head. I was afraid that my big brother, one of the toughest men I've ever known, was dying.

Before entering Columbia-Presbyterian, Frank removed his 1957 World Series ring and handed it to his wife. He didn't want to lose it there while undergoing tests. It was the first time he had taken it off his finger since he earned it thirty-nine years ago. The people at the hospital did a fantastic job. They stabilized Frank within two days with a drug that could only be administered intravenously. He felt comfortable, but his heart was giving out. Until a new one was located—the right match at the right time when his name moved to the top of the donor recipient list—Frank had to be tethered to a machine. There was nothing he could do but wait.

As Frank felt better, George felt worse. When our lead shrunk to eight games in mid-August, I could hear the first signs of panic in George's voice. He called me up one day at my office at Yankee Stadium with a warning. "Joe," he said, "if you blow this thing, they'll never let you forget it. You'll have to live with it the rest of your life. You'll be another Ralph Branca." I immediately thought back to Bobby Thomson's home run and the Dodgers' thirteen-game lead in mid-August. I just wanted to get it out of my mind.

I didn't dwell on it, but we still hit a slump. We lost one game in Chicago in which Jeter tried to steal third base in the eighth inning of a tie game with Fielder batting. He was thrown out. I was pissed, especially at myself. Even though Jeter had run on his own, I should have given him the sign *not* to run in that situation. I made the mistake of assuming that a rookie would know to let Cecil swing the bat in that situation. I was so mad that I didn't want to go over and talk to him, for fear I'd start screaming at him. I said to myself, He's still a kid; calm down. So what did Jeter do?

He came over and sat next to me in the dugout so I could yell at him and get it over with.

Jeter constantly impressed me with his poise. I liked him even before I met him. Before spring training I told reporters that he was going to be my shortstop. They were surprised, especially because we also had Tony Fernandez, an established shortstop. When asked about it, Jeter said, "I'm going to get an *opportunity* to play shortstop." I liked his answer better than mine. During a winter conference call with George and his advisers, Gene Michael, one of our scouts, said to me, "You're going to have to be patient with Jeter. He's made some errors in the past, but he'll get better. He may not be ready from day one." Then George said, "I better not come up to Yankee Stadium until July. I might not like what I see."

I was concerned about Jeter myself, only because when you rely on pitching you have to have a shortstop who can catch the ball. He worked very hard in spring training and I thought he would be okay. Late in spring training, though, George walked into my office and said, "My advisers tell me they don't think Jeter is ready to play." I said, "Well, it's too late for that now, folks." We had already made our commitment. And once the season started, it was as if he jumped into a phone booth and changed into a Superman costume. I received two pleasant surprises on opening day: a huge good-luck basket of goodies from my friend Big Julie Isaacson and a stunning performance by Jeter. The rookie made a great catch of a pop fly and hit a home run—signs of things to come. He played steady shortstop all year and stayed away from long slumps at the plate. There is one other thing about Jeter that I like: He always calls me Mr. Torre.

Like Jeter, Wetteland gave us invaluable consistency. But on August 16 we had to put him on the disabled list with a pulled groin muscle. Our starting pitchers tried to cover his loss by pitching better and longer, a dangerous mindset that often resulted in them getting tattooed in the first inning. By the time we left for a West Coast trip August 25, our lead was down to six games over Baltimore. The Mariners swept us three straight in Seattle, cutting it to four games. We had lost eight games off our lead in twenty-nine days. In the finale of that series Seattle kicked the crap out of us 10–2 and rubbed in the pain by throwing a pitch at Paul O'Neill. Paulie thought Mariners' manager Lou Piniella, his former manager in Cincinnati, had ordered the hit, and Paul started a bench-clearing fight when he challenged the Seattle dugout. O'Neill and Jeter were like knockdown dolls at a county fair all year; pitchers threw at them with regularity. Our pitchers didn't do a good enough job defending our own people. You can't let those knockdowns go unanswered, or else you're allowing yourself to be intimidated.

In this case Jeff Nelson did hit somebody, though I wish he had gone after somebody bigger. He hit a jockey: Joey Cora, their little second baseman. Our situation was getting urgent. For the first and only time all season, I held a meeting immediately after the game, trying to light a fire under my team.

First I told my pitchers they had to do a better job of

defending our hitters. "Don't let anybody ever think they can intimidate us," I said. And then I challenged my players.

"Now we'll see what we're made of, boys," I said. "This is a man's game. People are coming after you. Now let's see how you respond."

I guess my speech didn't exactly fire up the troops: We got clobbered the next night in California, 14–3. After that loss, with a six o'clock start scheduled for the next night, I announced in the clubhouse, "I don't want to see anybody in here until an hour before the game tomorrow. Don't even bother showing up before then. No batting practice, no nothing."

I sensed that the players were trying too hard. Pettitte made me look good by pitching eight strong innings that next game in a 6–2 win, running his record after losses to 12-2. The next time I want to have a meeting, I'll make sure I do it when Pettitte is my starting pitcher.

I felt so relieved about getting that win that I played golf the next day at Newport Country Club with Reggie Jackson, Gene Mauch (who played and managed in 4,245 games without getting to the World Series), and Zimmer. That was some foursome: Mr. October, Mr. Never Been to October, Mr. Wishing All His Life for October—and the little round guy we call Popeye. I'm not very good at golf, but it's a good getaway when you need a break from baseball. The season is such a long grind that I think it's necessary to occasionally make time for something else. I know that doesn't fit perfectly with George's thinking. He doesn't allow anyone on the club to travel with golf bags, which is fine—that discourages people from playing too much. But I and some coaches would pack golf shoes and balls and play once or twice on the longer trips. On the first West Coast trip Zim and I got up at five o'clock in the morning to play in Los Angeles. I found playing with rented clubs actually helped my game—I upgraded from terrible to bad.

On that same trip to Anaheim I decided we needed Bernie Williams to raise the level of his game. Bernie has tremendous skills, but he's such a quiet person that he was difficult for me to read sometimes. In fact, I called Don Mattingly, the former Yankee first baseman, once during the season just to talk about Bernie. Don had played with Bernie for several years and knew him much better than I did. He told me he noticed that Bernie played great toward the end of 1995, when he was moved from sixth to second in the batting order. Based on that conversation, I thought I had to keep Bernie high in the batting order—second or third, mostly—to get the most out of him.

In Anaheim I noticed that Bernie was stuck in one of these phases I would see from time to time where he doesn't play aggressively in the outfield. It's not that he wasn't hustling. He just wasn't getting good jumps on the ball. He wasn't making the plays he should make. I walked up to him in center field during batting practice and told him, "Bernie, I want you to know how important you are to this ball club. This team looks to you for leadership. I don't mean being vocal in the clubhouse. It's just the way you carry yourself. The rest of the team responds to your presence, just because of all the great things you can do on the field. That's the kind of player you are."

Bernie looked at me with those big, soft eyes of his like I had just told him a secret. He was shocked. He thought he was just another one of the guys on the team.

"I'd pay my own money to watch you play, that's the kind of special talent you have," I said.

He liked the sound of that. He smiled. Everyone else on the club was smiling, too, when David Cone returned to pitch September 2. We had a four-game lead, with twenty-six games to play. Coney gave us a big psychological lift by being back with us. No one expected he would throw seven no-hit innings in his first game in three months. I wasn't even close to letting him finish the game. I would have been jeopardizing his career, because he didn't have the arm strength yet to throw a complete game. I had had to do the same thing with a pitcher named Tommy Boggs when I was managing the Braves. He had a no-hitter going in his first start after rehabilitating his arm, but I had to take him out.

Cone is the kind of competitor who always wants the ball. After the seventh inning he told me, "If you leave it up to me, I'll stay in there. I understand it's your call." I told him, "I'm not going to risk losing you. Nice job." I later received a letter from somebody telling me I owed it to the fans to allow Cone to try for the no-hitter. That's too romantic. I have to be concerned about his health more than about fairy tales. My man Bernie, with his newly pumped-up ego, preserved the no-hitter with a great catch at the wall in center field. Mariano Rivera lost the no-hitter on an infield hit in the ninth inning, but we were thrilled to know that we had Cone back.

Surprisingly, the lift Cone gave us didn't last. We became

tentative. The Orioles seemed like they were winning every day, and we could hear their footsteps. On September 9, a travel day for us to Detroit, our lead was down to two and a half games, with twenty games to go. I didn't like the look of my team at that time. When guys walked into the clubhouse for work, they weren't holding their heads up high. We were timid. I decided I would have a meeting the next day.

Tiger Stadium has one of the smallest visiting clubhouses in baseball. With its narrow, chicken-wire lockers and pillars in the middle of the room, it probably hasn't changed much since Joe DiMaggio played there. I didn't mind that. It just meant my team would be huddled closer together when I addressed them.

"The only people we have are each other," I told them. "Everybody is looking to place blame, and if you want to do that, go ahead. It's there for you. Just be warned that you're going to be inundated with people trying to find out reasons why you're not winning and why your lead is cut. If you start pointing fingers, things are going to break down and get ugly.

"One thing I want you to remember: We're a better team than Baltimore. We've beaten them, and we're going to beat them. And do you know why? We have more heart than they do. We don't have any selfish players here. We're going to get this thing done. Believe me, we're going to win this."

As the players scattered to get ready to play, Zimmer said to me, "You lied."

"What are you talking about?" I said.

"You said we didn't have any selfish players here," he said.

"I know. Just leave this thing to me, will ya?" I said.

I knew what Zim was talking about. We did have a couple of players who may have been overly concerned sometimes about their own numbers. But you really don't have to tell your team that. The players know who among them has a selfish streak. Anyway, I believed my club was a lot tougher mentally than Baltimore. I remember back in April, when Davey Johnson took Cal Ripken out of a close game because he wanted a faster runner. I never thought anything about it; a manager tries to win every game he can. But I detected that a hush came over the crowd. And Cal just sat there on the bench through extra innings and didn't move, obviously upset about coming out.

I detected more individualism on their team than ours, probably because they had so many all-star players with strong personalities, beginning right from spring training, when Bobby Bonilla complained about being a DH. Later on they stopped the game and had a big ceremony when Eddie Murray hit his five hundredth home run. That's a great accomplishment, but anytime you stop the game and put the focus on an individual, that's distracting. It takes away from the flow of the game and contributes to the idea of an individual playing the game for his own rewards instead of for the purpose of winning. Knowing Eddie, he was probably more uncomfortable than anybody about the fanfare. As I told my ball club, I knew we had more heart than Baltimore. It's the one intangible that makes the difference between a first-place team and the rest of the pack.

We won that day of my speech—barely. Ruben Rivera saved a 9–8 victory with a diving catch in right field. I shudder to think what might have happened if the kid hadn't caught that ball. That win started us on a six-one trip, bringing us home to a showdown series with the Orioles. We had a three-game lead, with twelve games to play. We had to win at least one of the three games with Baltimore to hold them off. After a rainout we were two outs away from losing the opener when Bernie tied the game with a single. We won it 3–2, in the tenth inning, on a single by Ruben Rivera.

The next day, a doubleheader, I pitched Kenny Rogers in the first game against Mike Mussina and David Cone in the second game. I explained to Cone that I didn't want Kenny waiting around for the second game; I was afraid he would get too jumpy. Cone has the perfect attitude about those kinds of things. He's a confident professional who'll do whatever you ask. Kenny outpitched Mussina in the first game, a 9–3 win. I knew then the race was over. Even though we lost the second game of the doubleheader, we had a four-game lead with ten games to play. I knew we weren't going to blow that.

The official clincher happened on September 25, in the first game of a doubleheader at home against Milwaukee. We pounded the Brewers 19–2. I was thrilled that Ali, Andrea, and my sisters were at the game to share the moment with me. Streamers and confetti fell like snow from the upper deck. The standings and the Orioles didn't matter anymore. We were East Division champions.

The only decision I had to make in that clinching game was about who to pitch the ninth inning. I wanted somebody who had been with us all year. I thought it was the perfect spot for Jeff Nelson. Nellie is a six-foot-eight right-hander with nasty stuff, but he had been inconsistent. His ego could use the boost of being in the middle of the clinching celebration. It worked. Nellie came up to me a couple of days later and thanked me for the opportunity to get the clinching out. That's why it's important for a manager to know his players. You try to figure out what they need and put them in a position where they can succeed. That's one of Jimmy Leyland's favorite lines. I knew a small decision like that could pay dividends in the postseason.

After the clincher Wade Boggs and Tino Martinez asked me if they could have a beer. They weren't playing in the second game, so I said, "Sure, go ahead and celebrate." The rest of us made do with bottled water, saving the champagne for later. I felt elation and relief at the same time. The season had been grueling, especially because of the anxiety of the lead shrinking from twelve games to two and a half. I thought about the pain Frank's 1956 Braves team must have felt when it squandered a lead to the Dodgers, or how the 1951 Dodgers couldn't hold off the charge of the Giants— the race going down to the last swing of the bat. I was glad to avoid that kind of infamy.

While I was hugging my players, someone told me there was a telephone call for me in my office. I knew it was Steinbrenner, calling to congratulate me. I picked up the phone with a big grin on my face.

"Hello," I said, "this is Bobby Thomson."

CHAPTER 8

October, at Last

I WAS ELATED TO WIN THE EAST DIVI-
sion, but I felt relief more than anything after
spending the second half of the season cling-
ing to our lead. That long grind and the anxiety of watching our lead get sliced from
twelve games to two and a half didn't matter anymore.
Now, in the playoffs, everyone was even again. It would be a
matter of which team hit a hot streak. Of the three rounds of
playoffs, I felt the most pressure before our Division Series
against the Texas Rangers, because if we lost that series, very
few people would remember the 1996 Yankees. The Yankees
franchise has a tradition of excellence and high expectations.
Everything we accomplished during the regular season
would be diminished if we were bounced in the first round
by a team that was making its first trip ever to the postseason.

I had two major decisions to make for the series: Do I

pitch Jimmy Key or Kenny Rogers in Game Three? And do I start Darryl Strawberry or Cecil Fielder as my designated hitter in Game One? Key had been hit hard in his last start, and Rogers had pitched well in each of his past two starts. I decided on Key as my pitcher and told him and Rogers in the outfield during a workout on the next to last day of the season. I trusted Jimmy with the pressure of the postseason. He had been there before, and Kenny had not.

Before our workout on the eve of Game One against Texas, Darryl walked into my office and said, "Why don't you play Big Daddy, because I can handle not playing."

"I understand that," I said, "and I appreciate you telling me that. You've let me off the hook. But I'm still going to play you."

Strawberry had had good statistics batting against the Texas starter, John Burkett, when they played in the National League. I understood they were old numbers. But I looked for Strawberry to be pumped. I expected him to rise to the challenge of the postseason. He's not afraid of the competition. I was playing a hunch.

I explained my decision to Cecil and said, "I know you're not happy about it. I'm going to tell the writers that I'll make up my mind tomorrow. And tomorrow no writers are allowed in the clubhouse before the game, so you don't even have to deal with them. And unless Darryl just goes lights out, you'll be in there for Game Two."

I knew he was disappointed. As it turned out, I think it drove Cecil a little more. That wasn't the reason I did it, but I think it helped. Since then Cecil made some comments about being angry about not playing and having a problem with our communication. I pride myself on maintaining dialogue with my players. It took me a long time to make that decision about starting Darryl. I really wrestled with it. And when I did tell Cecil about it, I made sure I explained it and protected him from the media. Communication is very important to me. All year long, whenever I didn't play one of my regulars, I made sure to tell that player myself. I don't like sending one of my coaches to do that kind of work. It makes it easier to sleep. You do your own dirty work. If it turned out that I lit a fire under Cecil, it wasn't by design.

My hunch didn't pan out. Darryl was hitless in four at bats. We struggled against Burkett and lost 6–2. Burkett jammed the hell out of us, giving a perfect example of why it's important to pitch inside, to be able to get people out with pitches away. Too many pitchers today nibble at the outside corner of the plate with breaking balls. They're afraid to come inside, thinking if they don't get the ball inside enough, it can wind up in the outfield seats.

Burkett, by relying on a hard inside fastball, pitched the kind of game that used to be associated with the National League. As recently as about ten years ago, the American League was known as a breaking ball league and the National League as a fastball league. Ted Simmons, my old teammate with the Cardinals, struggled when he was traded to the Milwaukee Brewers in 1981 because every time he thought it was a fastball count, the AL pitchers would throw him a breaking ball. Now both leagues are breaking ball leagues. The biggest difference between the leagues is that the AL has more power, so managers tend to sit around and wait for home runs. Most AL teams don't send the runner with a full count on the batter. So-called running counts don't come into play in the AL like they do in the NL, mostly because of the DH. An AL manager doesn't have to worry about trying to score before the pitcher's spot in the lineup comes up.

My background, as well as Zimmer's aggressive style, gave us the look of an NL team. Some people criticized us in the second half of the season for being less creative after we acquired Strawberry and Fielder. But we fell behind early in a lot of games in the second half, which limits how bold you can be, and other teams began to catch on to us and did a better job anticipating when we would bunt, steal a base, or execute a hit-and-run play.

Steinbrenner walked into my office after Game One looking very distraught. "We've got to win three out of four now," he said.

"We can do that," I said. The truth is, I was scared to death after that first game. We were inept. I knew in a best-of-five series, we had to turn it around immediately. We had one more game at Yankee Stadium before the series moved to Texas, where we had lost five out of six games during the season. In Game Two, with Pettitte pitching, we fell behind 4–1 after three innings. Texas scored all of its runs on two home runs by Juan Gonzalez, his second and third of the series. Gonzalez was absolutely awesome. He hit pitches out of the ballpark whether we pitched him inside or outside. If I was ever going to walk someone intentionally with nobody on base, he would be the guy. But I didn't like the idea of putting one of my pitchers in a position where he has to throw strikes to the hitter coming up after him. It's a lot more comfortable to pitch when you don't have to throw strikes than when you do.

We chipped away at the Rangers until we tied the game at four in the eighth inning, on a base hit by Fielder. I had two thoughts at the time: We can beat the Rangers bullpen, and we should try to make Texas third baseman Dean Palmer handle the ball as much as we can. I noticed that he was having problems throwing the ball.

Texas put a scare into us in the twelfth inning. Graeme Lloyd started the inning for me, but I replaced him with Nelson after he gave up a base hit. Nelson struck out two batters, but then Gonzalez got a base hit. Then I replaced Nelson with Rogers because Will Clark, a left-handed hitter, was batting. Kenny walked Clark on four pitches. Then I replaced Rogers with Brian Boehringer. My only remaining relief pitcher was David Weathers, who had pitched two innings in Game One. Boehringer retired Palmer on a fly ball. We used four pitchers to get three outs in a half inning that took twenty-four minutes, and I came out looking like a genius. The reality is, I had no other choice but to use Boehringer in that spot. I was lucky. Those situations have a better chance of working out in Johnny Parascandola's basement with APBA cards than they do in the big leagues.

Derek Jeter, who started or finished as many big rallies for us as anyone, opened the bottom of the twelfth inning with a single. Tim Raines walked. Then I asked Charlie Hayes to bunt. He made the right play by bunting it to Palmer. The third baseman fielded the ball cleanly but threw it wildly to first base. The ball may have been slippery because of the light rain that was falling. Jeter came running home with the winning run.

It was almost two o'clock in the morning by the time we boarded the team buses that would take us to the airport for our trip to Texas. One bus was reserved for coaches, my staff, and front office personnel, including some women. I sat down in the first row on the right-hand side on the aisle. George was sitting in the row behind me, on the aisle. And then Reggie Jackson walked in.

"Here, sit next to me, Reggie," I said and scooted over to make room for him. Reggie hadn't been around the ball club often during the regular season. When the playoffs were about to begin, he had asked me if he should come in from his home in California. "Sure, come on in," I said. That was my mistake. I had wanted him there, but Reggie doesn't work for me. He works for George. I should have cleared it with the Boss.

"What are you doing here?" Steinbrenner snapped, sort of half kidding when he saw Reggie on the bus. George seemed miffed for a couple of reasons: He hadn't known Reggie would be traveling with us, and Reggie was sitting in front of him.

"You want me to leave?" Reggie said.

"No," George said, "but next time I want to know about your schedule—where you're going and where you plan to be every day."

I could feel Reggie bubbling like water on a stove. He jumped out of his seat and started going after George. I grabbed him around his shoulders, but Reggie threw me off him like a matchstick. He leaned down toward George, who was sitting down, and got right in his face.

"I'm sick of the way you talk down to me! Don't mess with me anymore!"

"Why don't you relax and sit down," George said.

Reggie went on for about two minutes, screaming at George about the way he disrespected him. George just kept trying to get Reggie to calm down and get out of his face. Willie Randolph and I also tried to get Reggie to sit down. Finally we steered Reggie into the seat where I had been sitting, away from the aisle. I sat down next to him and kept my hand on his knee.

Reggie had overreacted, and he knew it. It was something he shouldn't have done. This was my only peek into what the old battling Yankees of the 1970s and 1980s must have been like. Obviously, there was a lot of history that went into that confrontation. George is uneasy with Reggie's clout with the media. It's tough to take on Reggie in the newspapers and expect to win. I don't think George likes negative press that involves him and the Yankees. He's very sensitive to that stuff.

I love Reggie. I got to know him well when we were broadcasters together with the Angels in 1990. Reggie is the kind of guy who can offend people if you don't know him. He's a lot deeper than people think. He's a very sensitive person who, by the way he gets on people, sometimes doesn't think other people are sensitive.

Handling Reggie is a full-time job. He has a good eye for talent, and he has great knowledge and insights to share with my players, but sometimes he overloads them. It's not that what he says isn't good, but enough is enough. I liked having him around because he tells you what he thinks of players and situations. Reggie thinks he can detect fear in a person, almost like a dog's instinct to do that. He'd tell me, "I don't like the way this guy is walking around. I don't like his look." Then I'd go see for myself. I'd talk to that player and make my own judgment. Sometimes I'd come back to Reggie and say, "I think you're wrong," and he was fine with that. He didn't try to talk me into his way of thinking. One of the things I like best about Reggie is that he's been to the World Series and proved to be a clutch performer. I want to be surrounded by as many of those people as possible. When you watch from the stands or on television, you have no idea what's going on in the stomachs of the people on the field in that kind of pressure. I wasn't intimidated at all having Reggie around. It's comforting to be around people who've been in the foxhole.

We managed to make it to Texas without further incident. Later that day I ran into the maid as she was cleaning my hotel room. She noticed my Yankees suitcase and asked, "Are you with the team?" I said, "Yes, I'm the manager." She smiled and said, "Oh, yes. You're the one who sits next to that round guy." I guess Zim was becoming a cult hero.

When I arrived at the ballpark that night, Jose Cardenal gave me a plastic bag full of hot peppers. Jose has friends all over the world, and he told me these came from Mexico. He knows I like hot peppers. I thanked him and said, "Hope they bring me luck."

Jimmy Key pitched a gutsy ball game, but he wasn't

getting the calls to go his way. When I took him out after five innings, he had thrown 101 pitches and we were trailing 2–1. I turned the ball over to Nelson. Nellie was terrific, shutting down that powerful Rangers lineup with three shutout innings. As I watched him mow down Texas, I smiled, thinking how good I felt about my decision to let him get the last out of our division-clinching game.

We were three outs away from losing when—who else?— Jeter started a rally in the ninth inning. He advanced to third on a single by Raines and scored the tying run when Bernie hit a sacrifice fly. Three batters later, Mariano Duncan knocked in Raines with a single to give us a 3–2 lead. Wetteland took care of the ninth inning to put us one win away from the American League Championship Series.

After that game I went out to eat with my wife and some friends. People were lined up to get into the restaurant, so they sneaked us in through a back door to seat us. And who happened to be seated at the next booth? Jeter. The kid was everywhere. The people at the restaurant were great. They wished us luck and talked about how happy they were to have the Rangers in the playoffs for the first time. It was hard for their players not to feel the same way. The first time you get in, it's huge. But when you play for the Yankees, the first plateau is nothing. That's like waking up in the morning. Even though the Yankees had not been to the World Series in eighteen years, the fans and the media made it clear they expected us to get there. That's why I was eager to close out the series the next day.

Rogers, who had played for Texas before he signed as a free agent after the 1995 season, started Game Four. I knew he was in trouble before the game, when he came back from warming up in the bullpen with Mel Stottlemyre.

"The fans were killing him out there," Mel said. "They were taunting him and screaming obscenities at him."

"What did Kenny do?" I asked.

"He motioned to one of the fans and said, 'That's my neighbor up there,' " Mel said.

I didn't like the sound of that. Kenny was trying to make light of the situation instead of being mentally tough and blocking it out. He lasted only two innings. We fell behind 4–0 but rallied once again, with the help of two home runs from Bernie Williams, to win 6–4. I got choked up in the dugout after the last out and cried. That was such an important series for us because if we had lost it, people would not have known that we existed. When I sat down at the traditional postgame press conference, I saw my wife standing in the back of the interview room with Arthur Sando, my friend from New York, and Bob and Kate Devlin, friends from Houston who had flown in for the game. That really made me emotional, seeing how happy Ali looked. After years of hiding my emotions and guarding my feelings, here I was getting choked up in front of cameras and reporters. I couldn't help it. It felt great. And then Bernie walked in, and I grew emotional all over again. Bernie was playing like the star I knew he was. Watching him play at that level was like watching one of my own children talk or walk for the first time.

Before we left Texas, I made sure to pack the hot peppers in my baseball equipment bag. And I made sure to say something to Williams. "Bernie," I said, "I'm going to have to pay *more* money to watch you play the next series."

When Yankee Stadium filled up with 56,495 people for Game One of the American League Championship Series against Baltimore, I told Bernie, "Look at this place. All these people are here to see you." He smiled.

For the fourth straight game we rallied to victory after trailing as late as the seventh inning. Mr. Rally himself, Jeter, tied the game with one out in the eighth inning with one of the most unforgettable and controversial home runs of all time. A twelve-year-old kid playing hooky from school reached over the right-field wall and pulled Jeter's fly ball into the stands. The Orioles right fielder, Tony Tarasco, had thought he was about to catch it, to put Baltimore four outs away from a victory. Instead, we went on to win 5–4, when Bernie delighted the packed house with a long home run in the eleventh inning. I was three wins away from the World Series.

I don't blame the kid for reaching out to catch Jeter's fly ball. I would have done the same thing at that age. What bothered me was that the media turned him into a hero. There's no doubt that Richie Garcia, the umpire who awarded Derek the home run, missed the call. I'm not sure if Tarasco would have caught the ball, so maybe Garcia should have ruled a double. But that's just one of those weird things that happen in baseball sometimes—like Nippy Jones getting hit on the foot in the 1957 World Series. That in itself didn't decide the game. My sisters and my wife preferred to think of Jeter's home run as more divine than weird. Rocco, they said, was our angel in the outfield. Who could argue? Jeter's home run had come in the same ballpark and exactly thirty-nine years to the day that my brother Frank hit his home run in Game Six of the 1957 World Series.

We lost Game Two 5–3, when Nellie gave up a two-run home run to Rafael Palmeiro in the seventh inning. I beat myself up pretty good over that, because I should have talked to Nellie before that at bat. Jeff had first base open, so he didn't have to throw a strike, especially when the count was three-and-one. He tried to throw a strike with a back-door slider, the same pitch Kirk Gibson hit for his famous home run off Dennis Eckersley in the 1988 World Series. When a batter is hitting with a runner at second base with the game tied or his team down by one run, as Palmeiro and Gibson were, he's thinking about hitting the ball through the middle for a single. When you have that approach, you wait on the ball for a long time. And if the pitcher throws you a breaking ball, it seems as if the ball just stops for you. You wait all day for that ball, which is how you hit home runs: by not jumping at it.

As I packed after the game to go to Baltimore, I said to myself, Well, I've got to pack the peppers. With each passing day the peppers were getting more rancid. They were starting to ooze fluid. I thought, I hope to hell this plastic bag doesn't break open in my bag.

Before Game Three at Camden Yards in Baltimore, I saw Orioles third baseman Todd Zeile during batting practice. Todd, who had played for me in St. Louis, had hit a home run in Game Two. In feint anger I yelled at Zeile, "I've been waiting my whole life to get to the World Series! You've got plenty of time!" After we won the pennant, Todd sent me a telegram. It said, "I'm still young. Congratulations."

We rallied again in Baltimore. Mike Mussina, the Orioles' best pitcher, was four outs away from beating us 2–1, when we erupted for four runs in a span of four batters. Who started the rally with two outs and nobody on in the eighth? Jeter, of course. The tie-breaking run was scored on a bizarre error by Zeile, who spiked the ball into the ground when he tried to stop his throwing motion suddenly, after changing his mind about making a throw to second base. As the ball rolled away, Bernie alertly dashed home. We were ahead two games to one. I was two wins away from the World Series.

I was getting anxious about being so close to realizing my dream. I also knew we were 7-0 in Baltimore against the Orioles. How much longer could that streak continue? All my life Rocco had been a calming presence for me. And that night in my hotel room was no different. Rocco visited me in a dream. It was the first time I had dreamed about him since he passed away four months earlier. I dreamed that I heard a knock at my door. I opened it, and there stood Rocco. He didn't say a word. He just smiled in a peaceful, contented kind of way. I'll never forget that look on his face. I knew my dead brother was telling me something. He was telling me that everything was going to be all right.

We won Game Four without having to stage another comeback, 8–4. I was one victory away from the World Series. I was very determined the next day to close it out, but I was also extremely nervous. Pettitte, who had struggled in his previous two playoff outings, was my starting

201

pitcher. I told Jimmy Leyritz, the catcher that day, "Make sure you use the fastball. Don't fall in love with that cut fastball." Andy's youth had showed in his previous two starts; he thought he had to pitch differently in the post-season than in the regular season. Jimmy called a great game, and Pettitte, staked to an early 6–0 lead, pitched superbly for eight innings. Wetteland pitched the ninth.

At 7:20 P.M. on October 13, 1996, Cal Ripken, who was born one month and one day before my debut in the major leagues, hit a ground ball to Jeter. Derek threw the baseball in the dirt to first base to Tino Martinez, who made a great play to catch it for the final out of a 6–4 victory. Thirty-six years and 4,272 games since I put on a major league uniform for the first time, my dream had come true. Joseph Paul Torre finally was going to the World Series.

In my mind's eye I visualized where my wife and sisters were sitting in the stands. I thought about Frank in his hospital bed in New York. I thought about Rocco and felt his presence with me. I thought about all my friends who encouraged me to never give up my dream. A great, powerful wave of emotion just washed over me. It overwhelmed me. I cried, knowing what a fortunate man I was. I was truly loved by family and friends who wanted this for me even more than I wanted it for myself.

Then Reggie Jackson embraced me and whispered, "I'm happy for you." And then I totally lost it. I started bawling, because I knew that Reggie, this strong man who has been accused of being into himself so much, meant it from his heart.

I didn't go on the field. The celebration belonged to the

players. It was more satisfying for me to watch it rather than be mobbed in the middle of it. I thanked each of my players as they made their way through the dugout to the clubhouse. By the time I got inside, my family was waiting for me in the manager's office. I hugged my wife and baby tightly, and I saw the look of surprise on Ali's face at the way I completely broke down. She had never seen me cry so openly. After the Texas victory I did a decent job holding back many of the tears. But during the celebration in Baltimore they flowed freely. Then George called with congratulations, crying with happiness as he struggled for the right words. "You did a great job," he said, leaving out his usual "but we have more work to do." We had done everything we needed to do, and he knew it. A bit later the reporter for NBC, Jim Gray, asked me about Rocco. I didn't expect that question. And it started me crying all over again. Ali said I hadn't had time to grieve for Rocco during the season. She may be right. I guess I kept my deepest emotions about Rocco's death locked behind my responsibility to my players and the Yankees organization. But getting to the World Series caused me to let down my guard, and when I did, the sadness of losing a brother I loved and admired overpowered me.

I cried many years' worth of tears that day in Baltimore. (I did, however, remember to bring the peppers back to New York.) I felt so fortunate to be supported by so many loving people, including all of Ali's fifteen siblings and their spouses, which, including their children, is my midwestern fan club in itself: her brothers John, David, Michael, Preacher and his wife, Nancy, Jimmy and Jan, Joe and Gina,

Mark and Cheryl, Larry and Sharlene, Stan and Peggy, and her sisters Judy, Katie, Rosie and her husband Butch Putnick, Mary and Gary Even, Diane and Steve Bierman, and Lucy and Steve Borchers. And then, as if every last drop of water had burst forth from behind a dam, there were no more left. I stopped crying. I had reached my dream. Winning the World Series was the cherry on top of my hot fudge sundae. The pressure was off, and I was going to have fun being there. It's like all the athletes who go through years of training and several rounds of trials just to make the Olympic team. When they finally make the team, it's an honor in itself to be there and represent their country. I felt the same way about the World Series. And it was more fun that I ever could have imagined.

We waited to find out who would be our opponent. Either way, I would be facing one of my former teams, the Cardinals or the Braves. I didn't have a preference, though the Braves were the defending champions, and you always want to play the best. When that National League Championship Series went to a seventh game, I didn't watch. We had a team party that night at the Manhattan restaurant owned by my friend Joe Ponte. There was nothing I could do about that game in St. Louis. I preferred to enjoy the food and the company. Atlanta blew open that game very early. For the first time since I was a teenager watching Frank in his uniform number 14, the World Series would match the Yankees against the Braves.

On October 20, in front of 56,365 fans, Bob Sheppard, the voice of Yankee Stadium, introduced me before Game One of the World Series. I had one thought on my mind as I ran from the dugout to the first-base line: Don't trip. Reggie Jackson and Yogi Berra, two of the greatest World Series stars ever, had warned me that being introduced would be an emotionally powerful experience. It was even more emotional than I expected. A loud ovation shook the stadium. I had goose bumps on my arms. I looked up at the scoreboard in left field, and for the first time in my life I saw that no other games were being played or scheduled. I was at the center of the major league baseball universe. The excitement was incredible. All my years of dreaming about it didn't prepare me for the thrill of being introduced in a World Series. When I heard the crowd I knew I wasn't dreaming anymore. It was real. I was a little bit nervous, but more than anything I was thrilled to be there. When the game began, with Pettitte's first pitch, I was the happiest man alive. Normally I don't get caught up in the surroundings of the game. But on that first pitch I noticed a spectacular light show of hundreds of flashbulbs popping in the night all around the old ballpark. And for the rest of the night it was all downhill from there.

The Braves destroyed us 12–1. Atlanta rookie Andruw Jones, whose thirty-one career games were just slightly fewer than what it had taken me to get to the World Series, ripped two home runs. What bothered me was that both pitches Jones hit out of the park were up. Our scouts had specifically said he likes the ball up. Our pitchers made several mistakes like that. I met with some of my pitchers and catchers before the next game to emphasize the importance of our scouting reports. My players didn't know much about the Braves, but our scouts who had been watching them for a month did. We had to do a better job of relying on the reports.

Before Game Two the next night Bob Watson addressed the team. He told the players that he hadn't yet thanked them for the job they did all year and that he was immensely proud of them. I thought Bob sounded a little too much like he was delivering a eulogy, which is understandable because he had been listening to George all day. George can be very pessimistic. He likes to prepare himself for the worst. After listening to Bob, I decided I ought to say something as well.

"Listen," I said, "we've played and beaten better offensive teams than Atlanta—beat them with regularity. I'm talking about Cleveland, Baltimore, Texas. . . . There's no reason why we can't beat this team."

Deep down, though, I knew we were in trouble that night. Greg Maddux, the master magician, was pitching for Atlanta, and we still had rust on our bats after sitting out the five days since beating Baltimore. Steinbrenner walked into my office about ninety minutes before the first pitch, and said, "This is a must game." I barely looked up at him, and said nonchalantly, "You should be prepared for us to lose again tonight. But then we're going to Atlanta. Atlanta's my town. We'll take three games there and win it back here on Saturday."

George looked at me like I had two heads. He didn't say anything. He was dumbfounded.

Maddux threw a gem in Game Two, beating us 4–0. He's like a right-handed Whitey Ford—he dominates a game without being overpowering. We had lost the first two games of the World Series by a combined score of 16–1, the worst such showing among all ninety-two World Series ever played. There was only one thing to do: bring the peppers to Atlanta. A light drizzle was falling as I made the short walk from the exit gate at Yankee Stadium to the team buses that would take us to the airport and our charter flight to Atlanta. I actually felt good about going on the road. Not only had the six off days taken the edge off our game, but we also looked like a distracted team at home. The players hadn't gotten their World Series tickets until Friday, the day before the opener was rained out. Dealing with a constant barrage of ticket requests from friends and family can be a headache. Moreover, the pressure had been squarely on our shoulders at home. We felt like we had to hurry and get a win or two under our belts before going on the road. We didn't look loose because of that. Now we were back to being the under-dogs in a hostile environment. I liked my team under those conditions.

Small crowds of fans waited in the rain behind police barricades that had been set up for our walk to the buses. They started chanting, "Bring it back! Bring it back!" I smiled and thought, We will.

At about three o'clock in the afternoon, five hours before Game Three began, I was sitting at the desk in the man-ager's office of the visiting clubhouse at Atlanta Fulton County Stadium. I happened to be taking care of some very important advance work for the game—I was trying to come up with World Series tickets. It seemed like there was no end to the number of people I knew who needed tickets to watch my club, the New York Yankees, play the Atlanta

Braves. Every so often I'd call Bill Acree, the Braves' traveling secretary, and say, "Billy, I need four tickets." And then I'd write him a check and send one of the clubhouse attendants to run it up to his office. A little while later I'd get a call from someone else who wanted tickets, and I'd go through the same routine with Bill.

In between the phone calls and the check writing, I'd try to stay relaxed by doing a little self-hypnosis, just clearing my mind as I sat alone in the small office. When I was manager of the Mets, Father Joe Dispenza, a priest who traveled with us, taught me relaxation techniques. With that team a manager needed all the spiritual and mental help he could get. Now, outside my door in the main clubhouse, my coaches and players were also getting ready for what was a must-win game for us. My players were as loose as always; a bunch of them were engaged in a putting competition on the clubhouse carpet. Then my telephone rang.

"I have a phone call for Mr. Torre from a Mr. Steelbredder," the operator said. "Will you take the call?"

"Yeah, I'll take it," I told the stadium operator. I wasn't sure if it was actually George or not. I used to get crank calls during the season from jokesters who thought it was funny to call me up pretending to be George. About halfway through the season I started checking into hotels under the fictitious name Joe Russo—it was Italian and short, and people knew how to spell it. The calls stopped.

When George did come on the line, I could tell it was really him. That's because he doesn't say hello on the telephone. He just starts talking. I guess he's not interested in wasting even a second of his time.

"We can't be embarrassed," he said. That's one of George's favorite words: *embarrassed.* He uses it all the time. "We had the city to ourselves. New York was our town. But if we lose this thing, we're going to lose the city too. Let's not get embarrassed. Because I'll tell you one thing, Joe: If we lose, everything we've done up until now won't mean a damned thing. All that we've accomplished won't mean anything."

"Well, I don't think so, George, but don't worry about it," I said. "We're fine. We're fine."

"I hope you're right," he said. "I trust you."

I've always had the capacity to calm George. I talked to him the way I did my nervous troops back in basic training in 1962, when I was in the Air National Guard at Lackland Air Force Base in Texas. That was during the Cuban missile crisis. I was put in charge of about fifty guys—I guess because I had some leadership skills being a major league player, though I think being one of the biggest guys there helped too. We were on a march one night when my troops started moaning about going to war. So I said to them, "Don't worry. We're not going to war." I figured, what the hell could they tell me if I was wrong: "We told you we were going to war"? You might as well tell them, "Don't worry, we're not going." If you're right, everybody thinks you're real smart. And if you're wrong, nobody really cares, because by then they have too many things to worry about.

More than anything, I think George wanted us to avoid the embarrassment of getting swept. I don't think he was thinking about winning the World Series at that point. I found out after the Series that a few hours before he called me, he had traveled by himself to Atlanta on a flight from LaGuardia Airport. As he walked down the jetway to his first-class seat, he struck up a conversation with a writer he had known for years. "This series reminds me of 'seventy-six, when we got swept by the Reds," Steinbrenner said. "But we came back and won two world championships after that. Atlanta's a great team. They're the defending champions. You have to tip your cap to them. There's no shame in losing to a club like that."

Naturally, George didn't exactly leave our conversation at "I trust you." He had some recommendations about my lineup for the game that night against Tom Glavine, the Braves' left-handed pitcher. He asked me about playing Strawberry in right field instead of O'Neill. I had already decided to make that switch. O'Neill had been bothered for weeks by a pulled leg muscle, and in those first two games he didn't look to me like he had swung the bat with much authority. George also suggested the idea of using Fielder at first base instead of Martinez, which was another move I had already decided to make. I couldn't play both of them because we didn't have use of the designated hitter in Atlanta; you play under National League rules in the World Series when the National League team is home. Cecil had had base hits in his last two at bats in Game Two, while Tino had not driven in a run the entire postseason. It looked to me like he was pressing.

Then George said to me, "What about Kenny Rogers? Is there anyone else?" He was already worried about my Game Four pitcher.

"I could come back with Pettitte tomorrow on two days'

rest," I said, aware that Pettitte had thrown only fifty-five pitches before his third-inning exit in Game One. "But if I do that, then I'm still going to need a pitcher for Game Five. And if I use Rogers there, his confidence will be totally shot because I've just bumped him from starting Game Four. Don't worry about Rogers, George. We've won every game he's pitched in the postseason. He's pitching tomorrow. He'll be fine. Don't worry."

"Okay, I trust you," George said. We talked for another minute or so again about my lineup, and that was it. George, as he usually does, hung up without saying good-bye.

I was glad to have David Cone as my starting pitcher that night. I knew he had pitched in Atlanta before and would not pitch defensively in that small ballpark. I had held him out until Game Three because I wanted my left-handers, Pettitte and Key, pitching in Yankee Stadium in the first two games. Left-handers have a history of pitching better than right-handers at the stadium because they can take the short right-field porch out of play by matching up better against left-handed hitters. Atlanta was a weaker offensive club against left-handers anyway. I also used that order of pitchers because I knew that Game Three can often be a pivotal game in a series, and Cone is a great big-game pitcher. That's the very reason we signed him as a free agent in the first place: to pitch crucial games like this.

I remember on the eve of the World Series telling Pettitte, Key, and Cone their assignments. Jimmy looked surprised that he would start Game Two ahead of Cone. But David just told me, "I had a feeling you might go this way."

A lot of my decisions worked out in my favor over the course of the World Series, but deciding to pitch David in Game Three was probably the best decision I made.

I also knew that as long as we kept the game close, especially if we had a lead in the middle innings, we would win. All I thought about was winning that night. If you think about the magnitude of the overall task ahead of us— we had to win four times in no more than six games with Tom Glavine, Denny Neagle, John Smoltz, and Greg Maddux pitching for the Braves with full rest—you would be overwhelmed. I didn't necessarily think about beating their great starting pitchers, but I wanted to get them out of the game so that we could get into their bullpen. I liked our chances against their middle relievers. You have to think small: get a lead, protect it, win one game, and then play the next game.

I had another reason why I still liked our chances, though no hard-bitten baseball man would dare include this on his scouting report: I believed I was managing a team with destiny on its side. We were 5-0 on the road in the postseason, an almost unheard-of testament of resolve. From Jeter's kid-glove home run to five comeback wins already in the postseason to Cardenal's stinky peppers, I had a feeling good things were happening for us.

It was very important for us to get a lead in Game Three. So when Tim Raines led off the game with a walk, I flashed the sign to my third-base coach, Willie Randolph, that I wanted Jeter to bunt for a base hit. I didn't want Derek to give himself up totally, but if he did bunt for a hit, I figured the worst thing that could happen would be he'd get thrown

On November 2, 1995, I accepted the manager's job from the Yankees. Though some people thought I was crazy to manage in the "Bronx Zoo," I knew the Yankees were committed to doing whatever it took to get to the World Series. (STEVE CRANDALL)

My coaching staff: bullpen coach Tony Cloninger, pitching coach Mel Stottlemyre, me, hitting coach Chris Chambliss, third-base coach Willie Randolph, and bench coach Don Zimmer. (AP/WIDE WORLD PHOTOS)

Jose Cardenal was both my first-base coach and outfield coach. He is also responsible for providing my World Series charm—a bag of hot peppers.

The 1996 season started on a bizarre note—a snow-out in Cleveland. (AP/WIDE WORLD PHOTOS)

Zimmer, Bob Watson, and me. Watson helped bring in the talent we needed to get to the Series. (AP/WIDE WORLD PHOTOS)

One of the great stories of the year: Doc Gooden pitched a no-hitter at Yankee Stadium on May 14. (AP/WIDE WORLD PHOTOS)

In a season of incredible stories, David Cone added another one. On September 2, in his first game back from shoulder surgery, which some had believed would end his career, he pitched a no-hitter through seven innings against the Oakland A's. (AP/WIDE WORLD PHOTOS)

Hugging Mariano Rivera in the locker room after clinching the AL East Division title, September 25. (AP/WIDE WORLD PHOTOS)

In the playoffs against the Texas Rangers, Juan Gonzalez almost single-handedly beat us. I tried, unsuccessfully, to persuade the umpire that one of his five home runs was foul. (AL BELLO/ALLSPORT)

Down two games, I had no intention of pulling David Cone out in the sixth inning of Game Three with the bases loaded. He got out of the inning with our lead preserved.
(STEPHEN DUNN / ALLSPORT)

I wanted to meet Jane Fonda, Ted Turner's wife, so before the first game of the World Series I went over to be introduced. Unfortunately, she was in the ladies' room. Turner told me that if his Braves couldn't win the Series, he was glad that I would.
(AP / WIDE WORLD PHOTOS)

One of my proudest moments as a manager: John Wetteland hands me the game ball after we win our first World Series game against the Atlanta Braves, 5–2.
(AP / WIDE WORLD PHOTOS)

ON ROAD–OFFICIAL BATTING ORDER		
CLUB **CINCINNATI**	DATE	
ORIGINAL	CHANGE	ALSO ELIGIBLE
1 RAINES	B	~~(crossed out)~~
	C	~~(crossed out)~~
2 JETER	B	~~(crossed out)~~
	C	~~(crossed out)~~
3 WILLIAMS	B	~~(crossed out)~~
	C	~~(crossed out)~~
4 FIELDER	B fox	~~(crossed out)~~
	C Boggs	
5 HAYES	B	
	C	
6 STRAWBERRY	B	PETTITE
	C	
7 DUNCAN	B	KEY
	C	CONE
8 GIRARDI	B O'Neill	~~(crossed out)~~
	C LEYRITZ	~~(crossed out)~~
9 ROGERS	B SOJO	~~(crossed out)~~
	C MARTINEZ	~~(crossed out)~~
	D	~~(crossed out)~~
	E	~~(crossed out)~~
VISITING MANAGER'S COPY		

One of my prize possessions—the lineup card for Game Four. We forgot to bring our own, so we had to borrow an old Cincinnati card that was left in the visiting manager's office. I used every available player that game, except for three starting pitchers.

One of the turning points of the Series, without a doubt: Jim Leyritz's three-run home run to tie the game 6–6 off Mark Wohlers. I knew it was gone the moment he hit it.
(AP / WIDE WORLD PHOTOS)

One of the many heroes of Game Four, Cecil Fielder scores off a Charlie Hayes single in the sixth inning.
(AP / WIDE WORLD PHOTOS)

Wade Boggs manufacturing a walk off Steve Avery in the tenth inning of Game Four to put us ahead for good. He was the last available hitter in the dugout. (AP/WIDE WORLD PHOTOS)

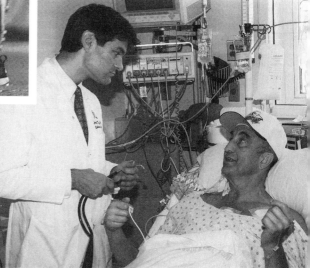

Frank somehow worked it out to get his new heart on the only off day of the Series—the night before Game Six. Dr. Mehmet Oz performed the successful operation. Frank called me that night asking for six tickets to Game Six. (AP/WIDE WORLD PHOTOS)

After we won Game Six and the World Series, I thought we should celebrate with the fans, so the team took a lap around the field. (STEVE CRANDALL)

Sister Marguerite celebrating with her kids at the Nativity School.
(AP/WIDE WORLD PHOTOS)

Support came from both sides of the family: Ali's father Ed, sister Rosie, and mother Lucille, with the trophy on my desk at Yankee Stadium.

At the parade in the Canyon of Heroes, in front of City Hall, with the mayor and the governor of New York.
(AP/WIDE WORLD PHOTOS)

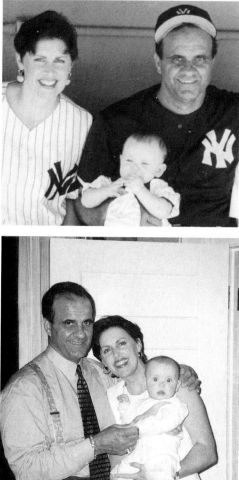

The spoils of victory: with my wife, Ali, our
daughter, Andrea Rae, and our dog Geena.

out and advance Raines to second base. That's exactly what happened, and when Bernie followed that bunt with a single to knock in Raines, I felt great. We had our first lead of the World Series. We made it 2–0 in the fourth, when we turned a leadoff error by Braves shortstop Jeff Blauser into a run.

Cone was magnificent. He had a three-hit shutout through five innings. I knew that if he could protect the lead through one more inning, our chances of winning were about as good as they get. We were 70-3 during the regular season whenever we had a lead after six innings. That's primarily because of the Formula. That's why the sixth inning was always the most important inning of our games. Cone needed to get us three more outs.

Bobby Cox, the Atlanta manager, allowed his pitcher, Glavine, to lead off the sixth inning. Cone committed a grave error: He walked the pitcher. Then Marquis Grissom singled. Mark Lemke tried to bunt but popped out. But then Cone walked Chipper Jones. I couldn't tell whether Cone suddenly was tiring—he had thrown only eighty-seven pitches, a low count for him—but somehow he had lost the command of his pitches. The bases were loaded. Fred McGriff, the Braves' hottest hitter, was the batter, with Ryan Klesko, another dangerous left-handed slugger, right behind him. I had a left-hander, Graeme Lloyd, ready in the bullpen.

The Braves were in position to blow us away. If they did break the game open—just one swing could do it—and take a three-games-to-none lead in the Series, well, even I would have to at least begin to question whether destiny had deserted us. I looked at the three runners on base and at McGriff walking to the plate, and I thought to myself, This is the whole World Series right here. If we don't stop them here, we just might get swept away.

I had a huge decision to make. Should I leave a struggling Cone in to pitch to McGriff, or should I play the percentages and bring in my left-hander, Lloyd? I turned to my bench coach, Don Zimmer, and said, "I'm going out there to the mound and see what he says."

As I left the dugout, I really didn't know what I was going to do. I jogged out to the mound. I didn't want Coney to think I had my mind made up to take him out. I had learned that lesson the hard way almost twenty years ago when I was managing the Mets. Jerry Koosman, a lefty, had been pitching a good game for us against Pittsburgh. We had a one-run lead. I had a right-handed pitcher warming in the bullpen. The Pirates had a right-handed hitter due up, but I knew they had John Milner, a good left-handed hitter, on their bench. So I walked slowly out to the mound, intending to tell Koosman that I wanted him to go ahead and pitch to the right-hander because I didn't want my right-handed reliever pitching to Milner. As soon as I got to the mound—and before I could say anything—Koosman reached out and handed me the ball. Shit, I thought. Now I had to take Koosman out of the game. He had effectively taken himself out, because he had convinced himself that he was out of the game by the way I walked to the mound. That made him lose his mental edge, and he was of no use anymore. After that I decided I would run to the mound whenever I just wanted to talk to the pitcher.

My gut feeling was that I wanted to leave Cone in the game. Cone is like Gibson, Koufax, and Maddux. They've earned the right to pitch in tough situations, no matter who's hitting. David has retired left-handed hitters his whole life. I hadn't kept him from pitching against the Braves just because they had McGriff. Now why all of a sudden should that make a difference? It would make a difference only if he was drained. What did he have left in his gas tank, if anything? I had to find out. And there was only one way to do it. I was going to stick my face as close as possible to his face and demand the truth out of him. I wanted to hear his words and look deep into his eyes.

"This is very important," I said to Cone, our eyes fixed on one another just inches apart. My catcher, Joe Girardi, was standing near us, but he might as well have been on the moon as far as I was concerned. It's never a good idea to ask the catcher about the pitcher while the pitcher is within earshot. You're unlikely to get an honest answer, because a pitcher will get angry at a catcher who says he's cooked. I told Cone, "I need the truth from you. How do you feel?"

"I'm okay," Cone said. "I lost the feel for my slider a little bit there, but I'm okay. I'll get this guy for you."

"This game is very important," I said. "I've got to know the truth, so don't bullshit me."

"I can get him," he said. "I can get out of this inning."

That was what I wanted to hear. And David didn't hesitate when he said it. But just as importantly, I liked the look I saw in his eyes. He was determined.

"Let's go get 'em," I said.

And then I left. I left the ball in Cone's hands. And I felt good about it. But I figured if McGriff got on base, I'd have to pull Cone.

David threw a strike to him, then got McGriff out on an infield pop-up for the second out of the sixth inning. That did it for me. Cone was fine, and so was I. This was his inning.

I spend a lot of my time trying to figure out what I can do better, and when things don't work, I really torture myself over them. But I felt good about this decision no matter what happened. Cone still had enough gas left. It was now a matter of execution. He then wavered a bit, walking Klesko to force in a run. It was a one-run game, 2–1, and Javy Lopez was batting for Atlanta. Cone responded. Lopez popped up an 0-1 pitch, and when Girardi squeezed it in foul ground, I knew the tide of the World Series had turned. Rivera and Wetteland, with two outs of help from Lloyd in between, nailed down what ended up a 5–2 victory. John gave me the ball from the last out, knowing it was my first World Series win.

All of a sudden, after serving as little more than bad props to the mighty Braves for two games, we were credible. We had some momentum. It's a good thing Coney pitched us through that sixth inning, because we played a courageous, historic game the next night that could only have happened with a win already under our belts. Game Four will go down in history as one of the most memorable World Series games ever and the signature game of the 1996 Yankees. But if Game Four had been Game Three— when we had yet to hold even a lead over the Braves—we could not have won it.

CHAPTER 9

Bulletproof

I FELT GREAT THE MORNING I WOKE up before Game Four. I knew winning one game in the World Series could easily turn into a second win—and then you'd be rolling. I don't think that applies to the regular season, but momentum seems much more important in the postseason. That's why I felt a lot of pressure in Game Five of the American League Championship Series in Baltimore. If we had let the Orioles up off the floor with a win there, who knew what would happen afterward? You can't put the other team back on the offensive. That's exactly what the Braves had done, though, when they failed to break out against David Cone with the bases loaded in that critical sixth inning of Game Three. They let us back in the Series, and we came charging back with confidence when they did.

I also felt relaxed before Game Four because I had no major decisions to make about the lineup. We had beaten

Tom Glavine, a left-hander, the night before with Wade Boggs, Tino Martinez, and Paul O'Neill on the bench in favor of Charlie Hayes, Cecil Fielder, and Darryl Strawberry. Atlanta was using another left-hander, Denny Neagle, in Game Four, so I wasn't about to change the lineup. The heat was off me. I'll admit, though, it did seem a little strange to be playing in the World Series with three guys in the middle of my lineup who hadn't even been with the club before the Fourth of July. It bothered me a little bit to be taking people out of the lineup who had been there all year. I reminded myself, though, that when you get to the World Series, you can't be concerned about reputation or hurting feelings. You have to decide who's going to help you win that day, which ultimately benefits everybody.

I had talked with Wade, Tino, and Paulie before Game Three—I didn't have to explain anything to them before Game Four because it was obvious I'd use the same lineup—and they handled it like professionals. Tino, however, looked more upset than the other guys. I think he was frustrated because he was having a bad postseason. He struggled because he fights himself so much. He wears himself out. He doesn't like you to say too much to him, either, so I stayed away from giving him any one-on-one advice. When I would see him walking by, though, I'd say something to somebody else loud enough that he could hear me. For instance, I'd grab O'Neill if I saw Tino next to him and say something like "Paulie, with this pitcher you have to . . ."

I felt the confidence in the clubhouse, too, before Game

Four. The guys were pretty loose the whole time, even after that ass kicking in Game One. But it's amazing what one victory can do for you, especially when you're playing the world champs and you're the underdog. Bernie Williams was happy because a shipment of his bats had arrived from New York. Bernie had forgotten to pack them after Game Two for our trip to Atlanta. How do you forget your bats for the World Series? That's Bernie, though. He's an intelligent guy, but he's so oblivious to pressure and his surroundings that sometimes I think he doesn't even know what planet he's on. Bernie had borrowed Joe Girardi's bat for Game Three and hit a home run with it. But he still switched back to his own bats before Game Four.

Speaking of forgetting things, no one on our club remembered to bring to Atlanta the generic blue visiting lineup cards. Most clubs stock them in the visiting manager's office, anyway. But the only cards in my desk at Atlanta Fulton County Stadium were left behind by the Reds. The cards had CINCINNATI printed in boldface on top. It would have to do. I scratched out CINCINNATI, though it remained legible on my carbon copy. And that's the reason the greatest game I ever managed is recorded with a Cincinnati Reds lineup card. By the end of the night, that lineup card looked more unkempt than I do if I skip a day of shaving. As I use players, I scratch their names off a list on the right side of my card. Every player's name eventually would be crossed out that night except three: Andy Pettitte, who was my starting pitcher the next night, and starting pitchers Jimmy Key and David Cone, both of whom I came so close to using in the late innings that I had to tell them to change out of their soft-soled shoes, which starters typically wear when they're not pitching, and into their spikes.

I kept that lineup card, as I did all the others from the World Series. It's a thing of beauty. It seemed like every move I made, no matter how strange it might have looked to others, turned out right. Game Four will go down as a classic. I believe it's the signature game of the 1996 Yankees because it showcased our greatest strengths: our bullpen, our depth, and above all, our heart. It was the second-greatest comeback in World Series history and a perfect example of why anybody who thinks baseball with the designated hitter is better is nuts. Having the pitcher bat presents the manager with a major decision every time his turn comes up. It was great being back in the National League. I used ten players just in the ninth spot alone in the batting order. Game Four ended at 12:36 in the morning after four hours and seventeen minutes of excruciating drama—the longest of the 543 World Series games ever played. It included so many strategic twists—and here I'll give you an inside look at the best of them—that I'm convinced a manager without National League experience could not have won it.

Kenny Rogers was my starting pitcher, a circumstance made possible by an act of God. No, Sister Marguerite had nothing to do with it. He started only because we had lost the first scheduled off-day, due to the rainstorm that postponed Game One. In fact, on the night of that rainout, I had petitioned acting commissioner Bud Selig to keep the off-

day between Games Two and Three and drop the one between Games Five and Six.

"Bud," I told him, "if you're going to give an off-day, I'd
rather have the first one—only because the Braves had an
opportunity to work out here at Yankee Stadium. We
should have the same opportunity to work out at their place.
Let's even the playing field."

"It makes sense," Selig said. "I'll think about it and get
back to you."

I didn't hear from him again about it. Bud had been
much easier to bargain with when he sold me that 1960
Thunderbird. The rainout was a real disadvantage for us. If
we had had the two off-days, Rogers would not have been
my Game Four starter. I would have used Pettitte on short
rest. So Rogers got the call in a matchup against Neagle,
who had been pitching much better for the Braves lately
than he did after his trade from Pittsburgh, August 28. I
told a couple of people before the game, "This is a game
we're going to have to win 8–6, 10–9, something like that."

I just thought, the way Kenny had been pitching, it
would be a high-scoring game. Also, the previous day Rogers had bagged the traditional press conference featuring the
next day's starting pitchers. Rick Cerrone, our director of
media relations, came to me and said, "Kenny doesn't want
to talk to the press."

"Fine," I told him. "Just tell the writers I think it's a
good idea, so it can take some of the pressure off him."

But then I learned that Kenny was just kidding with
Rick. By then it was too late to put the press conference

together, so Rick announced during the game that Rogers would be available to the media after the game. I just let it go and didn't talk to Kenny about it. That's Kenny. He's one of the most difficult players to read that I've ever managed. But I don't put him in that Ed Whitson category, the kind of guy who can't pitch in New York. He just needs more confidence in himself.

Several times during the season Kenny would come into my office, and I had no idea what he was talking about. I guess he was reading the newspapers and people were writing that I didn't like him and that he was in my doghouse and things like that. So he'd ask me questions about my confidence in him or lack of it. I'd tell him, "Kenny, I know your equipment. I know your stuff. But it doesn't do me any good to believe in you unless you believe in yourself."

Sports medicine is an amazingly advanced field. But with Rogers I wish they could invent some procedure to transfer confidence. Hook up some device to his left arm and just inject it. At least that way I would have felt, going into Game Four, that we were going to be all right. Instead, I felt like with Kenny pitching, we would have to knock their starter out of the game in order to win.

I noticed an omen about Rogers right from the start. When Tim Raines led off for us in the first inning, Rogers still was throwing in the bullpen. That's never a good sign. All that means is you're not loose. There's a certain tightness a player gets before a big game—which is fine. In the past players never admitted to the fact that they got nervous and jumpy. It's okay to admit it now, but not back when I played. You were a man, and you weren't supposed to be nervous. Consider the word *bravery*. It's contingent upon being nervous and afraid. If you're not afraid, there's no reason to be brave. It's what you do in spite of not feeling right that makes you brave.

Kenny, though, could not seem to conquer his anxiety. After Neagle set us down in order, Rogers fell behind on the count on his first three hitters. Zimmer turned to me and barked, "He won't throw strikes!" Rogers, though, did get a ground-ball out from each of those hitters. Whenever a pitcher is getting ground-ball outs, I'm happy. It means he's getting his pitches down, which makes it more difficult for a batter to get good wood on the ball.

Kenny wasn't so fortunate in the second inning. He fell behind Fred McGriff, three-and-one. Then McGriff launched a bomb over the center-field wall. Now, home runs to center field or the opposite field don't bother me. You can't put the total blame on the pitcher for those. If a pitcher flat out makes a mistake, such as hanging a curveball or grooving a fastball down the middle, a hitter is going to pull it. But if the hitter goes the other way or to dead center with a pitch, you just tip your hat to the hitter. And if you do give up dingers, you want to give them up with nobody on base. Kenny, though, obviously was shell-shocked after that blast. He went into his four-corner defense and refused to throw a strike. That's what drives me nuts more than anything. You can't be afraid to throw strikes. That's not giving yourself or your team a chance. After he walked Javy Lopez, I turned to Zimmer and said, "Shit. I better talk to him." My mission: Pump up Kenny's deflated ego.

Sometimes I can light a fire under a pitcher by challenging his manhood—really cursing him out and asking him to show me some guts. With Kenny I have to be a little more careful. He was still an enigma to me. As I walked to the mound, I decided to be firm with him but be careful not to go overboard. I didn't want to crush his confidence; I wanted to rebuild it.

"Listen, you threw the ball really well in the first inning," I told him. "Now, because of the home run, you want to start guiding the ball, and you're afraid to throw strikes. You've got to be the same guy you were last inning and throw strikes. You've got good shit. Don't be afraid to challenge people. Now let's go!"

Kenny didn't say anything. He just nodded. So what happened? He walked Andruw Jones. Now he really ticked me off. He had developed a mindset that he was not going to throw strikes. Your good pitchers don't throw strikes, but they throw pitches that *look* like strikes. Maddux is a master at that. Tom Seaver used the expression "pitching around the strike zone."

Rogers fell behind another batter, Jermaine Dye, but he did get an out on a fly ball long enough to advance both runners one base. With Jeff Blauser batting, I thought that Cox might squeeze in that situation, even if our scouting reports on the Braves said he didn't use the squeeze play. I knew better than that. I remember one game I managed against him in St. Louis when I called for three straight pitch-outs, with Rafael Belliard batting. On the third one Cox did have the squeeze play on, and we got the runner.

This time, though, Rogers was having such a tough time throwing strikes that I didn't want to pitch out. And if they did squeeze, big deal. This early in the game, I was willing to trade a run for an out. That time Cox squeezed with Belliard, it was late in the game, when one run is as good as five. It was only the second inning here. I'd take two outs and two runs in.

Sure enough, Blauser put down a bunt on a two-and-one count, and Lopez jogged home. The worst part of the play was that we didn't get an out. Mariano Duncan, my second baseman, failed to cover first base. He broke toward second because Jones was running on the pitch from first base. I couldn't get mad at Duncan about that; you don't want the shortstop covering second base with a pull hitter up. But that's why they say you never stop learning in baseball. We'll address that very play in spring training. The only thing a second baseman can do there to prevent leaving first base uncovered is to check the runner at third before breaking toward second base. If the guy on third is running, the second baseman has to get to first. You should react to the runner on third, not the one on first.

Neagle also bunted, sending Blauser to second, with Jones holding at third. Then Grissom smoked a double past Derek Jeter, making the score 4–0. Later on some writers asked me why didn't I walk Grissom to pitch to Lemke. Hey, I second-guessed myself when he got the hit, but analyzing it later, he hit the ball on the ground—hard, but on the ground. And that's what I wanted to see out of Kenny. When he's pitching well, he'll get a lot of ground balls because of the sink on his pitches. Anyway, I hate to walk people intentionally early in the game. You're just asking for trouble.

Rogers did get Lemke on a grounder, to temporarily stop the bleeding. He also managed our first hit off Neagle, a single in the third. Standing on first base, Rogers said to my coach, Jose Cardenal, "I'm glad I can hit, because I'm not pitching very good." Cardenal told me about it between innings. I didn't think that was real funny. It's that false mentality, trying to make light of the situation. Even when you're kidding, there's still that negative thought in your head.

When Kenny allowed singles to Chipper Jones and Mc-Griff to start the bottom of the third inning, I had to pull him. The one thing as a manager you have to stay away from is letting the game get blown out of shape. And I also had to remember that although Neagle is a good pitcher, he's not Maddux, Smoltz, or Glavine. We were still in this game. So I brought in Brian Boehringer. As Kenny left the field, I still felt the same way about him: I'm a Kenny Rogers fan. The problem is, he isn't.

Boehringer did a fine job, getting outs from all six batters he faced—one of those outs, a sacrifice fly, made it 5–0—before I had to hit for him in the fifth with Luis Sojo. As well as Boehringer pitched, I had to put up a better hitter for him when we were down by five runs. In the American League, because the pitcher doesn't bat, I would have stayed with him as long as he was effective. I had confidence, too, in relievers David Weathers, who had pitched most of the year with the Florida Marlins, Jeff Nelson, and Graeme Lloyd. I would not use Mariano Rivera and John Wetteland if we were trailing by a lot, so I could keep them for a game we could win.

The Braves tacked on another run in the fifth against Weathers. Chipper Jones had walked, moved to second on a balk, and scored on a double by Andruw Jones that bounced off Hayes's glove. I never saw that balk. I happened to be looking down at the time. But of course, that didn't stop me from mounting what might have looked on television like a vigorous argument with Jerry Davis, the National League umpire working second base who made the call.

"What did he do?" I asked Davis as I made my way across the field.

"He started to come around with the ball in his hand and then stopped," Davis said.

"You know, Jerry," I argued, "the problem is, you see somebody new, and something in his motion looks funny to you."

"Uh, Joe, he was with Florida all year."

I immediately recognized the folly of my argument. Florida is a National League team, and Davis, an NL umpire, was very familiar with the former Marlins pitcher.

"You know, that's a good point, Jerry," I said. "You're right."

I promptly wheeled around and headed back to the dugout, doing my best to surpress a chuckle and hoping my face wasn't too red.

When my team came off the field after that fifth inning, I delivered a message to them as they gathered in the middle of the dugout. Okay, things didn't look great. Neagle was throwing a two-hit shutout, and we were trailing by six runs. No Yankee team had come from that far back to win a World Series game. Ever. Only one other club had ever mounted a bigger comeback in the history of the Fall Classic: Connie Mack's 1929 Philadelphia Athletics. On top of that, we were only nine outs away from being down three games to one in the series, a virtually insurmountable deficit against the kind of starting pitchers the Braves had. But if you think that way, you're beat. So I didn't say a word of it. I reminded the players to think small.

"Let's cut it in half right here," I told them. "Take small bites. Do the little things to get one run at a time. Let's put a little pressure on them."

As had happened so often in the season, especially in October, a rally began with the unflappable kid, Jeter. He plays every game, including the World Series, like it's Saturday morning on the sandlots of Marine Park. After the first playoff game against Texas, after he left six runners on, all the writers were asking me, "Are you going to talk to him?" I didn't see any reason to. He just hadn't gotten a big hit. So what? He didn't seem to act any differently. That's why it's important for a manager to walk through the clubhouse a lot—to sense anything. I find out a lot in the trainers' room. I can sense tension there. How? Strained conversation, a looseness, what they're doing when you walk in, or if your walking in affects anything.

Jeter, though, doesn't seem to ever change. And I hope he never does. He'll now have a lot of forces pushing him in different directions: his agents, the media, and of course, all the women. Keeping up his work habits will be the key. I'll notice right away this spring if he's changing. If he stops working, he'll have a problem.

What I like about Jeter as a hitter is, he uses the whole

field. He became even more right-field conscious against the Braves because their whole damned pitching staff lives on the outside of the plate. Check out their outfield alignment sometime. They overshift more to the opposite field than any club I've ever seen, and they do it on everybody.

So naturally, Jeter hit a fly ball near the right-field line. Dye didn't seem to have a good line on the ball, but umpire Tim Welke didn't help his cause either. The umpire never made an effort to get out of Dye's way. Dye had to run around the umpire like a basketball defender trying to get around a pick. What should have been the first out dropped into foul territory. Given another swing, Jeter blooped a single in front of Dye.

I know that Cox beefed about Welke for the rest of the Series, calling it the turning point of Game Four. I don't know about that. I don't know if that was the umpire's fault. I guess he has to be out of the way, but he was looking at the two infielders coming at him. And that didn't turn the series around. Even after that ball landed foul, the Braves still were ahead 6–0 and Neagle still hadn't given up a hard hit. Welke had nothing to do with all the hits and walks that came after that.

For me, it was a good sign. We had come from behind so many times during the year, especially in the postseason, that whenever something as lucky as a misplayed pop-up went our way, I figured more breaks would follow. I just wanted to get into Atlanta's middle relief. Of course, I took for granted that our pitching was going to shut them down. That's the way you have to think. That's why, when you're managing a team like Detroit, with its raggedy pitching staff, it's tough to figure out how many runs you need. That's a helpless feeling.

So I never thought this game looked over. You can't lose sight of the fact that this is the World Series and there are only four games left to play. This is it. Jeter was as good as anybody feeling that we were never going to lose. I'd go out to change a pitcher, and he'd come to the mound and say, "We're going to win this game." I love that. If you say it enough, you believe it.

Neagle walked Bernie Williams, and now it looked like all of a sudden he was running out of gas. I had my big man up, Cecil Fielder, with runners at first and second. He's the kind of slugger who can cut the lead in half with one swing, but in this series Fielder suddenly became much more than a power hitter. He was simply a tough out, a guy who was really locked in.

Soon after we traded for Cecil, I had asked him about having a game plan when he went to the plate, including the thought of driving the ball to the opposite field. "I can't do that," he said. Cecil didn't want to think too much up at the plate; he just wanted to go up there and mash. But he had one at bat in August against Randy Johnson that stuck with me. Randy can blow his fastball past Cecil, especially if he gets it up. With two strikes, though, Cecil hit one of Johnson's heaters up the middle for a two-run single. That told me he knows what he's doing up there, even though he may not understand some of the things I was trying to tell him.

Cecil wound up with nine hits in the World Series: three to left field, three to center field, and three to right field.

Now he collected one of those opposite-field hits against Neagle, drilling an outside pitch so hard to right field that it ate up Dye after one wicked bounce. As the ball bounced away from Dye, Derek and Bernie scored; third-base coach Willie Randolph made a terrific call in sending Williams home. I think Willie so surprised the Braves' defense by sending Bernie with no outs that Bernie scored without a throw to the plate.

Now it was 6–2, Cecil on second, and Charlie Hayes was up. His job was to get Cecil to third base. I can't tell you how proud I am of these guys because they never lost sight of what they had to do. Charlie did hit the ball to the right side—so well, in fact, that he wound up driving in Cecil with a single.

I was so pleasantly surprised about Charlie Hayes. I had never been crazy about watching him play on other teams. I didn't like his body language on the field. I'd had chances to get him in trades before and said no thanks. Then on August 30 Bob Watson asked me if I had interest in Hayes. At that point Boggsy was struggling a little bit, so it was tempting. The guy who turned me around on Hayes was Jim Leyland, the Pirates' manager at the time. I called him up and asked him about Charlie. He said, "You'll love him, and he'll help you." He was right.

Just as I had asked the guys in my dugout meeting, we cut the lead in half. Now I was greedy and wanted more. Why not? When Darryl drew a walk off Terrell Wade, we once again had two on and nobody out.

Cox brought in Mike Bielecki, a right-hander whom Zimmer had managed once in Chicago. Do I pinch-hit for

Duncan, who is one-for-eleven, with a left-handed hitter like Boggs? No way. Duncan came up with too many big hits for us all year. Besides, you just can't run yourself out of players. It's still only the sixth inning. You still have to manage the whole game. I remember a game I was playing with the Mets in Cincinnati. Joe Frazier was the manager. I was leading off the ninth inning when he pinch-hit for me with a left-handed hitter. The game ended with one of our pitchers, Skip Lockwood, hitting for himself with a couple of runners on because he had no players left. You really have to project what could happen, to think where you're going to need your players. That's especially true in the National League. In the American League you can't run out of players because of the designated hitter.

Do I ask Dunc to bunt? No way, again. I know Mariano is a lousy bunter. He's just not comfortable doing it, so I'm not going to ask him. So I let him hack. Mariano is such a freewheeling first-ball hitter that you could throw the resin bag up there and he'd swing at it. Bielecki struck him out.

I then decided to pinch-hit for Girardi, who was hitless in the series to that point, with O'Neill. I wasn't sure what Cox would do. If he had brought in a left-hander, Steve Avery, I would have sent Leyritz up. I think at that point Cox already was committed to bringing in his closer, Mark Wohlers, in the eighth inning. Why did I feel that way? I thought Cox felt the game was close to slipping away, and he didn't have anyone he trusted to pitch the eighth inning. Even if it meant Cox would not have Wohlers rested for Game Five, he wanted to be up three games to one. This had become a huge game for him because he had that big lead.

Bielecki was throwing gas. Zimmer told me, "I've never seen him throw this hard." He whiffed O'Neill and Tino Martinez, who batted for Weathers.

It was 6–3 then. Zim gave me a nudge. "Check out your sister," he said. I looked behind me in the field boxes, and there was Sister Marguerite dancing in the aisles. She was doing the macarena.

Then I asked Jeff Nelson to keep the Braves in check. He did a perfect job, keeping the game at 6–3 with two hitless innings, bringing us to an eighth-inning showdown with Wohlers. I heard later that Bobby Cox took some heat for pulling Bielecki, who looked like Nolan Ryan out there. But it was the right move—he had gotten out of Bielecki what he wanted. It used to be managers brought in their closer with a runner on second base, leaving the guy no breathing room. Now most managers prefer to give their horse the ball with a little room for error. I'm with Bobby on that one.

Hayes led off against Wohlers, and I couldn't afford to pinch-hit for him. I was down to Aldrete, Fox, and Boggs. If I led off with Boggs, who would I have to knock in the run? Fox? Aldrete? They weren't yet proven hitters in those clutch situations. I knew Boggs had trouble knocking in runs, but I still had to save him for that kind of situation. Plus, I was committed in my mind to starting Hayes the next day against Smoltz. But if he was going to play against Smoltz, why not use him against Wohlers?

Then something happened that made me think once again that this was meant to be. Hayes topped a ball down the third-base line. It clearly was rolling foul. It even crossed over onto the chalk line. But suddenly, amazingly, the damned thing took a right-hand turn. It wound up fair by more than a foot. It was so absurd that Charlie stood on first base laughing. Like Jeter's divine home run against the Orioles, it's easy to believe that Rocco had his hand in that hit as well. I admit that at that point I was thinking about destiny, that we were destined to win this thing. There's nothing wrong with thinking that way—you just have to make sure you don't get caught up in it to the point where you stop working. You have to continue to work at it. But that kind of thinking keeps you from getting anxious. You start saying, "Whatever's going to happen is going to happen, but it sure looks good for us."

Darryl came up with another hit, a single that put runners on first and second. And more good things happened for us. Duncan hit a smash to shortstop. It was a sure double-play ball, especially because Cox had put his defensive specialist, Belliard, in the game. Whoops! He couldn't handle the hop. Belliard did get an out at second base, but he lost the double play. "Wow," I said to myself. "I love this." Our whole dugout was buzzing with excitement. The dugouts in Atlanta Fulton County Stadium are terrible—the seats are way too low. So everybody was standing up or sitting on the front ledge of the dugout.

Leyritz was the batter, but I started to think about who should pinch-hit for Nelson, whose spot in the lineup was coming up next. Aldrete? Boggs? If Leyritz got on, it would be Boggs. If not, Aldrete. Jimmy had a pretty good hack at Wohlers's first pitch, a ninety-eight-mile-per-hour fastball, and fouled it back. Wohlers had this strange look on his face, one that said something like, "Wow, I just gave him my best bullet, and he was right on it." I thought Jimmy was slightly behind the ball, but the damage to Wohlers's psyche was done. He wasn't sure if he could get Leyritz out with his best heater. I thought about that time I pinch-hit for Jimmy and he was pissed off, telling me he was a better hitter in big situations.

After that, Wohlers tried to trick Jimmy with two break-ing balls, neither of which was a strike. So Wohlers tried another fastball again, this one at ninety-nine miles per hour. And again Jimmy fouled it back. I still think that if Wohlers had thrown his fastball a little higher—at least as high as the belt—Jimmy wouldn't have been able to catch up to it. Wohlers has one of the best fastballs on earth. He is so intimidating with that heater that Leyritz decided to use Darryl Strawberry's bat against him; Jimmy had only a couple of his own bats left and was afraid of breaking them against Wohlers. Straw's bats were expendable. I found that to be pretty funny. I mean, it was the fourth game of the World Series. What was Jimmy saving his bats for?

After that second foul ball, Wohlers had seen enough. He said later that he thought Leyritz was "right on my fastball," so he eliminated the pitch from his thinking. With the count two-and-two, Wohlers threw a nasty slider, breaking it off down and away. Leyritz reached out and tapped the ball foul past third base. Sometimes great hitting isn't always about hitting home runs or putting the ball in play. Hank Aaron, for instance, was great at fouling off tough pitches to extend at bats. That's what Jimmy did. Wohlers decided to come back with another slider. If the previous one had been nasty, he tried to make this one even better. But when you try to do that, usually you wind up throwing a hanger, which is what Wohlers did. Jimmy connected solidly. I know how well the ball carries in the Launching Pad, and I've seen enough home runs to recognize them by the way they jump off the bat. I knew this one was out as soon as Jimmy hit it. Wohlers got beaten with his third-best pitch. Our whole dugout emptied to congratulate Jimmy. Believe me, I wanted to go out there too. But it's not proper protocol for a manager to be celebrating on the field, unless you're Tommy Lasorda and you can get away with hugging people. I'm not about to look for that kind of attention. And anyway, the game wasn't over. It was like I was numb at first. It took a moment for it to sink in that the score was now 6–6. It was still only the eighth inning.

I wound up using Aldrete as my pinch hitter. He grounded out. But I liked where this game was going. If you were the Braves, you had to believe you still had the hammer; you were still the home team in a tie game. But I figure they had to know the momentum had slipped away from them. It showed too. The Braves never again had a lead the rest of the Series. I think the sixth inning of the night before, when Cone had withstood the Atlanta rally, turned the Series around. It gave us momentum and confidence. But Jimmy's home run was nearly as big. It convinced us not only that we had played our way into a competitive World Series with the Braves, but also that we were going to win it.

Rivera shut down Atlanta for another inning by throwing

his best pitch, the fastball, almost exclusively. Wohlers, meanwhile, should have been second-guessing himself. As Tim McCarver pointed out on the television broadcast after two men were out, "You haven't seen a slider yet from Mariano Rivera, have you?" Rivera was doing what he was supposed to be doing—he was throwing heat. It reminded me of the time I caught Steve Carlton and called for every pitch to be a fastball. When a pitcher is on with that kind of live fastball, it doesn't matter if the batter knows it's coming. He doesn't stand a chance.

Wohlers recovered in the ninth by getting out Jeter on a strike-out and Williams on a ground ball. We had two outs and nobody on base when Cecil cracked another hit—to right field yet again. Zim turned to me and asked, "What about pinch-running with Fox? We could steal second base easily off Wohlers's high leg kick." It wasn't a bad idea, but I really didn't like taking Cecil's bat out of a tie game. I also didn't like the idea of having to play Mariano Duncan at first base, an unfamiliar position for him, with the score tied. Before I had time to make a decision, Charlie Hayes smacked the next pitch into left field for a single.

Do I pinch-run for Cecil now? I really wrestled with that call. Cox went out to talk with Wohlers, and I still hadn't decided by the time he walked back to the dugout. Then Wohlers threw a pitch to Darryl. Finally I figured, hell, I've *got* to run for him. If Straw gets a hit and Cecil can't score from second base, I'll never forgive myself. So I sent Fox in to run for him. Straw did get a hit, though not the kind that could have scored Fox, it was another one of those blessed infield dribblers.

Now we had the bases loaded and two outs, and Duncan was facing Wohlers. Do I finally use Boggs here? Nope. Boggs was the only player I had left. If I used him and he didn't get the run in, then I might be in a situation in the tenth inning where I would have to let my pitcher hit. If this were the American League, I could have sent Boggs up there for Duncan. But I couldn't do that with the National League rules, not when my pitcher was batting and I'd need a pinch hitter. Duncan hit a rocket, but Dye, thanks to that overshifted alignment, caught the line drive in right field.

I planned to put Fox at second and Duncan at first base for the bottom of the ninth, but then Hayes came over to me and said, "Do you want me to play first base?"

"Have you ever done it?" I asked him.

"Yeah, this year with the Pirates," he said.

"Go ahead then," I said.

I liked that alignment better, with Duncan at second and Fox at third. Rivera went back out for another inning, even though he had thrown thirty-five pitches the night before. This was the World Series. I thought about all those times in April and May when people had asked me, "Did you think about using Rivera for another inning?" And I'd said, "If it was the World Series, I would." Well, here we were. It was something I never was faced with before. I had used that comment long enough, so now I had to put my money where my mouth was. I didn't like the idea of having him throw so many pitches, but there really was no decision, at least not until McGriff came up with two on and one out. That was when I brought in Graeme Lloyd, who some people, including our own media relations department, probably felt shouldn't even have been on our postseason roster. The media relations people didn't bother including a bio of Lloyd in our postseason media guide.

Lloyd had struggled big-time after we acquired him from Milwaukee in August. It turned out his elbow was killing him, but he didn't tell us. One day in Seattle he gave up a home run to Jeff Manto that cost us the ball game. Finally he admitted he was hurt. That really upset me. I told him, "Hell, you cost me a ball game." Pitching hurt or playing hurt is one thing. Playing stupid is something else. And Lloyd had been playing stupid.

In late September, as we were putting our postseason roster together, I called all my coaches into my office. I said, "All right, give me your ten-man staff." Everybody picked Dale Polley over Lloyd.

A few days later Zimmer said to me, "Give me your gut feeling. If you had to choose between Polley and Lloyd, who would you pick?"

"Lloyd," I said.

"So you have to do that," Zim said.

The next time we were voting on ten-man staffs, everybody picked Lloyd. I smiled. I knew Zim had been working the underground coaches' network. This is the way I saw it: Why had all of our scouts said Lloyd was the guy when we were looking for a left-hander? Once I found out he felt all right, I had to go back to the big picture and the scouting reports. And I talked to Phil Garner, who managed him in Milwaukee, and Bob Uecker, who worked as a broadcaster with the Brewers, and they gave me glowing reports on him as a person. So that was the gut call I made on the eve of the playoffs. He was healthy, and I wanted him.

I never dreamed he'd be *this* good, though. Lloyd had faced fifteen batters in October and retired fourteen of them, including McGriff on an inning-ending double play to get out of that ninth-inning jam. Welcome to extra innings. Cox decided not to push Wohlers into a third inning, so he brought in Steve Avery, the left-hander, to start the tenth inning. I assumed Cox had lost confidence in his other relievers, particularly Greg McMichael, who had given up a single, a home run, and a double to the three batters he faced in Game Three. So he gave the ball to Avery. Lloyd, who had never batted in the majors before, was due to hit second in the tenth inning. Zimmer asked me, "Who's going to hit?"

"Lloyd," I said.

"What about one of your other pitchers?" he asked.

Good point. If Leyritz, the leadoff batter, reached base, I was going to use Cone, who had experience batting in the National League, to bunt him to second. "Go put your spikes on," I told Cone, who dashed into the clubhouse to get ready. Then I thought if the score was still tied, I might use Jimmy Key to pitch two innings and save Wetteland, who was warming up, for later. I wanted to be prepared if this turned out to be a long extra-inning game. So I told Key to put his spikes on too.

Leyritz grounded out, so I left Lloyd in to hit, knowing that Cox still had Klesko, his big left-handed power threat, on his bench. But then I talked some more with Zim and

Mel and decided to get Wetteland up again. "Hell, let's use him for two innings," I said. "Let's hope we score in his first inning and he'll save it in the second." Lloyd actually had a decent hack but grounded out.

Avery then ignited our rally with a huge blunder, considering he had two outs and nobody on: He walked Tim Raines, who had been 0-for-5 that night, on four pitches. I gave Raines the green light to steal—the sign that says take it when you want it. But Raines, to my disappointment, played it cautious and never made a break for the bag. The ice-cool kid, Jeter, fell behind 0-and-2 before working the count to two-and-two, then he rapped a single to left. I loved it. Now I had Bernie Williams hitting right-handed, which is by far his better side of the plate. Cox had two choices: bring in right-hander Brad Clontz to turn Williams around, or walk him. He knew I had Boggs to hit for Fox, who was due to hit after Bernie. I think Cox made the right call. He walked Bernie. Williams had been Mr. October for us, and one of the cardinal rules of managing is don't let the other team's best hitter beat you.

I stood there and said to Zim, "This is it. I've got Boggs." And he just said, "Yeah." Finally, that was the time to use my last player, a future Hall of Famer. I think being patient with my usage of players—making sure I didn't run myself out of players by holding on to Boggs like a trump card—helped win the game for us. "Boggsy!" I yelled, and he took off his jacket and got ready to hit. Now, I knew Boggs had struggled this year with runners on base and two out (.146). But you can throw those stats out the window in the post-season. I also knew he doesn't chase bad pitches. And I wondered what was going through his head. Ten years ago with the Boston Red Sox, the guy had been one strike away from being a world champion. Now here he was with a second chance.

As a manager, you almost never sit back and watch, unless it's the ninth inning and we have a lead. You always have to be thinking ahead. As Boggs walked to the plate, I was thinking about who the hell was going to pitch the bottom of the inning for us. Wetteland had been up and down like a Yo-Yo in the bullpen. In fact, after the game I felt so bad about that that I apologized to him for warming him up so many times. John just said to me, "I understand. You had no choice."

I figured if the game was still tied in the bottom of the tenth, I would use Lloyd. If we scored, it would be Wetteland. That whole time Zimmer was yacking away at me, firing questions left and right: "Where's the pitcher hitting? Who's pitching next inning? Who do they have left?" Sometimes I just had to say to him, "Shaddup." It was like a nutty Marx Brothers routine in the dugout.

Boggsy is a professional hitter. He didn't nibble at Avery's sliders off the plate, especially a dangerously close one—it was low—at two-and-two. With a full count and the bases loaded, Avery threw a fastball not nearly close enough in the strike zone to even tempt Boggs. Wade watched it for ball four and what had to be the biggest RBI of his great career. We had the lead for the first time all night, 7–6. Then Zim, Mel, and I all agreed: Wetteland would start the bottom of the inning. But then Cox made a move that put an end to our waffling about who should start the ninth inning. He pulled a double switch, putting Klesko at first base leading off and Clontz on the mound. Now it was obvious what to do: Lloyd for Klesko, with Wetteland after that.

Then Hayes hit a feeble little pop-up that, fittingly, Klesko dropped for an error, giving us another run. Beautiful. Now we were up 8–6, and Klesko would have to face Lloyd with nobody on base leading off the tenth. Naturally, Lloyd struck him out. As Zim said, "Klesko will be seeing that big lefty in his sleep." One thing we did perfectly in the Series was, we made Klesko a nonfactor. I knew he had done some damage against Cleveland in the 1995 World Series. But we completely took him out of this Series by starting a left-hander in five of the six games and by getting matchups against him late in the games with Lloyd, our suddenly invincible left-hander.

The rest of the game belonged to Wetteland. Big John added his usual flair for the exciting. The first batter, Andruw Jones, singled. I'm usually very cool in the dugout. I don't even pace. I've never showed a lot of emotion as a manager because I remember managers who cursed out loud or threw something if a guy struck out with the bases loaded or made an error. That always bothered me. Hell, I've been out there playing the game, and I know how hard it is. And the players on the bench are seeing their manager lose his cool, so they know when they're out there and mess up, he'll be doing the same thing. With two outs to go, though, I was nervous and jumpy in that dugout. I rearranged things in there, asking our trainer, Gene Monahan, "Wasn't the Gatorade bucket over there yesterday when we won?" Of course, I'm not superstitious. Not at all. It was just in case somebody else was superstitious.

I was also a little nervous about Wetteland. He had struggled sometimes during the year after I would get him up and down a few times in the bullpen. Thankfully, he now closed the door, even if he did so somewhat gently rather than slamming it. He got two fly balls to the warning track in left field. On the second one Tim Raines looked for a moment as if he had misjudged the ball. He wound up falling backward on the track as he squeezed the last out. We won 8–6, the kind of score I had predicted before the game, with Rogers going to the mound. I had never seen my team with so much energy as it showed after that last out. I felt it too. That comeback was so stirring, I couldn't fall asleep that night until four-thirty in the morning.

In the clubhouse I hugged everybody in sight and yelled things like "How about Graeme Lloyd! How about David Weathers! How about Jeff Nelson! You guys are great! This is a great team!" I made sure I hugged Kenny Rogers too. I thought about that great Game Six of the 1975 World Series, when Carlton Fisk wrapped a home run around the fair side of the foul pole, and I told Zim, who had been coaching third base for the Red Sox then, "This is going to go down as one of the greatest ever, just like that Carlton Fisk game! Except we're going to win this damned thing!"

I was just so excited. I wasn't even thinking about tomorrow. The Series was tied two games to two, but I felt so good about it because we were guaranteed to go back to New York, which was huge for us, even though we had lost the first two games there. After we lost the first game, I had said all we had to do was win two out of the next four to get it back home. I knew there would be less pressure on us for Games Six and Seven than there had been for games Games One and Two.

The feeling I had after Game Four was unbelievable. I felt bulletproof. There are things you do right and things you do wrong—like when I was trying to decide about pinch-running for Fielder. I'd made up my mind after that first pitch to Straw. But if that first pitch had been a base hit and Cecil hadn't scored, I would have looked like a dummy. Now nobody noticed it. When you're hot, you get away with things like that. That's what made me think I was bulletproof.

After the celebration in the clubhouse, I just sat there at my desk in the manager's office with a smile on my face and talked with some friends on the phone. Everything seemed to be happening for a reason. Leyritz hit that three-run home run, and it didn't even surprise me. Hayes hit that dribbler that took a right-hand turn fair, and strange as it was, it seemed that was the way it was meant to be. It was weird. I had had this little thought in my head throughout the playoffs and the World Series that would not go away. It was never so strong as in those euphoric moments after Game Four. Over and over again it went like this: I always see good things happen for other people. Why can't they happen to me now? I've waited so long for this. At this point everything is equal. Why *not* me?

CHAPTER 10

On Top of the World

I WAS SO EXHAUSTED, WHEN I WOKE up after Game Four, that I didn't want to leave my hotel for lunch. Then my friend Ed Maull called me up and reminded me that we had gone out to lunch before both Game Three and Game Four—and both games had turned out to be victories. "We *have* to have lunch," he said. I agreed. I wasn't going to screw it up now. My wife went shopping, with her sisters Mary, Katie, and Rosie, and I went to lunch at the Buckhead Diner with Ed and two other friends, Arthur Sando and Dr. Joe Platania. As we drove to the diner I sensed that Dr. Joe wanted to provide his usual help to me regarding my lineup.

"So, what are you going to do tonight?" he asked me.

"I don't know," I lied. I didn't want to tell anybody.

"I've got your lineup for you," Dr. Joe said, and he proceeded to run through his batting order. We were facing a tough right-handed pitcher, John Smoltz, that night, so he had most of my left-handed hitters, including Boggs, back in his lineup. "Now, who are you going to play?" he asked me.

"I'm not going to tell you," I said.

Deep down, I knew I had some very tough decisions to make that were guaranteed to make somebody very unhappy. When I got to the ballpark around three o'clock, I asked Zimmer, "Who would you play?" He said, "O'Neill, Boggs, Martinez . . ." I looked at him and shook my head. "Nope. Can't do that," I said. I told him I had decided I was going to leave Hayes, Fielder, and Raines in my lineup. He gave me that bug-eyed look of his. I knew he was very surprised. Against Smoltz, the 1996 Cy Young award winner, who was twenty-eight and eight, including his four postseason wins—I was keeping three of my best left-handed hitters on the bench: two batting champions (Boggs and O'Neill) and our top RBI guy over the course of the season (Martinez).

I've never been the type of manager who just posts the lineup in the clubhouse without explanation, not when I have these kinds of decisions to make. So one by one I called the players who weren't starting into my office. First I talked to Boggs. I explained that I liked the way Hayes was swinging the bat, and that Hayes had had decent success against Smoltz when he played in the National League. I could tell Boggsy was disappointed, but he took it pretty well. Then I talked to Tino. I told him Cecil looked like he was so locked in and was swinging such a hot bat that I had to play him. Tino was clearly angry. He listened to what I had to say and walked out, hardly saying a word.

And then I brought in O'Neill. That was the toughest call for me. I was upset with Raines. In Game Three we had been leading 2–0 in the fifth inning when Raines, with one out, got doubled off first base on a fly ball that was caught in right-center field. He was past second base when the ball was caught, so he stopped, looked at the outfielder who caught the ball, and figured "I can't get back." Then he realized he *could* have made make it back, but it was too late. He had made a mistake, and he knew it. Since then he had gone 0-for-7. I decided I wanted Raines batting leadoff anyway, as he had in our wins in Games Three and Four. When I broke the news to O'Neill, he was devastated—just crushed. Paulie had been busting his ass for us for weeks with a bad leg, and here I had just slapped him in the face. His reaction was totally different from Tino's. Tino was mad. Paulie was just resigned. He looked very down. He walked out of my office with his head bowed and his shoulders slouched.

Only a few minutes later Zimmer walked into my office. "Paulie's down," he said.

"Yeah, I know," I said. Then I started to kick an idea around in my head. I said to Zim, "Let's play him. Let's play O'Neill."

"Instead of Strawberry?" Zim asked.

"No. Instead of Raines," I said.

"Yeah, you can do that," he said.

"Tell Paulie I want to see him," I said.

Zim went for O'Neill. When O'Neill came back into my office, I said to him, "Manager's prerogative. I changed my mind. You're playing."

I had changed my mind because of what I read out of Paul's body language. What it told me was that by not playing him, I might have lost him completely. His confidence and his energy might have been so shot at that point that he might not have done me much good for the rest of the Series. But Paulie had been too important to our club all year for that to happen.

A manager has to be very flexible reading players and reacting to situations. I may have been a better manager in 1996 than before only because some things worked out, but I always felt that I've managed with the intent to win the game at hand as opposed to managing to answer questions afterward. As George Kissell taught me, you can't go by "the book" just to cover your ass. The manager is the one who's with the players every day and gets a sense of what they're all about. And there are days when they're not the same as they were the day before, and you have to have a feel for that. I will say that I probably spent more time hanging around the players in the clubhouse and the trainers' room in 1996 than I had in the past. It brought me closer to the players and that meant a lot to me, especially after my relationship with the St. Louis players had soured in 1995.

Game Five, like Game Four, turned out to be another one of those classic chess matches where I had to rely on my experience and instincts, not just the comfort of percentages. Smoltz started off in typically dominant fashion by striking out six of our first nine batters. But then in the fourth inning, two of my surprise starters, Hayes and Fielder, combined to get us a 1–0 lead. Hayes hit a fly ball into right-center field, where Marquis Grissom and Jermaine Dye converged. Neither one really took charge of the play, and the ball wound up bouncing off Grissom's glove for a two-base error. Then Bernie Williams, playing perfect situational baseball, moved Charlie to third with a grounder to the right side. Then Cecil smoked a double off the left-field wall to put us ahead.

Andy Pettitte was even better than Smoltz. He had a four-hit shutout through eight innings. Everybody expected me to give Wetteland the ball in the ninth inning to close out a 1–0 game. But Pettitte hadn't even thrown a hundred pitches, and Chipper Jones and Fred McGriff, both of whom hit right-handers better, were Atlanta's first two batters of the ninth inning. I wanted Pettitte to face them. There was one potential problem, though: We were playing under National League rules and Pettitte was due to bat fifth in the top of the ninth. Should I take him out for a pinch hitter if his spot came up?

After two outs Mariano Duncan was on first base with Jimmy Leyritz batting against Mark Wohlers, with Pettitte on deck. I gave Duncan the steal sign, figuring if he was thrown out it was no big deal, and I wouldn't have to decide whether to pinch hit for Pettitte. It was worth the gamble. I guess I was on such a roll that everything was going our way. Duncan was safe. Naturally the Braves decided to walk Leyritz. Wohlers, however, threw ball four all the way to the backstop, advancing Duncan yet another base. Now we had runners on first and third, two outs, and my pitcher was up.

I made up my mind to let Pettitte hit, even though I had Boggs and Raines on my bench. I explained to Zimmer why I wanted Andy to stay in the game. "Am I crazy or what?" I asked Zim, who said, "No, it makes sense."

One obnoxious fan next to the dugout apparently didn't agree. He was screaming, "Hey, Torre! What about Boggs? What about Boggs, you dummy!" Zim, as only Zim can do, turned around and snapped, "Sit down you asshole!"

Meanwhile, back in New York, Frank was probably questioning me, too, as he watched the game from his hospital bed. A friend of mine from New York, Jack Kennedy, was sitting with Frank during the three games in Atlanta. Frank would scream at the television whenever I made a move he didn't like. "You idiot," he'd say. "You moron. Why did you do that?" Poor Jack. He kept one eye on the game and one eye on Frank's heart monitor, worried sick about both of them.

Ali was at the game, sitting next to Pettitte's wife, Laura. When Laura saw Andy walking to the plate to hit, she said, "Oh, no. Oh, no. Andy never pitches the ninth inning. He always takes him out. What is he doing?" Laura had seen enough excitement for eight innings and wanted to relax for the last three outs. My wife didn't have an answer for her. Like a lot of people, she didn't know what I was doing either. But she told Laura, "Don't worry. Andy will be fine."

More important, Andy had thought he was coming out of the game too. I didn't find that out until later. I figured I had given him the message when I left him in the on-deck circle with Leyritz batting. The message was, This is your game. I guess Andy didn't get it. If I had known at the time that he expected to be taken out of the game, I would talked to him, because once you think you're out—like Koosman did back with the Mets—you let your guard down. Andy actually had a couple of decent hacks up at the plate, but he eventually flied out for the third out.

In the bottom of the ninth Pettitte really put me on the hot seat when he hung a pitch to Jones, who knocked it into left field for a double. The tying run was on second base with no outs. I let Pettitte face McGriff, and he got him out on a grounder, though Jones moved to third. Then I called for Wetteland. Big John got an out and kept Jones at third with one pitch, getting Javy Lopez on a grounder to Hayes. Now we needed one more out to win the game. Bobby Cox had two pinch hitters ready: first Klesko, and then I figured it would be Terry Pendleton. I decided it was time to walk out to talk to Wetteland. I remembered a game we had lost to Boston in July and I didn't want to repeat the same mistake that cost us that game.

Wetteland had pitched the ninth inning in Boston with an 11–9 lead. He walked Tim Naehring with one out, so I sent Mel Stottlemyre to the mound to remind him to be aggressive. That was the big mistake. Mike Stanley hit a double, but then Wetteland struck out Kevin Mitchell. Two outs. Now what do I do? Pitch to Reggie Jefferson, who was batting .375, or Troy O'Leary? I couldn't talk to Wetteland about it, because if you visit a pitcher twice in the same inning, you have to take him out. I held up four fingers, telling Wetteland to intentionally walk Jefferson. I could see John slump; his body language told me he didn't like

253

the idea. With the bases loaded John grooved a fastball to O'Leary on the first pitch. He later said he was trying to get ahead of O'Leary with no room on base to put him. But that's where he was wrong. Even if he walked O'Leary, he still would have had a one-run lead. I would have told him that, if only we had not already used up that first visit to the mound. O'Leary ripped a double, tying the game. Jeff Frye then hit a single to give Boston a 12–11 win. I felt absolutely awful that night. I decided then that whenever Wetteland was in position to walk someone intentionally, I would talk to him.

When I got to the mound, I said to John, "I'm here to ask you a question. Would you feel better pitching to Klesko or Pendleton?"

"Um . . ." John hesitated. That was enough for me.

"Put him on," I said. "Go get Pendleton."

So John walked Klesko. I didn't worry about putting the winning run on base, not when it's a guy like Klesko, who can hit a home run at any time. Cox surprised me a little by sending up Luis Polonia to bat instead of Pendleton. Polonia fouled off about six fastballs in a row. Zimmer turned to me and said, "Wouldn't it be nice if John threw one of those curveballs right now?" I said, "Yeah, but I don't want one in the dirt that goes back to the screen either." I think John was worried about that, too, because a passed ball would have easily scored Jones and would have tied the game. He kept pumping fastballs until Polonia finally put one in play, a flyball to right-center field.

"That's an out," I thought to myself. But then I saw O'Neill keep running back for it. And then it looked like he stumbled—I thought he stepped in a hole or something. And then, with every ounce of strength that was left in those gimpy legs, O'Neill made one last stride at the edge of the warning track. He extended his arm and opened his glove. If he catches the ball, I thought, we win 1–0 and take a three-games-to-two lead in the Series. If he doesn't, we lose 2–1, the Braves take a three-games-to-two lead, and I will be skewered for letting Pettitte bat in the ninth inning. O'Neill, who wasn't supposed to be in the lineup, whose body language had caused me to change my mind about playing him, caught the ball. We were an amazing 8-0 on the road in the postseason, needing only one more win at Yankee Stadium to be world champions.

I felt great flying back on our charter flight that night— taking with me those unsightly peppers, still in the same unopened bag, of course. It's funny how when you win and hardly get any sleep, you still feel terrific. When you lose, you can sleep all night and still feel lousy when you wake up. By the time I got to the door of my house, it was five-fifteen in the morning. Thirty minutes later the telephone rang. It was Columbia-Presbyterian. They had a heart for Frank. A twenty-eight-year-old man from the Bronx had died from a brain disease and had donated his major organs. It looked like a good match. They were taking Frank down to surgery at six-thirty. I was terrified at first, thinking about the operation. But then I thought, Hell, this is what we'd been waiting for. There was nothing I could do but wait. Dr. Eric Rose called me twice to tell me how the operation was going. I'd doze off a little in between calls. And then, at eleven-thirty, he called to tell me it was over.

It looked good. Dr. Mehmet Oz, who had placed the heart in Frank's chest cavity, said the heart took to Frank like a fish to water. I couldn't believe what was happening. We were one victory away from the World Series, and Frank had received a heart from a man named Oz. I didn't know whether to laugh, cry, or click my heels three times. Dr. Rose told me Frank was in recovery, still not alert because of all the drugs in him. I left for the ballpark for our voluntary workout, after about ninety minutes of sleep.

I went to see Frank at about seven o'clock that night. Reggie Jackson and his agent, Matt Merola, were there too. Frank had tubes in him all over the place. He couldn't talk, but he nodded to my questions and wrote me notes. "Nice going," he wrote. And "No visitors." I was there about twenty minutes when I decided to let him rest. I bent over and kissed him on the cheek. Soon after we left, Frank's wife slipped his 1957 World Series ring back on his finger. Everything seemed right in the world.

I drove home and picked up Ali, who had taken a commercial flight back to New York, and we went out to dinner. When we came home, Ali checked the messages on our machine.

"Joe, you've got to listen to this," she said. "Someone is saying he's your brother, but it doesn't sound like him."

I played the tape. She was right—it didn't sound like Frank saying, "This is your brother. I just wanted to talk to you." It was a sick trick if someone else was pretending to be Frank. So I called the hospital and asked, "Did Frank try to call me?" They told me yes, he did. They arranged for Frank to call me back. And when he did, this is what he told me: "I need six tickets to tomorrow's game for my new friends here. I'll send somebody over there tomorrow to pick them up." Great! I thought. The old wheeler-dealer is back. I knew he was starting to feel better already.

I didn't sleep much that night either. I was so thrilled about Frank and the World Series that after about two hours of sleep, I woke up full of energy. I was running on fumes just about the entire postseason. I look at pictures of myself taken during the World Series, and I can see I'm totally exhausted—I just didn't know it at the time. I arrived at Yankee Stadium at eleven-thirty in the morning on Saturday, more than eight hours before Game Six. The first thing I did when I sat down at my desk was to call my wife and ask her if we had enough champagne in our house for a party. Ali said no, we would need more. So I called a wine shop in Bronxville run by Alfredo Cruz, whom Rusty Staub had introduced me to during the season. I ordered two cases of champagne to be delivered to my house. Confident? The way I looked at it, nothing would be open until Monday if I waited after the game to order champagne. But I have to admit that I felt like I was on a roll. If you can't feel confident after winning three games in Atlanta and with your brother finally getting a heart transplant, when can you?

And then it really hit me, sitting in my office before Game Six: My team could win the World Series tonight. Suddenly, I became as nervous as I've ever been in my entire life. Reggie Jackson had been checking on me throughout the postseason. Every once in a while he'd say to me, "Joe, you look so calm. How do you feel?" And I'd say, "I'm fine.

I'm all right." But when I saw Reggie before Game Six, I didn't even wait for him to ask.

"Reggie," I said, "I'm not calm anymore."

He smiled. Reggie liked that. He had played in enough big games to know that a little nervousness is a natural reaction.

Zimmer must have been confident. He came in my office and said, "You know, when we won our division title with the Cubs, we took a victory lap around the field. I thought that worked out great. You might want to think about it."

The best feeling I had coming into the game was knowing that our pitching was virtually at full strength. Everybody in the bullpen had had two days off except for Wetteland, and I knew he was fine. He had had one day off after pitching in the ninth inning of Game Five. The only one I was uncertain about was Jeff Nelson. We could not use him in Game Five because his elbow bothered him, and we weren't sure if he was available for Game Six. I was relieved that I had a fresh Mariano Rivera. And I knew that even if we didn't win, we could come back the next day with the same relievers available.

The matchup of starting pitchers was a repeat of Game Two: Jimmy Key against Greg Maddux. As Jimmy walked out to the mound for the first inning, I had one thought on my mind: Get me through the sixth inning. If we kept the game close through the sixth, and especially if we managed a lead, I loved the idea of turning the game over to Mo and John.

Maddux was sharp again. When he cruised through the first two innings in perfect order, he had faced thirty-five batters in this World Series while allowing the ball out of the infield only eight times. But then, leading off the third inning of a scoreless game, O'Neill came through. He ripped a hard double into the right-field corner. That made me feel even better about changing my mind about playing Paul in Game Five; now he was there when we needed him. With no outs, Duncan did a perfect job of moving the runner to third when he grounded out to second base. With Girardi batting, Maddux proved that even the greatest pitchers make mistakes. He left a pitch up in the strike zone, and Girardi belted it to the wall in center field for a triple and a 1–0 lead.

I was so happy for Joe. I hadn't had much to do with constructing the Yankees after I was hired—George and Bob had done most of that work while asking my opinion on some players. But being a former catcher, the one thing I pushed for was getting a good defensive catcher who knew how to handle pitchers. Mike Stanley had been the Yankees catcher before I got there. I knew he was a good hitter, but he looked inconsistent behind the plate, from what I saw on television and some videos the Yankees gave me. I've always liked my catcher to give me defense first, offense second. I talked with Zimmer, who had managed Girardi with the Cubs, and Mel Stottlemyre. We agreed Girardi was the best defensive catcher in the National League. I liked his approach to hitting—he sprayed the ball to all fields—and he could run a little bit. As I had been, Girardi was a player rep during the strike. I think that's one of the reasons the Colorado Rockies made him available to us in a trade. The New York fans had hated the deal because Stanley, whom we allowed to leave as a free agent, had been a popular player. Joe was heckled when he came to our fan festival in January. But he won over everyone with his consistency, his hustle— and especially his big triple off Maddux.

We kept the rally going. Cox thought I would squeeze on the first pitch to Jeter—he called a pitch-out—but Derek was swinging too hot a bat for me to give up an out. Jeter knocked the next pitch into center field for a single, to drive in Girardi. Then Jeter stole second base and, after Boggsy flied out, scored on a single by Bernie. We had a 3–0 lead on Maddux.

Jimmy was pitching a gutsy game. He decided he wasn't going to come close to making the kind of mistake Maddux made to Girardi. If he was going to miss with his pitches, it was going to be outside the strike zone, where he wouldn't get hurt. He threw the majority of his pitches with that mindset, which usually bothers me, but he stayed out of a big inning. He really nibbled in the fourth inning, when he forced in a run for Atlanta with a bases-loaded walk. With our lead down to 3–1 and the bases full with one out, Jimmy got Terry Pendleton to ground into a double play. That was enormous. Jimmy was one pitch away from com- ing out of the game; if he had thrown ball four or allowed a hit, I would have gone to my bullpen.

The biggest inning for me, as usual, was the sixth. There was magic in the number six for me, a guy who switched from uniform number 9 in St. Louis to number 6 in New York, trying to win the world championship in '96 in six games. See what I mean about destiny? In Game Three Cone had pitched out of that jam in the sixth inning; in Game

Four we had started our comeback from a 6–0 deficit in the sixth inning; in Game Five Pettitte had preserved the 1–0 lead with two exceptional fielding plays in the sixth inning; and in Game Six I would need three pitchers to get me through the sixth inning.

Key gave up a leadoff double to Chipper Jones. I immediately started David Weathers and Graeme Lloyd throwing in the bullpen. Jimmy got McGriff out on a ground ball on a play in which Chipper advanced to third. With Nelson still a little tender, I called on Weathers to get Javy Lopez. Weathers was magnificent. He struck out Lopez on three pitches for the second out. He made good pitches to Andruw Jones next, but the rookie was patient and drew a walk. When the Braves sent Ryan Klesko to bat, I called on Lloyd one more time. This matchup was a little too exciting. Lloyd threw ball one. And then ball two. And then he left a slider on the inside part of the plate. It was a mistake pitch. Klesko is strong enough to have knocked out a bulb atop the right-field light tower with a pitch like that. He had the pitch to hit but just missed it. He popped it up. We had dodged a bullet. I let out a big sigh of relief. We had made it through the sixth inning with a 3–1 lead. My work was almost over. It was as easy as sticking to the Formula after that.

I did make one more move. I took Boggs out of the game in the seventh inning and put Charlie Hayes at third base. I had started Boggs over Hayes just on a hunch. It was a move based totally on a feeling I had, not on statistics. After Boggs batted three times without a hit, I needed my best defensive team on the field to protect the lead. While

Boggsy has very good hands, he doesn't have the same range that Charlie does. I knew Wade had been with us all year and wanted to be on the field for the last out, but he should know as well as anybody that there is no room for sentiment at a time like that. He played on the 1986 Red Sox team that was one strike away from winning the world championship against the Mets. Boston manager John McNamara left Bill Buckner and his wobbly legs at first base, even though during the regular season he had regularly replaced Buckner with Dave Stapleton, a better fielder, to protect late-inning leads. This time McNamara wanted Buckner to be on the field for a world championship celebration. I was surprised to see Buckner out there, especially because Johnny Mac had made the defensive change all year. Of course, the Mets won the game when Buckner let a ground ball through his legs.

Rivera, after walking his first batter on four pitches, blew away six straight hitters to get us to the ninth inning. I turned to Stottlemyre and said, "What about Rivera in the ninth?" Mel looked at me as if he were about to have a heart attack. I smiled at him, letting him in on my little joke. "We haven't done it all year, have we?" I said.

The ninth inning belonged to Big John. He struck out Andruw Jones. One out. Klesko hit a ground ball to Jeter's left. Jeter has a problem with balls to his left because he tries to catch everything with two hands, rather than stabbing the ball with his glove hand. Two hands are preferred for balls hit right at you, but you can't reach as far to balls at your side if you reach with both hands rather than one. Derek, with his abbreviated reach, saw Klesko's grounder kick off the end of his glove for a base hit. Then Pendleton stroked a single to right field, sending Klesko to third. The tying runs were on base. The next batter was Polonia, who had battled his ass off against Wetteland before making that last out of Game Five. This time John overpowered him, striking him out quickly. Two outs. One out to go for the world championship. I was sitting on my hands in the dugout, nervous as hell on the inside. I grew more nervous when Marquis Grissom grounded a single into right field. Klesko scored to cut our lead to 3–2. Well, I thought, we've been doing it all year like this. Another one-run game. Why should this one be any different?

Mark Lemke batted next. The tying run was on second base and the go-ahead run at first. Lemke is one of those tough hitters you hate to see up there in these situations. He's a clutch postseason player who puts the ball in play. Lemke lifted a pop-up next to the Atlanta dugout on the third-base side. Hayes reached over the railing of a photographers' well and barely missed catching the foul ball. I turned to Zimmer and asked, "What do you think? Should I go out there or send Mel out there just to give John a breather? Settle him down?"

"Naw," Zimmer said. "He's going to get him out on this next pitch."

Then John threw a great pitch: a hard fastball away. Lemke lofted another pop-up near the Braves dugout. As soon as that ball went up, I knew this one was in play. I've watched too many games from the same seat at Yankee Stadium not to know when a ball is going in the stands and when it's not. I held my breath. I had waited thirty-seven years since I'd signed my first big league contract for this very moment. And now it seemed like it took another thirty-seven years for the baseball to come down. Finally it landed in Hayes's glove. And then I couldn't see anything. Zimmer, Stottlemyre, and the rest of my coaches jumped on me and started beating on me. I started screaming—just screaming with joy.

As soon as I got out from under the pile in the dugout, I ran on the field. This celebration was one I definitely was going to take part in. After all those years of painfully watching other people have their fun, now it was my turn. Months after it happened, I still get choked up when I see videos of our celebration after the last out. It was always Michael Jordan and the Bulls, or the Dallas Cowboys, or so many other teams piling on each other. Now whenever I see video of my Yankees team doing it, I think, Wow, that's us. That's really us. It gives me goose bumps.

After a minute or two of hugging my players, I remembered Zimmer's suggestion about a victory lap. I told Leyritz, "Let's take it around the field!" We headed toward the right-field seats, but when we turned around, no one was following us. So Jimmy and I went back to the crowd of players and said, "Let's go," and they all took off for left field. I was a little frightened as we ran near the mounted police, who were on the field for crowd control. The previous year, after I had been fired by St. Louis, I visited the paddock area of Saratoga and learned you should never walk behind a horse—if it gets scared it can kill you with one swift kick. I made sure to keep a safe distance from those horses.

We ran around the edge of the warning track, waving to

the fans. I'll never forget seeing such happiness on their faces. As much as they loved the victory lap, I think we enjoyed it even more. We ran all the way around the outfield and along the first-base seats. I stopped when I got next to our dugout and my box, where my daughters Tina and Lauren and my son Michael were sitting. Tina was crying like a baby. I hugged all of them. My wife and Andrea were sitting farther back; I always made sure my baby was protected from foul balls by the screen behind home plate.

Zimmer came up to me after he finished the lap. He was breathing heavily. "Joe," he said, "remember when I told you about that lap we took with the Cubs? We walked. You damn near killed me out there."

The next two or three hours in the clubhouse were a blur of interviews, hugs, kisses, champagne showers, and cigar smoke. I was so busy running around that I missed the congratulatory call from President Clinton, though he did track me down the next day in my office. I do remember standing on a wooden platform in the back of the clubhouse holding the World Series trophy with George, when I heard someone hollering louder than any one else, "Wooooo!" I recognized my wife's voice. I turned, and when our eyes met as she ran to me she yelled, "Yes! Yes!" I started crying all over again with her in my arms.

It was close to two o'clock in the morning before I decided to leave. Ali had long since headed home with Andrea and made sure our nephew Jeff had taken my car keys. I was going to take a shower, but then I thought, Why bother? I walked out of Yankee Stadium in my champagne-soaked uniform. I had taken about five or six steps when the crowd that was still milling around outside started cheering. I jumped into the back of a car waiting for me, a beat-up BMW belonging to Dr. Joe. Arthur Sando was sitting in the front. Fans quickly surrounded the car. They pounded on it in excitement, and for a moment I feared they were going to turn it over. With some police help we were able to make it out of there and back to my house. I walked in the door to see my home packed with people. And I had no idea who half of them were.

I didn't talk with Frank until the morning after our game, Sunday. He was in intensive care, so I couldn't call him. I had to wait for his call. When he did call, it was one of the rare times when I heard his voice crack with emotion. For years Frank used to have fun needling me about never having been to the World Series. Anytime I thought I was smarter or better than him, he'd remind me, "I've been to the World Series twice and got my ring; you don't have any." What could I say? He was right. This telephone call was the first time I could talk to my brother like I was on the same level as him. This time he had nothing to complain about with me.

In a soft weakened voice, Frank said, "Nice going, kid." Those three simple words meant more to me than all the thousands of flattering stories, headlines, and pictures ever devoted to me.

The next day, Monday, I was invited to appear on *The Late Show with David Letterman.* I wore the same suit I had worn to the press conference when I was introduced as manager of the Yankees—only five days shy of exactly one year that I had gone from Clueless Joe to national celebrity. I brought Cardenal's lucky peppers with me, which by then were grotesquely shriveled, and Letterman's people placed them between David's and my chair before the taping in anticipation of making them a topic of discussion. I never did get around to talking about them. Toward the end of my interview I was ambushed with champagne spray by Leyritz, Boggs, and O'Neill. I had no idea they would do that. I just threw my hands up as if to say, "Go to it, guys." After the show I figured I would go home to change clothes before I met Ali, Joe Molloy, and Bob Watson and his wife for dinner. But Letterman's people had a complete new outfit waiting for me, including socks, underwear, shirt, tie, and a blue double-breasted suit. Amazingly, other than the pants being an inch too long, the clothes fit perfectly. A few days later they delivered my freshly cleaned suit to my home—but not the peppers. They still may be rotting next to David's desk, for all I know.

On the morning after the Letterman show, I had the honor of ringing the bell to open trading on the New York Stock Exchange. I signed so many autographs and posed for so many pictures that it took an hour just to walk across the floor of the exchange. It was a thrill to be there, and it made me wonder: If Frank hadn't encouraged me to be a catcher in those days when I was working for the American Exchange, I would be working on the floor instead of being congratulated on being a world champion.

I had to hustle out of the exchange because I had an important date: a ticker-tape parade for the team down lower Broadway in Manhattan. While we waited in a tent for the parade to start, I was thrilled to meet one of my favorite recording artists, Placido Domingo. I was happy to see my mother-in-law and father-in-law there too. I'm sorry my parents were not alive to share in my happiness, but Ali's parents have become such special people in my life that it was wonderful for me to see them at the parade.

I rode on a float with Bob Watson and my coaches. I was stunned at the sheer number of people who had turned out along the parade route. The police estimated that three million people were there. I saw nothing but smiling faces as far as I could see. When we reached each intersection, I would look down the cross street and see people lined up for what must have been a quarter of a mile just to get a glimpse of us as we rode by. As a native New Yorker, I recall the ticker-tape parades given to General Douglas Mac-Arthur and to the Apollo 11 astronauts, though I must say, as a St. Louis Cardinals player at the time, I didn't pay much attention to the one for the 1969 world champion Mets. I was awed by those parades as they made their way through what is known as the Canyon of Heroes. No city in the world but New York can put on such a spectacle. To be a part of one myself—one of the biggest such parades ever—made me proud to be a New Yorker and proud to be a Yankee. Add me to the list of people who believe there's no better place to win than in New York, especially when it's your hometown. I had to ask myself, Is it really you? Are you really a part of this? It was like an out-of-body experience.

For days, even weeks, I floated in a thick, dreamy haze of utter happiness. I wore a silly grin on my face every waking moment—probably in my sleep too. I was the honorary starter with Mayor Rudy Giuliani of the New York Marathon, then took a helicopter ride over the Verrazano Bridge in the brilliant light of a crisp morning as the mass of runners spilled like water from one side of the bridge to the other. I attended a Knicks game at Madison Square Garden with Ali, David Cone, and his wife. We received an overwhelming standing ovation when we were introduced to the crowd. We were touched by the way people responded to us. Whenever I went out in public, even shopping with Ali, I felt people's eyes following me all the time.

The high still hasn't worn off. I feel a thoroughly satisfying sense of accomplishment and exoneration. The most amazing part is that it is so lasting. Not a day goes by where I don't feel it, whether I'm reminded by others or feel it myself. It's with me from my first cup of coffee in the morning to my last sip of wine at night. It's so powerful that I'm glad such happiness came to me later in life. I can understand how people get carried away with success. At fifty-six, I'm too old to change.

I have never been happier in my life, and yet when I say those words I feel guilty. It's difficult to admit feeling so enchanted when I know that Rocco died in the middle of my championship season. I thought about him often during our drive to the World Series. In the ninth innings of tense games, when all I could do was watch, I would think about Rocco and the way he showed me what a loving husband and father could be. I thought about how, as children, my friend Matt Borzello and I would bring him sandwiches and plates of food from home when he was on police duty; he always was happy to see me, but never more than I was to see him. Whenever I thought about Rocco in those moments of anxiety in the dugout, I became calm and relaxed. I wish he could have been there to feel the excitement of every victory and to taste the sweetness of the champagne. But the way I see it, maybe he had to be up there in heaven for all of this to happen. Maybe in his own way Rocco made possible all the wonderful things that we clumsily ascribe to destiny.

Ali preferred that I quit this managing grind after the World Series, though she knew I would honor my contract. I understood what she was thinking. I had reached my lifelong dream and we had a beautiful girl nearing her first birthday to take care of. But there are more people to think about than just me. We won as a team. I didn't want to walk away from the players, the staff, and the special feeling we created in New York. I want to defend our championship. It will be invigorating to go back out there on the field as a world champion. It's like buying a beautiful new suit. Now you want to wear it.

One day in December, with the glow of the coming Christmas everywhere, George called me to a meeting in his office at Yankee Stadium. It was the meeting for which I had been waiting my whole life. I sat down in a chair at his conference table, the same chair in which I had been sitting when George told me we didn't dare go into a doubleheader in Cleveland with two rookie starting pitchers. Bob Watson and Arthur Richman were sitting with us. On the table before us, sparkling like long-lost treasures, nearly a dozen styles of World Series championship rings shimmered against the smooth polish of the wood table. Some of them were inscribed "Watson," some of them were inscribed "Steinbrenner," and most of them were inscribed "Torre." It was real now. It was time to choose what style of ring we wanted.

"After we decide on this one," I told George, "then we're going to decide on Tuesday's ring, right? One for every day of the week?"

George laughed. Then I turned serious for a minute. George understood about my promise, twenty-four years ago to Frank, that I would replace his 1958 World Series ring with one of my own someday. I didn't want to leave anything to chance though. I wanted to be on record as requesting a ring for Frank.

"Don't forget," I told George, "I want to buy an extra ring for Frank. I've got to have one for Frank."

"Don't worry," George said. "We'll make sure of that."

I had told Frank, a short time after we won the World Series, that I intended to make good on my promise. I told him I was going to order a second ring inscribed "Torre" and give it to him. I knew he planned to give it to his son, Frankie. Frank pretended it was no big deal.

"Aw, you don't have to worry about getting me a regular ring," he said. "Just get me a cheaper one."

"Don't you worry about it," I said. "I'll handle it."

It was fun playing with the different styles of rings. Bob, George, Arthur, and I slipped them on and off our fingers, holding our hands out to admire the beauty of each one. We all kept coming back to the same ring. The interlocking "NY" of the Yankees was highlighted in diamonds on the top. One side featured a raised replica of the world champi-

271

onship trophy and the number 23, representing the number of world championships won by the franchise. The other side was inscribed with three words that characterized the spirit of our ball club: "Courage. Tradition. Pride." George especially liked that touch. This was going to be the ring.

I liked it, too, but I had one small change in mind, a change everyone else immediately agreed on. I thought about the way my Yankees never gave up, the way no deficit, no matter how big or how late, was too big for us to conquer. And I thought about the connection my team shared with my two brothers: Rocco, how he died, and Frank, how he lives. The words will be forever etched in gold.

"Courage. Tradition. Heart."

About the Authors

Joe Torre was born and raised in Brooklyn, New York. A nine-time all-star for the Milwaukee and Atlanta Braves, the St. Louis Cardinals, and the New York Mets, he retired in 1977 to become a manager. On November 1, 1995, he was named manager of the New York Yankees. He lives in New York with his wife, Alice, and their daughter, Andrea Rae.

Tom Verducci is a senior writer for *Sports Illustrated.* He lives with his wife, Kirsten, and two sons, Adam and Benjamin, in New Jersey.